MODERN
SMALL
ARMS

MODERN
SMALL
ARMS

Ian V. Hogg

Bison Books

Published by
Bison Books Ltd.
176 Old Brompton Road
London, SW5
England

ISBN 0 86124 123 1

Printed in Hong Kong

Reprinted 1986

CONTENTS

The Model 45 'Carl Gustav' submachine gun in Swedish army use.

INTRODUCTION

In writing about *modern* small arms, we have to begin by defining what we mean; the principles upon which most small arms work are far from modern, and, indeed, there are only a scant handful of weapons in this book which have broken new ground on the technological battlefront. It would have been too easy to simply make a list of what is currently on offer from the major manufacturers of the world; but this would not have been a collection of entirely modern weapons, since most manufacturers are sensible enough to stick to a good design when they have one, and there are many weapons on sale today which, in essence, are the same as the ones the firm were selling in the 1900s.

The criterion has therefore had to be somewhat fluid, and I have selected weapons which represent the latest manufacturing techniques; which reflect the latest fashions in shooting (for there are fashions in this as there are in anything else); which represent a new departure for a particular maker; which introduce a new or unusual cartridge into a company's line-up; which are being evaluated by various military forces throughout the world for possible adoption; which represent some new military concept; or which have introduced some totally new method of operation.

Even this attempt at selection led to some borderline cases, and the final result has thus left plenty of room for argument; there will be questions as to why 'A' went in and 'B' was left out; to which the only answer can be that this is a very subjective field, and no two writers will agree upon their order of priorities. These are the ones I think are interesting; another compilation by a different hand could well produce a totally different answer.

The demands of space have led to unavoidable condensation in many cases, and I would like, therefore, to use this introduction to discuss one or two aspects of modern small arms which cannot easily be brought up under the heading of any specific weapon.

There is, of course, a great deal of interreaction between military and civil firearms design, and as in many other fields – electronics, plastics, ceramics for example – the commercial market benefits from the 'spin-off' from the military developments. Many calibers now in regular sporting use started life as military cartridges, though the bullets and loadings used for sport bear little relationship to their military forebears apart from caliber. A potential area for development in the future is the propellant charge; in many cartridges the propellant is now occupying as much space as it can in the case, so that improvements in power are out of the question. For some years writers have been hinting at imminent breakthroughs in propellant chemistry, though nothing concrete has been seen and some of the 'high energy' propellants postulated make little chemical sense. But it does now seem that we are on the verge of some advance in this area, largely as a by-product of research into the caseless cartridge.

As explained elsewhere, the German firm of Heckler & Koch, confronted with an extremely difficult demand from the West German Army, came to the conclusion that it could only be achieved by a weapon using a caseless cartridge, a round of ammunition in which the conventional metallic case was not used. There is nothing really new in the concept of caseless ammunition; there were German designs in 1944 and the U.S. Army spent some time exploring the concept in the 1950s, but all these used conventional nitrocellulose propellant bound together into a rigid shape by some plastic cement, and all of them gave rise to over-heating in the weapon. Heckler & Koch ran up against the same problem, but elected to solve it not by modifying the weapon but by changing the characteristics of the propellant; reducing the temperature would have reduced the power, so a new composition, known to the outside world only as 'HITP' for 'High Ignition Temperature Propellant', was developed. This burns with much the same temperature, develops the desired power, but is much more resistant to external heat, so that when loaded into a hot chamber the

An example of the spread of military technology to the civil market – the Heckler & Koch 300 sporting rifle, built by a firm who are famed for their military weapons.

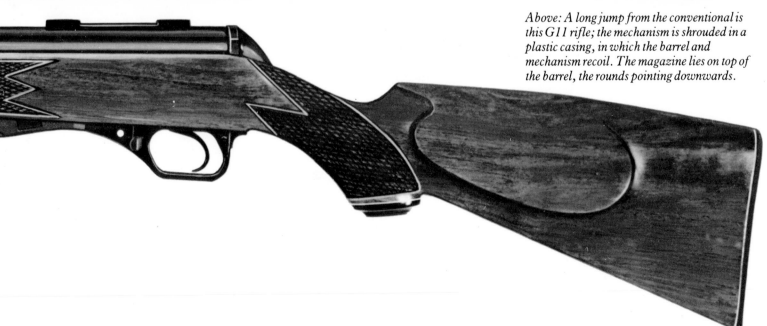

Above: A long jump from the conventional is this G11 rifle; the mechanism is shrouded in a plastic casing, in which the barrel and mechanism recoil. The magazine lies on top of the barrel, the rounds pointing downwards.

Caseless cartridge 4,7 mm

Bullet weight = 3,4 g
Cartridge weight = 5 g

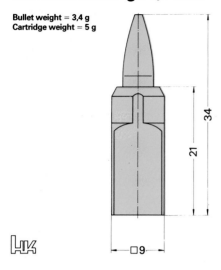

A scale drawing of the caseless 4.7mm cartridge developed for Heckler and Koch.

cartridge does not 'cook off' and explode prematurely. This has been done by moving away from the traditional nitrocellulose composition and developing a propellant based on one of the members of the Hexogen family of high explosives. By suitably moderating this substance it can be given the burning characteristics of a propellant, rather than its normal detonating characteristic, and into the bargain develops a greater amount of power per cùbic centimeter of powder. This substance also burns cleaner than the traditional powders, leaving less residue and generating less smoke. It seems likely that the long awaited 'breakthrough' in propellants is about to begin, using moderated high explosives as the starting point. If these substances can be perfected, then it should be possible to obtain a fresh lease of life from a number of sporting cartridges.

Provided, of course, that the weapons themselves are not worn out too fast by the

application of new propellants giving higher velocities. Here again there have been a number of useful pointers from military usage, particularly the adoption of chrome and stellite liners for chambers and throats to combat wear in those areas where most of it takes place. This becomes a very important question as calibers decrease; some of the early work on 5.56mm machine guns ran into trouble with barrels wearing out after three or four belts of ammunition had been fired, and though these problems have been solved in an empirical manner there remains much experimental and research work to be done. There seems to be some sort of a cross-over point between reducing caliber and increasing velocity at which barrel wear suddenly leaps to unacceptable levels, and until this is more thoroughly understood, the development of smaller calibers will be very much in a cut-and-try mode.

It is possible though, that this trend to smaller calibers has now reached its limits, or indeed gone beyond them. Ten years ago there was enormous enthusiasm for the .17 caliber, but this appears to have evaporated. Undoubtedly .17 delivered some extremely accurate results and promised flat trajectories and high velocities, but it also brought the wear problem along in some cases, and though widely touted as a hunting round it proved sadly deficient in killing power. It should be borne in mind that military and commercial requirements in killing power are vastly different; the soldier hunts only one animal, and his cartridge can thus be optimized against his specified target. But the average sporting hunter has a variety of possible targets and there is no chance of optimizing one bullet

Right: The FN 'Minimi' is one of the first successful 5.56mm machine guns and shortly begins production for the American army. Below: The Swedish 4.5mm Interdynamic rimfire military cartridge compared with the center-fire 7.62mm and 5.56mm NATO rounds.

to deal effectively with everything he may feel constrained to shoot at. So that while the 5.56mm and even smaller calibers have some validity in a military context, they have rather less advantages as hunting cartridges.

Speaking of reductions in caliber brings to mind the recent abortive search for a 9mm replacement for the much-respected Colt M1911A1 automatic pistol as the standard U.S. military sidearm. There is no argument that what the .45 ACP hits, it stops; but there has been long argument for many years over the problems of training the average soldier to be a competent shot with the pistol. There were also questions of supply, of spare parts, of economizing by adopting a standard arm to replace the multiplicity of revolvers which have been procured in small lots at various times, and so on and so forth. And, of course, there was the question of NATO standardization

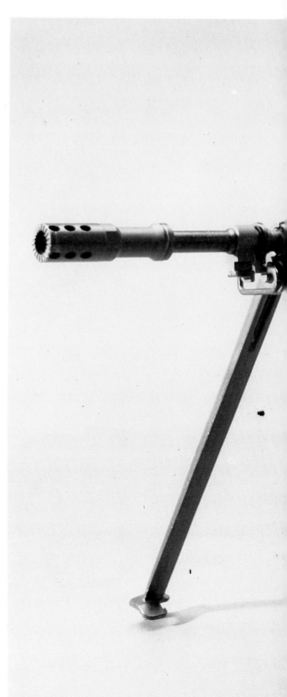

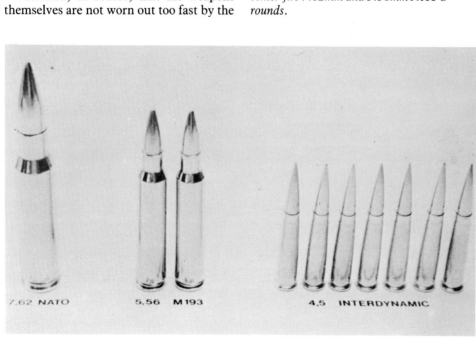

7.62 NATO   5.56   M193   4.5   INTERDYNAMIC

on a universal caliber for pistols and sub-machine guns. And, finally, there was the unaswerable argument that no matter what the relative ballistic values were, the 9mm bullet has killed far more people than has the .45 ACP, so it cannot be entirely useless.

The U.S. Air Force opened proceedings by conducting comparative tests of a selection of military 9mm pistols, including such names as Beretta, Browning, Heckler & Koch, SIG and other well-known makes. Then the U.S. Army declared an interest and the Department of Defense moved in; the Air Force tests were discarded as presumably not sufficiently scientific, and a new program was begun. Finally all the contestants were thrown out, the report saying, among other things, that 'none of the pistols met all the 71 major requirements . . .' The most recent information is that the whole program has now been dropped and presumably the U.S. armed

forces will have to wait for a new handgun for several more years. What worries most onlookers is that, on this showing, three-quarters of the armies of the world are walking about with substandard handguns. The other question which several European commentators would like answered is what were the '71 major requirements' and if there were so many major requirements, how many minor ones were there?

The commercial pistol field seems to be seeing a reduction in the progress of the big battalions; in the 1970s new 'Magnum' calibers were appearing every week and disappearing with similar regularity as every would-be designer tried to outdo the opposition with a more powerful cartridge. At one stage it began to look as if the ideal would be a pistol nobody could handle because of its excessive recoil. But the mania has now died down leaving only those calibers which manage to ally accuracy with

force and yet remain controllable in conventional weapons. On the other hand the increasing interest in metallic silhouette shooting over the last seven or eight years has done wonders for the powerful target pistols such as the Remington XP-100 and the Thompson Center and has stimulated interest in weapons capable of accurate results at long range, which has led to a revival of the Auto-Mag and the development of the Wildey automatic with its allied Magnum cartridges. It has also set the hand-loaders and wild-catters to work at their benches in search of the elusive combination of accuracy and power which will unfailingly knock over iron boars at 200 yards range. After studying some of these proposals I am more than ever convinced that success awaits the man who realizes the potential of the 7.62×39mm Soviet cartridge.

Similarly the tendency for commercial

Top: One military application of heavy-barreled rifles is for use as light machine guns; these Canadian troops form a tank hunting team – the 84mm 'Carl Gustav' recoilless gun operator is protected by a trooper using a heavy-barreled FN automatic rifle.
Above: Heavy rifles find favor in military circles as sniping weapons; this Parker-Hale Model 82 is fitted with a Pilkington 'Sniper Mark II' image-intensifying sight, capable of detecting a man at 350 yards range in dim starlight.

rifles to creep ever upwards into magnum calibers appears to be lessening. This is doubtless due to the gradual restriction on hunting which is creeping across the entire world; gone are the days when one could go off to Africa or India and proceed to decimate the animal population without let or hindrance. Ecology and economy alike have cut deeply into that activity. Instead, today's would-be hunter must consider carefully where he will be able to hunt and what he is likely to find there, after which he selects his rifle and cartridge accordingly. And except for a few cases, he finds that a medium caliber will do all that is necessary, with the result that the demand for the 'elephant gun' calibers is slowing down. So too, as we have already noted, has the tendency towards micro-calibers; many of these have been outlawed by conservation authorities due to inexperienced shots trying to do too much and, in the end, wounding game without killing it. The application of these small calibers to target shooting is circumscribed by various regulations covering minimum calibers, weights and so forth, some of which might be considered due for overhaul by those anxious to try something new, or not so considered by those reluctant to give up familiar equipment. In this respect we find great disagreement over the worth of 5.56mm (.223) as a target caliber; some swear by it, others at it. I suspect that the right answer lies in the correct relationship between bullet and pitch of rifling, and that what suits military

applications does not necessarily prove to be the optimum for anything else. It is notable that no military authority in search of a sniping rifle has yet adopted a 5.56mm weapon for this role.

To go back to the military scene again, this question of the 5.56mm bullet versus something heavier has caused some dissent in Europe when considered in relation to machine guns. By selecting 5.56mm as the new NATO standard caliber, many western armies have committed themselves to a 5.56mm squad machine gun in order to avoid the problem of having to carry two types of ammunition and then have problems when the machine gunner runs out and the riflemen still have plenty. The West German Army, however, has roundly condemned the 5.56mm for machine gun use and has said it will adhere to 7.62mm in that role; since it is now also committed to adopting 4.7mm as its rifle caliber in 1990, once again NATO standardization seems remote.

The argument against 5.56mm for machine guns is by no means trivial; in general, the soldier expects his light machine gun to have that little bit more reach than his rifle, and also to have useful armor-piercing, tracer and possibly incendiary bullets as well, particularly in view of the number of infantry-carrying light armored vehicles which the battlefield of the 1980s will see. And there can be no argument that 7.62mm gives more room for piercing cores or tracer loadings than does a

The M16A1 Carbine, a shorter version of the standard US service rifle. Attempts to make shorter 5.56mm weapons have been unsuccessful, since the cartridge demands a minimum length of barrel in which to burn its powder.

Below: The new 'Mini-Uzi' submachine gun can be fired single-handed, like a pistol, or, with the stock extended as here, makes a compact submachine gun. With the stock folded it is a fraction over 14 inches long.

Below: A Laser Aiming Spot mounted on an M16 rifle; this electronic sighting aid delivers a tight beam of light which is aligned with the bore, so that the shot will fall wherever the spot of light is directed.

5.56mm bullet and carries more weight behind it at the target. What we have here, in fact, is the classic case of the tail wagging the dog; there seems little doubt that the 5.56m cartridge was chosen less on its ballistic merits than on its availability and on the existence of machinery for its mass production, and several people are belatedly realizing that something slightly larger might have been a more sensible choice.

The selection of the 5.56mm bullet has had one significant effect on military machine gun design; it has begun a move away from the 'general purpose machine gun' concept and back to the separate 'light machine gun' and 'medium machine gun', or the squad weapon and the company support weapon. The GPMG was acceptable in 7.62mm caliber, since it was intended to function on a bipod as the squad weapon or on a tripod as the supporting gun, having the range and weight of bullet to perform the latter function adequately. But in 5.56mm caliber it would only be effective as the squad weapon, and most armies intend to retain 7.62mm guns in the support role. In truth, the GPMG was more popular with the planners and theorists than it ever was with the soldiers; no machine gun draped in belts of ammunition could be considered 'light', and the reversion to a really lightweight magazine-fed weapon will be welcomed.

Where the submachine gun is today is a question many analysts are avoiding; several years ago it was freely predicted that the submachine gun was on the way out, to be replaced by light and short assault rifles, but this doesn't seem to have come about quite as quickly as expected. Early in 1981 the US Army stated a requirement for a new submachine gun to replace the aged M3A1s which are still in reserve, but very little has been heard of any progress. Sterling, Uzi and Beretta guns are still being made and sold, and in spite of one or two attempts to shorten 5.56mm rifles and call them submachine guns, there appear to have been few enthusiasts for this concept. What seems to have saved the submachine gun is the rise of international terrorism and the need for police and security forces to have some compact firepower available to deal with terrorists. Police forces, particularly in Europe, who have traditionally either been unarmed or have had nothing more serious than a 7.65mm pistol are now to be seen with 9mm submachine guns, sniping rifles, image-intensifying sights, laser aiming devices and all the aids which modern technology can give them. The submachine gun is also the preferred close-range weapon of the various semi-clandestine military forces of the major nations, such as the British Special Air Service who use Heckler & Koch MP5s.

Another weapon which has begun to appear more regularly in police forces is the shotgun; this is, perhaps, no stranger in America, but the introduction of riot shotguns into European security forces has been a considerable innovation. The sporting shotgun is not the best weapon for riot control, and therefore neither is a simple adaptation of a commercial model. The principal defect from the police point of view is that sporting guns are invariably choked to produce the best possible pattern of shot for some particular game application, whether that be taking partridge at tree-top height, high-flying ducks or clays at rigidly-defined ranges. The policeman, on the other hand, requires a fast and wide spread of shot for instant immobilization of an adversary at close range, and he also wants the ability to fire solid slugs or gas projectiles if necessary, all of which argue a cylinder-bored gun. He also wants a short and handy weapon which he can use inside a building without getting it jammed across doorways, and he wants a rapid repeat shot or two if the first fails. Consequently the past year or two have seen a sudden interest in specialized shotguns, and we are now beginning to see the first fruits of this from European manufacturers.

Terrorism has also been responsible for an increase in the bodyguard business, leading to demands for powerful but small pistols which can be concealed more easily than the traditional heavy service-pattern pistol but which can still drop the adversary with the first shot. Early attempts at cutting-down standard pistols were not entirely successful, and we are now seeing a number of carefully thought out designs in which the cutting has been done in a more scientific manner so that the power is not reduced to ridiculous levels. Some of the early weapons went so far in reduction of barrel length that the .45 ACP bullet arrived at the target with less energy than the average .38 Special fired from a stock revolver, a situation which was obviously not cost-effective.

Forecasting of trends is a difficult business, particularly in the firearms field; one is reminded of Josh Billings' immortal precept 'Never prophesy; for if you prophesy right, nobody will remember, and if you prophesy wrong nobody will forget.' Nevertheless, certain tendencies do seem to be apparent, and will probably continue for some time. The military automatic pistol has now totally replaced the revolver, and the design has coalesced into a 9mm Parabellum with double-action lockwork and a magazine containing at least a dozen cartridges. Not all armies have a weapon meeting this specification, but we suggest that by the end of the century this will be the universal standard sidearm.

Police forces are less certain of what they want; many still adhere to their time-tested revolvers, others have adopted a wide variety of automatic pistols. The difficulty here is that their objective is not so clearly defined as that of the soldier, and they are required to use weapons in circumstances which can, and often do, involve innocent bystanders. So problems of ricochet and penetration loom large in their considerations; these are problems which do not affect military users, and thus simply trans-

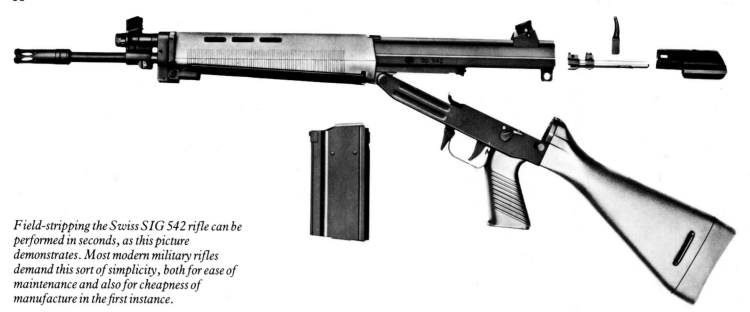

Field-stripping the Swiss SIG 542 rifle can be performed in seconds, as this picture demonstrates. Most modern military rifles demand this sort of simplicity, both for ease of maintenance and also for cheapness of manufacture in the first instance.

ferring military arms across to police forces is not the entire answer, as several British police forces have discovered. Much work is being done, and much more remains to be done, on deciding which is the best ammunition to use, ammunition which will meet the conflicting requirements of effectiveness and safety, lethality and freedom from ricochet, and many other factors.

For sporting use the range of available pistols remains as wide as ever, with something for every taste; 'combat' pistol shooting has risen in popularity during the past five years or so, and this has led to specialist companies developing 'improved' versions of stock pistols, with better sights, better grips, tightened actions and so forth, all aimed at improving accuracy or speed of response to a simulated combat situation. Metallic silhouette shooting is another fast-rising sport which is beginning to show results in actual hardware.

Sporting rifles will, we suspect, show little change; we have already commented on the gradual decline of the really heavy calibers, due to the changes in hunting patterns. Rifles, as a general rule, are circumscribed by such facts of life as weight, size, and the immutable ballistic laws, and where competition is involved by the rules of the particular type of contest, and given all that there is very little room for innovation.

Military rifles are unlikely to make any major steps over the coming two decades.

Most armies have, during the past three or four years, decided on their next generation of rifle, a choice which has been conditioned by the NATO acceptance of the 5.56mm cartridge as their standard. Though NATO rules do not, obviously, apply world-wide, the fact of an item's acceptance by NATO is generally sufficient of a guarantee of its worth to ensure its adoption by many other armies. Even the Soviets appear to have accepted the reduction in caliber, though they have chosen to go their own way in the matter of cartridge design.

Machine guns, as I have outlined above, are in something of a flux due to the conflicting demands made on them; several armies appear to accept 5.56mm as their machine gun caliber, while others have reservations and may well stick to 7.62mm. An interesting feature of the past few years has been the resurgence of interest in the Browning .50-caliber machine gun; this had lain dormant for many years and has been restored to its place by demands for a weapon capable of dealing with the proliferation of light armored vehicles now appearing on the battlefield. In fact, the Browning is not the best choice, but it is the best available weapon; what is really needed is a new cartridge in the .50 region, and then either a redesigned Browning or a totally new gun. When all is said and done, the .50 cartridge is some sixty years old and far beyond any worthwhile revamping.

As to the submachine gun; I really hesi-

tate to say how that is going to develop. There does seem a strong likelihood that it is in for a revival in some armies, but there is an equally strong chance that in others it will be totally extinguished. However there seems little doubt that as a security force weapon it will remain in service. The most likely move will be to a miniaturization of existing designs, borne out by recent news of a 'Mini Uzi', shorter and lighter than the standard Uzi but firing the same ammunition; unfortunately further details have not been received, so I have been unable to include it in the body of the book. Another interesting trend in this field is the adoption of .22 Long Rifle as a submachine gun caliber; I have included the American 180 gun, and stop press news of a Bingham design in .22 calibre has also just been received, a lightweight weapon intended for such tasks as urban policing.

In the sections which follow I have adhered to a standard format, and the facts presented are based on manufacturer's information whenever possible; where this has not been possible it is based upon informed reports or upon examination of the weapons in question. I have tried to handle and fire as many of the weapons described as I could, but this has not always been possible. The opinions are my own, presented in a spirit of constructive analysis; others may differ, since firearms often differ and another student with a different weapon might reach different conclusions.

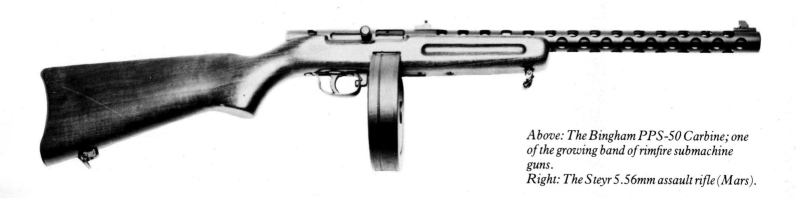

Above: The Bingham PPS-50 Carbine; one of the growing band of rimfire submachine guns.
Right: The Steyr 5.56mm assault rifle (Mars).

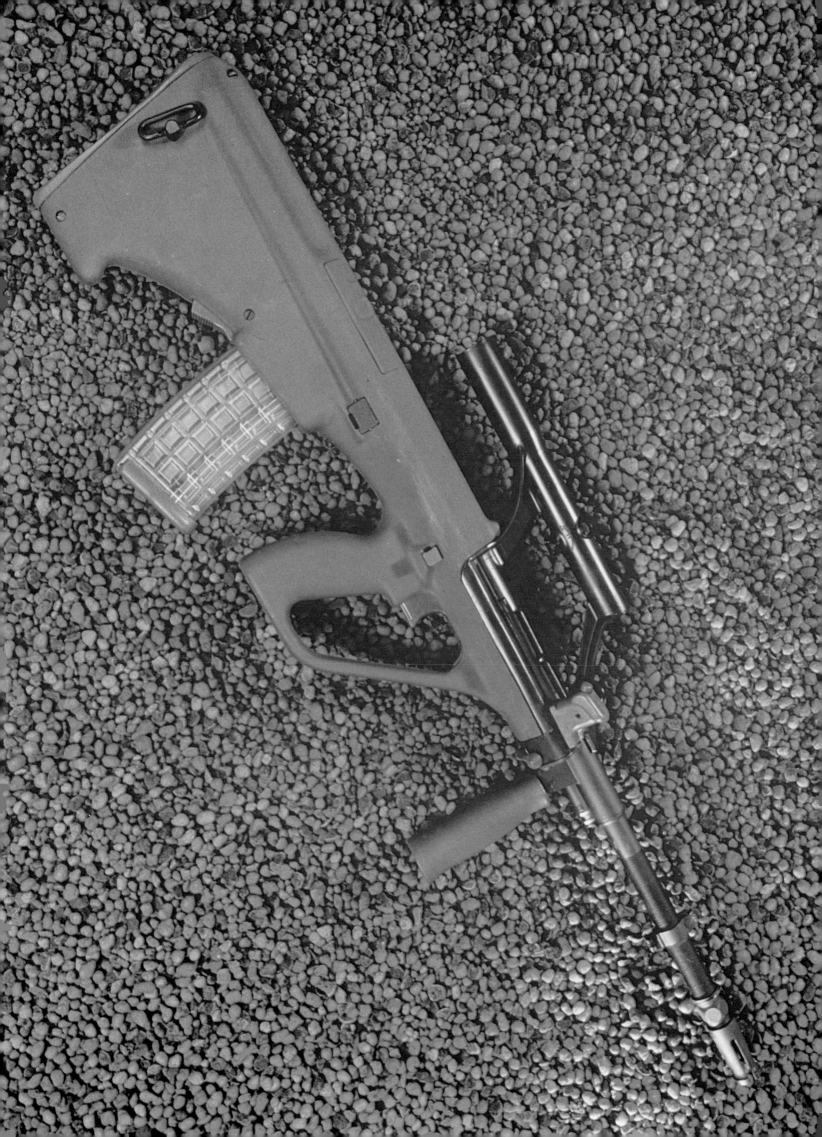

A Swedish Army patrol armed with a 'Miniman' antitank gun and carrying Heckler & Koch G3 rifles.

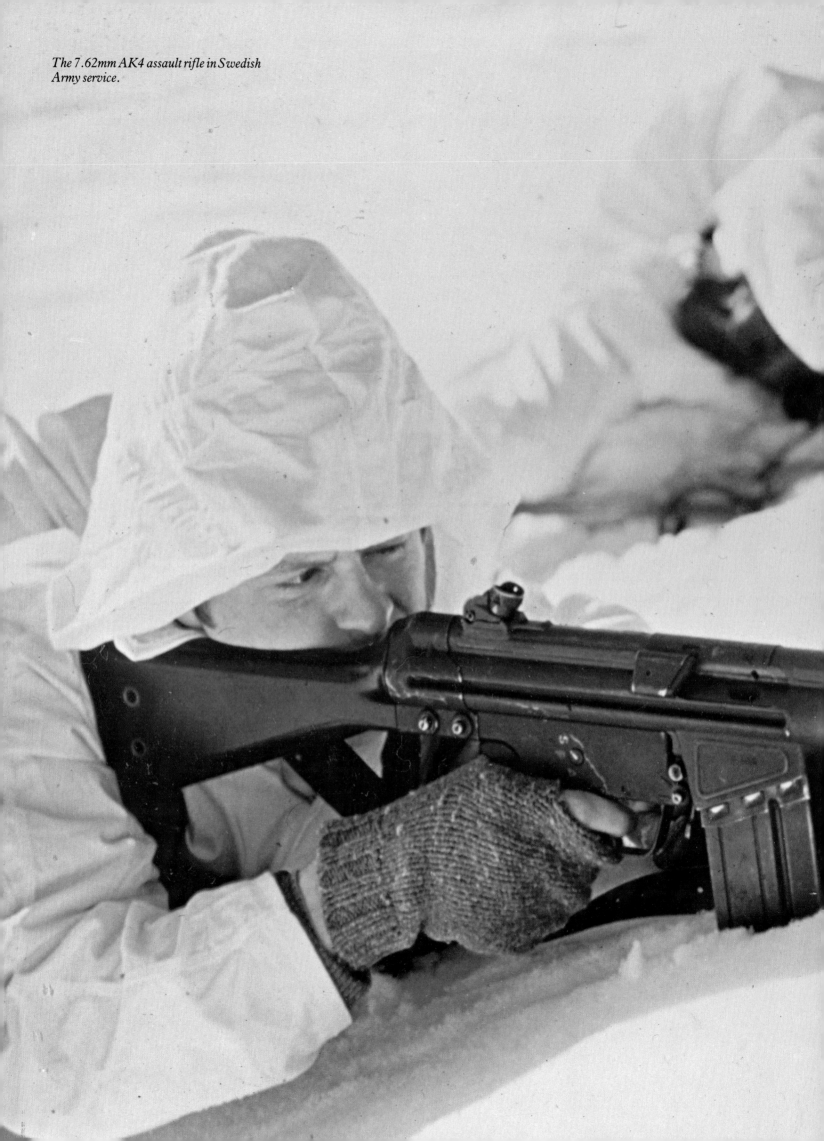

The 7.62mm AK4 assault rifle in Swedish Army service.

British troops firing an L7A1 7.62mm General Purpose Machine Gun (GPMG) in its sustained-fire role.

*Above: The Armi Renato Gamba .38Sp
Trident revolver is based on a German design.*

*Above: The 9mm Walther PPK automatic
pistol – one of the most popular weapons of its
type.*
*Left: A British paratrooper fires a Sterling
L2A3 9mm submachine gun.*

Above: A REXIM submachine gun.
Below: A French infantryman takes aim with his FAMAS 'Trumpet' assault rifle. Note the folded bipod and the long protected sight lying within the carrying handle.
Right: A Steyr MP1 69 machine pistol

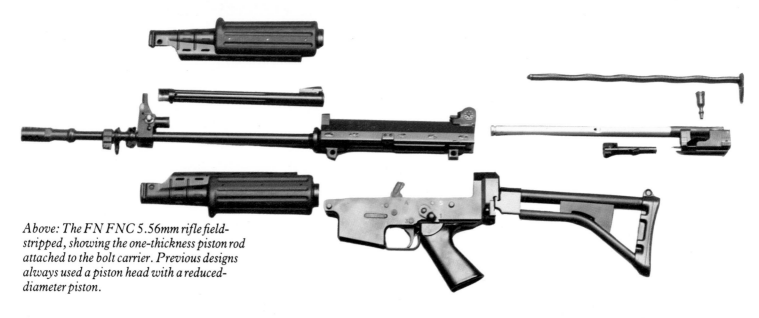

Above: The FN FNC 5.56mm rifle field-stripped, showing the one-thickness piston rod attached to the bolt carrier. Previous designs always used a piston head with a reduced-diameter piston.

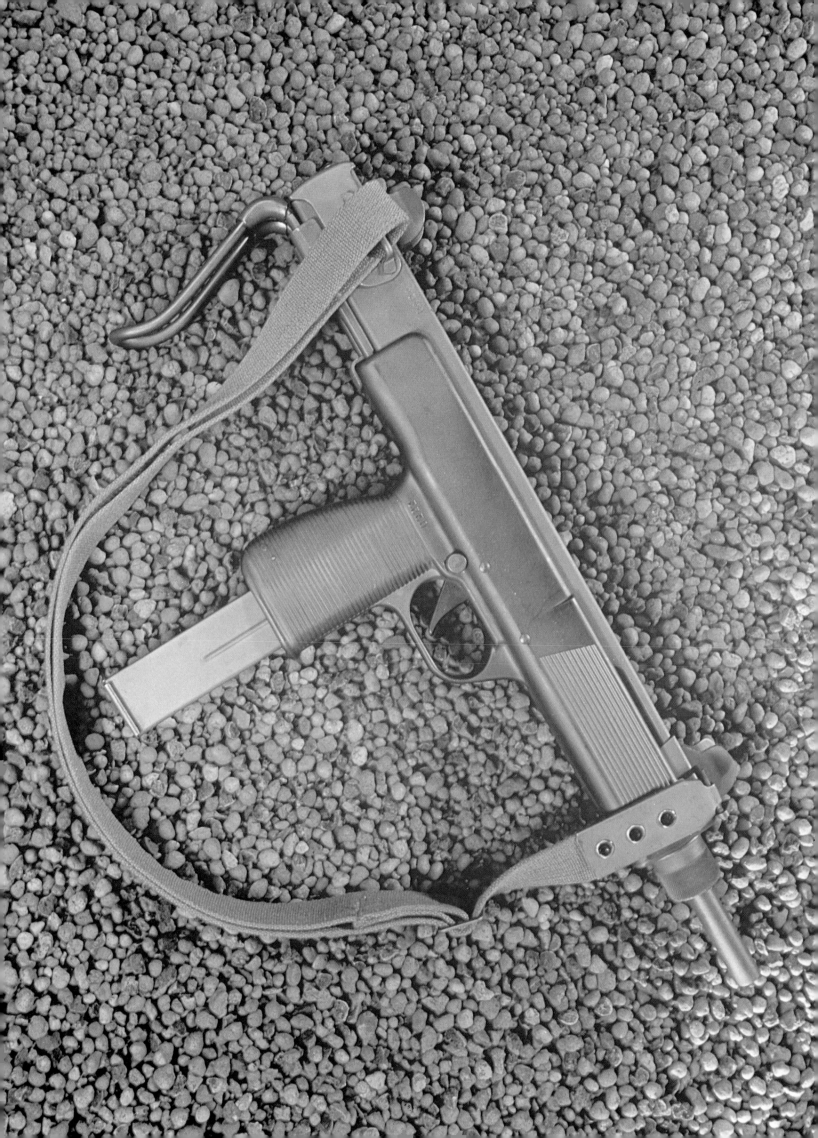

Above: Favorite weapon of terrorists and guerillas, the Soviet AK47 Kalashnikov assault rifle. This particular version is a Chinese-manufactured copy, offered for sale in the world market.

Right: An adapter which allows the firing of blank cartridges at full automatic in a light machine gun. Since there is no bullet, there would be no gas pressure to actuate the gun, so this adapter restricts the muzzle, chokes back the gas, and permits sufficient pressure build-up.

Below: The FN FNC rifle with an anti-personnel grenade slipped over the muzzle and ready to be launched. This combination has a range of up to 550 meters when the rifle is elevated to 45°.

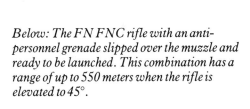

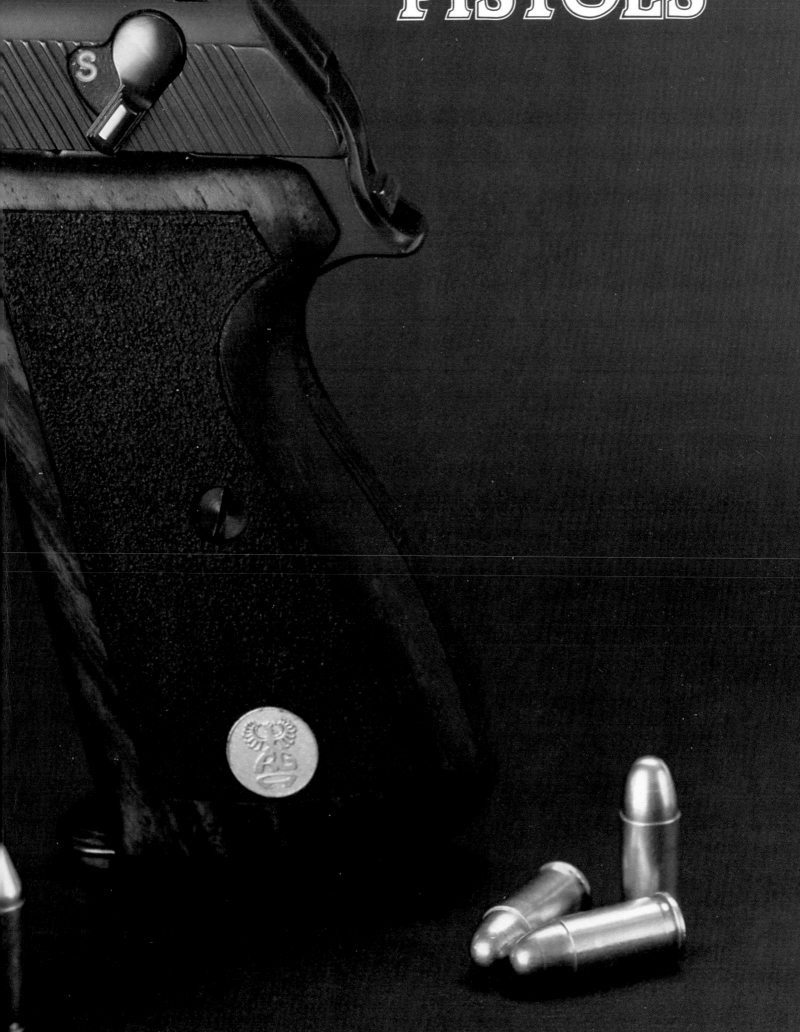

PISTOLS

ASP 9mm Auto Pistol

Manufacturer Armament Systems and Procedures, Appleton, WI 54911, U.S.A.
Type Semi-auto, locked breech, double-action
Caliber 9mm Parabellum
Barrel 3.25in (82.5mm)
Weight 24oz (680gm)
Magazine capacity 7 rounds

Almost 20 years ago the clandestine services of the US Government stated a requirement for a concealable but powerful automatic pistol, and the first response was a cutdown .45 M1911A1 Colt developed by the CIA. While this worked, it could hardly be said to be an elegant solution. It was noisy, had excessive muzzle flash, a magazine capacity of only four shots, and less target effect than the average .38 Special revolver. Another solution was sought, which was to be based on the 9mm Parabellum cartridge, and this led to the design which is now commercially available as the 'ASP', named for the company who make it.

The ASP is actually a re-manufacture. It begins life as a standard Smith & Wesson Model 39 which is then severely cut about. The butt, slide, slide stop and safety catch are all dimensionally reduced and lightening cuts are made in the slide so as to distribute the balance correctly. The barrel is shortened, throated and polished, the feed ramp smoothed and polished, and a custom-built barrel bushing pressed into the slide. New recoil spring and guide are fitted, every edge of the weapon hand-smoothed, and the entire surface coated with 'Teflon' to give a smooth, black, resistant finish. The butt plates are replaced with special models, with that on the left side having a transparent panel which allows the contents of the magazine to be checked. The trigger-guard is given a forward hook and the magazine floor given a finger rest, both aiding the holding of the pistol in combat mode. Finally a 'Guttersnipe' combat sight unit is fitted to the slide. This is a trough with the interior walls colored yellow, and if the sight picture is correct, the target can be seen within three equally-proportioned walls. If the aim is off, then the walls of the sight display an unbalanced picture which indicates the sighting error.

The resulting weapon is not cheap; it is necessary to buy the Model 39 first and then add $350 for the conversion. But for those whose life could depend upon quick and accurate firepower, the price is immaterial and the ASP promises to be the right answer.

Astra Model A-80 Auto Pistol

Manufacturer Astra, Unceta y Cia, Guernica, Spain
Type Locked breech double-action semi-automatic
Caliber 9mm Parabellum
Barrel 3.75in (95mm)
Weight 34.2oz (970gm)
Magazine capacity 15 rounds

The Astra company has been manufacturing automatic pistols since 1908. It has been providing Spanish military and police pistols since 1913 and has thus gained valuable knowledge of practical requirements as opposed to theoretical desires, and this shows in their latest pistol the A-80.

The A-80 is very much in the modern idiom – a double-action weapon with a large magazine. It is compact, simply built and easy to disassemble, yet it is also of a respectable weight so that it points well and balances nicely in the hand. The breech is locked by the normal Browning swinging

Above: The ASP 9mm combat pistol, showing the visibility of the magazine contents.
Right: The 'Guttersnipe' sight, used on the ASP 9mm pistol.
Previous pages: The 7.65mm Mauser HSc mod. 80 produced under license by the Italian firm of Renato Gamba.

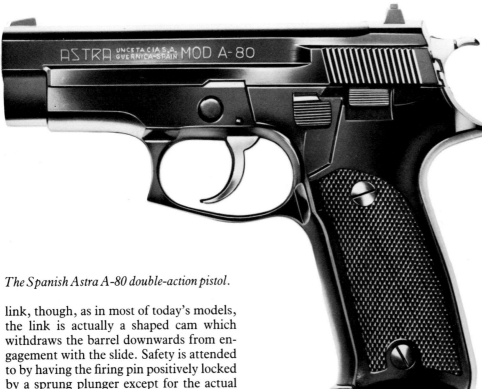

The Spanish Astra A-80 double-action pistol.

link, though, as in most of today's models, the link is actually a shaped cam which withdraws the barrel downwards from engagement with the slide. Safety is attended to by having the firing pin positively locked by a sprung plunger except for the actual moment that the hammer is released by trigger action, at which time a portion of the trigger linkage lifts the plunger out of engagement and frees the firing pin. There is a de-cocking lever on the left side of the frame, its thumb catch just behind the trigger guard. Depressing this drops the hammer to be caught on the rebound notch, after which pulling the trigger will double-action the hammer to full cock and then drop it. An interesting point is that this de-cocking lever can be moved across to the right side for left-handed shooters.

The foresight is a blade with whitened rear face, and the backsight has a white line below the ample notch, so that they can easily be picked up and aligned in poor light. But the rear sight is fixed, except that it could possibly be drifted sideways for zeroing. Even so, the sights appear to be well aligned from the factory and the range performance with a stock model was satisfactory.

The A-80 is also manufactured in .38 Super and .45 ACP chambering; in the latter case the magazine holds nine rounds.

Astra .357 Revolver

Manufacturer Astra, Unceta y Cia, Guernica, Spain
Type Six-shot, solid frame, double-action
Caliber .357 Magnum
Barrel 3, 4, 6 and 8.5in (76, 102, 152 and 216mm)
Weight 40oz (1134gm) (6in barrel)

Astra Unceta have a long history of automatic pistol manufacture, having made the Spanish Army's service sidearm since World War One, but they did not enter the revolver field until the late 1950s, and then

with a relatively cheap line under the name of 'Cadix.' About ten years later, having gained some practical experience, they then produced this .357 Magnum model, an excellent revolver which will stand comparison with anyone's.

Like most Spanish guns, it has a striking resemblance to the Smith & Wesson family. It is a conventional solid-frame weapon with swing-out cylinder, floating firing pin, and with a safety bar included in the lockwork. An unusual point is that the shorter (3 and 4 inch) barreled models have smaller grips than the longer-barreled models; it seems that their theory is that those who buy the short guns want a handy defensive weapon, while those who buy the longer

barrels are looking for target guns and deserve target-style grips. All have fully-adjustable Patridge-style rear sights and ramp foresights.

The fit and finish is first-class; all have fully recessed chambers which enclose the cartridge heads, the walnut grips are neatly checkered, and the metal is well blued and polished to a deep luster. Both hammer spur and trigger are deeply grooved to give them non-slip properties.

The accuracy and reliability of these Astra revolvers is in keeping with their quality of finish. They can be expected to group as tightly as the shooter is capable of holding, and they show no signs of loosening after long wear. Though not inexpensive, they are good value and cost less than many comparable pistols.

Astra .44 Magnum Revolver

Manufacturer Astra, Unceta y Cia, Guernica, Spain
Type Six-shot, double action, solid frame
Caliber .44 Magnum
Barrel 5.93in (150mm)
Weight 45oz (1275gm)

As stated the Astra Unceta company have a long record of manufacturing automatic pistols but they did not go into the revolver business until 1958, and it was several years before they went as far as a .357 Magnum. They have now gone to the limit in revolver calibers in this model, which can also be had in .41 Magnum, .45 Colt and .45 ACP calibers.

The Astra uses a new large frame and, in basic features, follows the Smith & Wesson pattern; a shrouded ejector rod, left side push-forward catch for releasing the cylinder crane and double-action lockwork.

The Astra .357 revolver bears some resemblance to elements of Smith & Wesson design.

The Astra .44 Magnum revolver.

The grip is somewhat large, though this may be felt desirable with such powerful cartridges, but it appears not to be everyone's taste as far as the shape goes, being too broad at the foot.

The foresight is a blade set on a ramp, while the rear sight is an open notch adjustable for elevation and windage. With walnut grips and well-blued metal, it is an impressive revolver and is finished to a high standard. It shoots well, has a smooth trigger action, and is capable of making regular two to three inch groups at 25 yards.

Auto-Mag .44 Auto Pistol

Manufacturer Arcadia Machine & Tool Co., El Monte, CA 91732, U.S.A.
Type Locked breech, semi-automatic
Caliber .44 Auto-Mag or .357 Auto-Mag
Barrel 8.5in (216mm) or 10.5in (267mm)
Weight 3.5lbs (1587gm)
Magazine capacity 7 rounds

The Auto-Mag pistol first appeared in 1970, having been developed in order to fire the .44 Auto-Mag cartridge, a wildcat round based on the .308 Winchester case cut down and fitted with a .44 caliber bullet. The design oscillated between manufacturers for some years, and it finally disappeared from the market in about 1977. It has now been revived and a limited number are to be built until the supply of compo-

nent parts runs out, whereupon the Auto-Mag will finally retire.

The Auto-Mag is a locked breech pistol relying upon a rotating bolt which is controlled by cam tracks in the pistol frame. On firing both barrel and bolt/slide recoil together for a short distance until the bolt is unlocked and the barrel brought to a stop, after which the slide and bolt continue rearward to cock the hammer and begin the cycle over again. The original models were produced with 6.5-in barrels with ventilated ribs; the new models will be offered with 8.5 or 10.5in barrels without ribs. Manufacture is of high-quality stainless steel and the pistols are immensely strong, as they need to be with the loadings involved.

The pistol was originally intended as a powerful hunting weapon, but it appears to have been largely instrumental in assisting the sport of metallic silhouette shooting to gain credence in the U.S.A., and the new models are principally aimed at that sport, hence the longer barrels. The sights are, of course, fully adjustable and the pistol is capable of excellent shooting at 200 meters range.

The two cartridges for which this pistol is made are the .44 AMP and .357 AMP. Both are based on the case of the .308 Winchester (7.62mm NATO) rifle cartridge, cut down and either fitted with a .44 bullet or necked to a smaller mouth diameter and fitted with

a .357 bullet. Either way the result is an extremely 'hot' cartridge; the .44 AMP has a velocity of 1500ft/sec with a 200 grain bullet, the .357 AMP 1725ft/sec with a 140 grain bullet. The only problem is that neither round is commercially manufactured, and anyone contemplating an Auto-Mag should realize that he will have to make his own ammunition.

Bauer .25 Auto Pistol

Manufacturer Bauer Firearms Corp, Fraser, MI 48026, U.S.A.
Type Blowback, semi-automatic
Caliber .25 (6.35mm)
Barrel 2.125in (54mm)
Weight 10oz (284gm)
Magazine capacity 6 rounds

Automatic pistols in .25 calibre arouse mixed feelings; some critics claim that they are liable to annoy an adversary, others claim that provided they are properly used they can be an effective defensive weapon. There is no gainsaying the fact that the .25 cartridge generates about one-third less power than does a .22 Long Rifle cartridge, but on the other hand even 100 Joules of energy (74 foot-pounds) can be lethal if it hits a vital spot. The moral is that if you insist on using a .25 pistol, learn to shoot straight.

The American demand for .25 pistols was usually satisfied by European manufacturers, but the 1968 Gun Control Act, with its minimum size restrictions, put a stop to much of that. This gap is now being filled by native manufacture, and the Bauer is among the best of them. It is modeled on the Browning 'Baby' but unlike that weapon is manufactured in stainless steel. It is striker fired, and has both manual and magazine safety devices. There are fixed sights on the slide, a blade at the front and a notch at the rear, but they appear to be no more than a concession to appearance, since they are very difficult to align due to their small size.

No .25 is particularly accurate, due to their short barrels, and the bullets have a habit of tumbling in flight, but the Bauer puts up a good performance for its class;

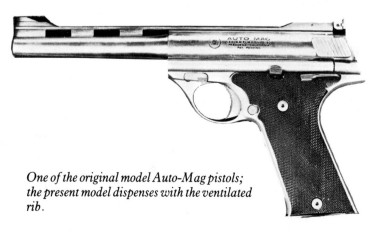

One of the original model Auto-Mag pistols; the present model dispenses with the ventilated rib.

The Bauer .25 pistol, a design based largely on the prewar 'Baby' Browning model.

groups of about five inches can be managed at 10 yards range. Its great asset is conceal-ability; it can be tucked into a vest pocket or carried in a lady's purse, to be produced with considerable moral effect at an appropriate moment.

Benelli Model B-76 Auto Pistol

Manufacturer Benelli Armi SpA., Via della Stazione 50, I-61029, Urbino, Italy
Type Locked-breech double-action semi-automatic
Caliber 9mm Parabellum
Barrel 4¼in (108mm)
Weight (empty) 34oz (970gm)
Magazine capacity 8 rounds

This weapon was introduced in 1977 and was the first military-style pistol to appear from this maker. Benelli have a high reputation for their sporting weapons and this model is produced to an extremely high standard of fit and finish. There are reports that it is to be adopted as a military pistol by some unnamed 'Third World' armies.

The Benelli uses an apparently conventional configuration of slide and frame, with external hammer, double-action lock, and a box magazine inserted into the butt. Mechanically, though, it is unique, having an unusual toggle-locked breech system and a fixed barrel. The breech-block is a separate unit inside the slide, retained by a latch plate at the rear end through which the firing pin passes. Behind the breech block is a small toggle which lies between block and slide, and the block is free to move downward so that a shaped heel can

The Benelli Model B-76 pistol.

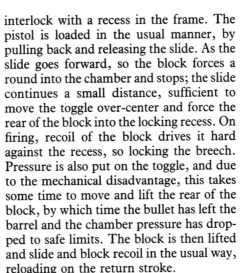

interlock with a recess in the frame. The pistol is loaded in the usual manner, by pulling back and releasing the slide. As the slide goes forward, so the block forces a round into the chamber and stops; the slide continues a small distance, sufficient to move the toggle over-center and force the rear of the block into the locking recess. On firing, recoil of the block drives it hard against the recess, so locking the breech. Pressure is also put on the toggle, and due to the mechanical disadvantage, this takes some time to move and lift the rear of the block, by which time the bullet has left the barrel and the chamber pressure has dropped to safe limits. The block is then lifted and slide and block recoil in the usual way, reloading on the return stroke.

In spite of the apparent complexity, the Benelli is easily and quickly field stripped. The grip is placed at a good shooting angle and the barrel lies close to the hand, reducing the tendency to lift on firing. As a result it handles well and shoots accurately. The sights are combat-style fixed blade and square notch, though the rear sight is in a dove-tail slot and can be moved sideways for zeroing.

The Beretta Model 84 pistol in 9mm Short (.380 Auto) caliber; on the right is the magazine, showing the double-column arrangement of cartridges.

Beretta Models 81 and 84

Manufacturer Armi Beretta SpA, I-25063, Gardone Val Trompia, Italy
Type Blowback double-action semi-automatic
Caliber 7.65mm ACP (Model 81); .380/9mm Short (Model 84)
Barrel 3.81in (97mm)
Weight (empty) 23.5oz (665gm) (Mod 81); 22.5oz (640gm) (Mod 84)
Magazine capacity 12 rounds (Mod 81); 13 rounds (Mod 84)

These two pistols are members of the double-action family which appeared in 1976. They have met with considerable success both in adoption by police and security forces in many parts of the world and in commercial sales.

In many respects they are updated versions of the well-known Model 1934 Beretta which armed the Italian forces until 1945, robust blowback weapons with fixed barrels and with the unique Beretta configuration of cut-away slide over the barrel. However, bringing them up to date has added double-action lockwork and magazines of much greater capacity, with a better-shaped butt frame and walnut grips. The magazine release is in the forward edge of the butt beneath the trigger guard and can be located on the left or right side, as preferred. The safety catch is at the rear of the slide and can be operated from either side. When the chamber contains a cartridge the extractor protrudes on the right-hand side of the slide and shows a red indication; it can also be checked by feel in the dark.

The two models are identical except for their caliber and magazine capacity; due to changes in the magazine follower, the 9mm

Model 84 actually manages to take one more round in the magazine than does the 7.65mm Model 81; the 84 is also slightly lighter, due to the barrel having similar external dimensions but a larger bore.

Beretta Model 92 Auto Pistol

Manufacturer Armi Beretta SpA, I-25063, Gardone Val Trompia, Italy
Type Locked breech, double-action, semi-automatic
Caliber 9mm Parabellum
Barrel 4.92in (125mm)
Weight (empty) 33.5oz (950gm)
Magazine capacity 15 rounds

This appeared in 1976 as the third member of the new double-action family, and it has since been adopted by the Italian forces and by several other armies as their service pistol.

Breech locking is performed by a dropping block beneath the barrel, very similar in operation to that familiar to most people on the Walther P-38. It is a shaped block which is connected at its front to the underside of the barrel and, by lugs at the rear, to the slide, so locking the two together. A shaped heel rests on a transom in the frame, so that the block cannot unlock from the slide. After firing, recoil forces the slide to pull back, but it is restrained by the fact

that the block cannot move down; as the entire barrel and slide unit moves rearward, against the recoil spring, so the locking block moves off the transom and is then free to fall, releasing the slide while the barrel stops. There is ample delay time to permit the bullet to leave the barrel. The return of the slide, reloading the breech, forces the barrel forward and so lifts the block back on to its transom and also into locking engagement with the slide once more.

The extractor is mounted laterally, on the right side, and when the weapon is loaded it protrudes, revealing a red 'chamber-loaded' indication; this can also be felt in the dark, so that there is always a positive indication available. The safety is on the left side and locks both trigger and slide, and there is a half-cock notch on the hammer. The front sight is a simple blade, integral with the slide, while the rear sight is a square notch unit riding in a dovetail slot so that it can be laterally shifted for zeroing.

The Beretta 92 is a well-made, robust and functional military or police weapon. It is also sold in North and South America as the 'Taurus PT-92', marked accordingly, by Taurus S.A. of Sao Paulo, Brazil.

A variant model is the Model 92S which has a slide-mounted safety which, when applied, deflects the firing pin from alignment with the hammer, releases the hammer and breaks the connection between trigger bar and sear. A further variant is the Model 92SB which has the safety lever on both sides of the slide and moves the magazine release from its usual European position at the bottom of the butt to the American position in the front of the butt, just below the trigger-guard; this is normally on the left side, but can be switched to the right if required. Broadly speaking the Model 92SB was developed in response to U.S. military demands and it is doubtful whether it will be continued in production.

The Beretta Model 92S, one of the most reliable military pistols in existence.

Beretta Model 93R Machine Pistol

Manufacturer Armi Beretta SpA, I-25063 Gardone Val Trompia, Italy
Type Locked breech, double-action, semi-automatic with burst-fire facility.
Caliber 9mm Parabellum
Barrel 6.14in (156mm) including muzzle brake
Weight (empty) 41.2oz (1170gm)
Magazine capacity 20 rounds

This is an advanced weapon based on the Model 92 but with several additional features which place it in the 'machine pistol' category. It has been adopted by Italian Special Forces and security police and interest has been expressed in several other countries.

Basically, the pistol is similar to the Model 92 in that it uses a dropping-block locked breech. The principal visible change is the use of a longer barrel which protrudes in front of the slide and has a prominent muzzle brake; there is also a folding front grip, hinged to the frame so that it lies beneath the frame front when not in use or can be folded down to act as a grip for the left (or disengaged) hand. This proves to be more practical than one might think, giving a steadier hold than the more common two-handed butt grip. In addition there is a light metal folding stock unit which can be clipped to the bottom of the butt, and which then converts the pistol into something approaching a light carbine. Finally, the magazine has been lengthened to hold 20 rounds, so that it extends below the bottom of the butt. For those preferring a more elegant shape, the normal Model 92 15-shot magazine can be used.

The reason for all these changes is that under the right butt-plate is a three-round burst controller. The frame-mounted safety catch offers three positions: Safe, single shot, and 3-round burst; placing the catch in this last position permits the firing of three rapid shots for one pressure on the trigger, the cyclic rate of fire being about 110 rounds per minute. This is low by machine pistol standards and therefore there is less disturbance of the aim; moreover the forward hand grip and shoulder stock, used either separately or together, and the damping effect of the muzzle brake, allow the firer firm control of the weapon, and high-speed photography shows that there is relatively little 'climb' during the firing of a burst.

Browning BDA Auto Pistol

Manufacturer Armi Beretta SpA, Gardone Val Trompia, Italy
Marketed by Browning Arms, Rt #1, Morgan, UT 84050, U.S.A.
Type Blow back double-action semi-automatic
Caliber .380/9mm Short
Barrel 3.8in (97mm)
Weight (empty) 23oz (652gm)
Magazine capacity 13 rounds

This pistol resembles the Beretta Model 84 in most respects, and is actually made by Beretta in Italy, but there have been one or two modifications to bring it to the specification demanded by Browning. Another plus feature is that, in the U.S.A., it costs considerably less than an imported Model 84.

The BDA is a conventional blowback automatic pistol, perhaps unusual in having a larger magazine capacity than is common in American pistols. The principal difference between this and the Beretta 84 is the use of an enveloping slide and the addition of a slide-mounted safety and de-cocking lever which operates from both sides of the slide. Depressing this lever lowers the hammer from full- to half-cock position and locks it; once the safety is down the pistol cannot be cocked by thumbing the hammer back. Pulling the trigger allows the hammer to fall from the half-cock to the fired position, without touching the firing pin. Re-

Above: The Beretta 93R in handgun form; the selector is set for single shots and the forward hand grip folded out of the way.

Above and below: Adding accessories makes the Beretta 93R into a machine pistol; here the forward grip is folded down into its action position, the selector is set for three-round bursts, and the buttstock unfolded beneath.

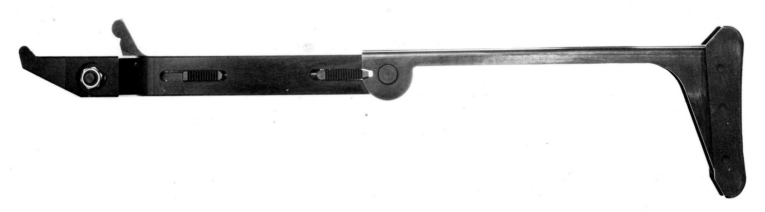

The Browning BDA pistol is a re-worked Beretta, using an enveloping slide instead of the Beretta open-topped design.

leasing the safety allows both thumb-cocking and double-action cock-and-fire action with a single pull on the trigger.

Sights consist of a fixed front sight and a non-adjustable rear sight which is held in a dovetail groove and can be laterally shifted for zeroing. Accuracy is satisfactory, the pistol grouping within a five-inch circle at 50 yards. Finish is excellent, with walnut grips inlaid with the Browning medallion.

Centrum Free Pistol

Manufacturer Centrum, East Germany
Type Competition free pistol, single shot
Caliber .22 Long RF
Barrel 10in (254mm)

Free pistols are principally a European avocation, being specialized single shot .22 weapons designed solely for national and international competition shooting. It is specifically intended for the UIT .22 free pistol contest in which the 10-ring of the target is 2 inches in diameter and the range is fifty meters. In short, it is the ultimate test of shooting ability, and the rules permit virtually any sort of pistol in order to evade any mechanical restriction and concentrate entirely on the shooter's skill. Hence the phrase 'free pistol,' which refers to the lack of restriction on style or type. In general these are hand-built and expensive weapons, vehicles for their owners' and designers' pet theories, but there are a few European gunsmithing firms who make 'stock' free pistols which can be the basis for individual modification.

One of the most recent is the Centrum made in East Germany. It is a single shot weapon using a falling block breech operated by the trigger guard. The breech is opened and the cartridge loaded until it touches the extractor; the block is then closed and seats the cartridge firmly in the chamber. After firing the block is lowered, which ejects the empty case about one-tenth of an inch, after which a separate extractor, on the left of the chamber, allows the case to be pulled a further quarter of an inch from the chamber, after which it can

be flicked out with the finger-nail. Rapid fire is, obviously, not a requirement in this type of contest.

The pistol has a set trigger which is set by a lever on the left side; the trigger itself can be adjusted for reach, travel, backlash and slack without having to dismantle anything. The foresight is mounted on a large ramp, and the blade is secured in place by a screw so that it can easily be changed. The rearsight is fitted on a dovetail extension over the grip; its location can be altered to suit the individual, and it is capable of adjustment for elevation and windage by click-stopped knobs.

The grip is anatomically shaped so that the barrel is low to the hand and thus there is practically no jump or recoil effect. There is also a wooden fore end, though this is for balance and appearance.

Practical firing shows that this weapon, which is a precision machine, needs to be fed with the best ammunition; it appears sensitive to the ammunition used and does not perform well with cheap cartridges. Each gun is supplied with a test target and a five-year guarantee, the target usually showing four or five shots in the 10-ring. These pistols are capable of doing whatever the shooter is capable of, and more than many shooters can manage without some intensive practice.

Charter Arms 'Pathfinder' Revolver

Manufacturer Charter Arms Corp., 430 Sniffens Lane, Stratford, CT 06497, U.S.A.
Type Six-shot, solid-frame, double action revolver.
Caliber .22 Long Rifle RF, or .22 Winchester Magnum RF.
Barrel 6in (152mm)
Weight 22.5oz (638gm)

This is an enlarged version of the .22 Pathfinder introduced in 1972; the earlier weapon had a 3-inch barrel and proved popular as a pack gun. Now with the adoption of a 6in barrel the gun becomes even more versatile.

The pistol uses a steel solid frame and an attractive point is that the walnut grips are of a good size to allow a firm grip, a feature frequently overlooked in this caliber. The swing-out cylinder is released by a catch on the left side of the frame or by pulling the ejector rod forward. The six chambers are individually counterbored and the ejector rod is long enough to push the empty cases well clear of the cylinder face. The foresight is a broad blade and the rear a wide slot; the rear sight is fully adjustable for elevation and windage, though demanding a small screwdriver to make the adjustment. The double-action trigger pull is light and smooth, while the single-action release is

sharp, requiring 3-4lbs pressure to let off. Firing is by a floating firing pin and transfer bar system, by means of which the hammer cannot possibly contact the firing pin unless the trigger has been correctly pulled.

The pistol is available in either .22LR or .22WMRF chambering, though the cylinders are not interchangeable. The .22RF version will, of course, shoot .22 Long and .22 Short equally well. Either chambering gives perfectly good accuracy; tests show that 1½-inch groups at 25 yards can be considered the normal performance in skilled hands. The length of barrel and angle of grips make this a good pointing pistol.

Charter Arms .44 Target Bulldog

Manufacturer Charter Arms Inc., Stratford, CT 06497, U.S.A.
Type Five-shot, solid frame, double-action
Caliber .44 Special
Barrel 4in (102mm)
Weight 20oz (567gm)

Charter Arms started their career by producing robust no-frills revolvers for lawmen and others, and one of their notable innovations was the .44 Bulldog, a short-barreled but powerful pistol which revived the .44 Special cartridge. This is a highly serviceable round which has tended to be overlooked in recent years, being edged out by the .44 Magnum, and it had a good reputation for accuracy. In response to various enquiries and requests, Charter have now redesigned the Bulldog to take maximum advantage of the cartridge's capabilities.

The Target Bulldog differs from the original Bulldog in having a one-inch longer barrel, complete with shroud for the ejector rod, and in having a fully adjustable rear sight. It is also slightly heavier, and the net result of the extra length and weight is a revolver which is rather more controllable than the original and which is sufficiently accurate to shoot two-inch groups at 25 yards all day. Lengthening the barrel has improved the velocity and consistency and has also cut down slightly on the muzzle blast, making the pistol more comfortable to shoot.

For those who consider the .44 Special a little too much, the Target Bulldog is also available in .357 Magnum caliber.

The Charter Arms 'Pathfinder' revolver in basic form.

Chinese Type 64 Silenced

Manufacturer Chinese State Arsenals
Type Selective semi-automatic or single shot, blowback, with integral silencer
Caliber 7.65mm (.32, special chambering)
Barrel 4.88in (124mm)
Weight 44.8oz (1270gm)
Magazine capacity 8 rounds

This remarkable weapon is quite unique and appears to have only one function in life, that of assassination. It is chambered for a special 7.65×17mm rimless cartridge with a low-velocity loading; it cannot be used with commercial .32 ACP semi-rimmed ammunition.

The Type 64 can be used either as a manually-loaded single shot pistol or as a

The Charter Arms 'Target Bulldog'.

The Chinese Type 64 silenced assassination pistol, showing the bulbous appearance of the integral silencer.

Dan Wesson's 'Pistol Pac', showing the alternative barrels which can be rapidly fitted to the basic frame.

blowback semi-automatic. For the utmost silence a selector bar in the upper part of the slide is pushed to the left and this rotates the bolt, locking it into lugs in the breech. When the pistol is fired the breech remains closed and can be opened only by pushing the selector across and manually retracting the slide. If the selector is left in its right-hand position, then the bolt does not rotate, nor does it lock, and when the pistol is fired the slide blows back in the conventional manner.

Silence is achieved partly by the special ammunition, which ensures sub-sonic velocity of the bullet, and partly by the built-in silencer. The casing which surrounds the barrel extends in front of the muzzle; the gases escaping from the muzzle behind the bullet are expanded into a wire-mesh cylinder surrounded by an expanded metal sleeve, while the bullet passes through a number of rubber discs which prevent the following gas escaping to the outside. When the breech is locked, the pistol is extremely quiet; with the breech unlocked the noise is somewhat greater due to the clatter of the slide moving backwards, but the report is still silenced.

Czech CZ75 Auto Pistol

Manufacturer Ceskoslovenska Zbrojovka a.s., Uhersky Brod, Czechoslovakia
Type Locked breech, double-action semi-automatic
Caliber 9mm Parabellum
Barrel 4.72in (120mm)
Weight (empty) 34.5oz (980gm)
Magazine capacity 15 rounds

This is a military-style pistol produced for commercial sale throughout the world; it is not known whether it has been officially adopted by the Czech Army but this is extremely doubtful, given their adherence to Soviet patterns and calibers for military arms.

The CZ-75 uses the familiar Browning action of locked breech in which the barrel has lugs above the chamber which engage in recesses in the slide; a shaped cam in a lump beneath the chamber moves across the slide stop pin during recoil, thus pulling the

barrel down and withdrawing the lugs from the recesses, so freeing the slide to move to the rear and complete the extraction and reloading cycle. The pistol differs slightly from the usual Browning design by having a deep-waisted frame and the slide guide rails on the inside of this section, so that the shallow rear portion of the slide moves within the frame.

The external hammer is cocked during the recoil stroke in the usual manner, but there is a double-action lock which permits firing the first round from a hammer-down condition. The safety is on the frame and merely locks trigger and hammer; there is no hammer-drop facility. The sights are fixed military pattern, and the foresight is rather small, making deliberate shooting rather difficult. Nevertheless, the CZ-75 is accurate and consistent, and with adjustable sights fitted would make a reasonable competition weapon. The fit and finish are good and the double-action trigger movement is particularly good, being light and with consistent pull-off points. In practical tests it has been shown that the pistol will accept practically any military or commercial ammunition without malfunction.

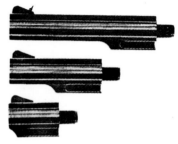

Dan Wesson Pistol-Pac

Manufacturer Dan Wesson Arms, Monson, MA 01057, U.S.A.
Type Six-shot, solid frame, double-action
Caliber .357 Magnum
Barrel 2, 4, 6 and 8in (See text) (51, 102, 152 and 203mm)
Weight 36oz (1020gm) (4in barrel)

Dan Wesson revolvers are not new, but the Pistol Pac concept is so different that it deserves a place in any listing.

The Dan Wesson Company began in 1968 and rapidly made a name for its unique revolvers. The unusual feature was that the barrels were removeable and could be changed for others of different length, so

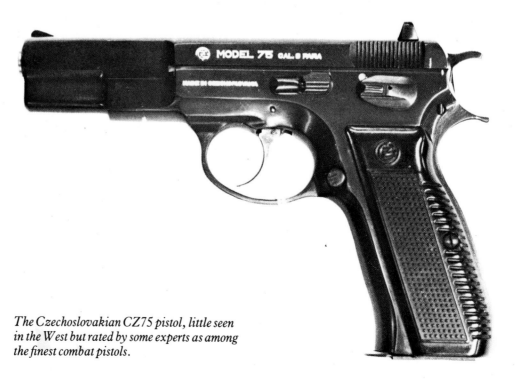

The Czechoslovakian CZ75 pistol, little seen in the West but rated by some experts as among the finest combat pistols.

The Dan Wesson revolver is a handsome weapon; this view indicates the barrel and jacket construction.

that, for example, one could have an 8 inch barrel for target shooting and a 2 inch barrel for home defense, changing them around as required. The basic action is a solid framed double-action revolver; the barrel screws into the front of the frame in conventional manner, but it is then concealed by a jacket, carrying foresight and ejector rod shroud, which slips over the barrel and is then secured by a retaining nut screwed on to the muzzle of the barrel so as to hold the jacket firmly in place and place the barrel under tension. The jacket is automatically aligned with the foresight upright, and sight placement remains constant when barrels are changed. The use of a feeler gage allows the user to ensure that the correct breech-to-cylinder clearance is maintained.

While producing a variety of revolvers in calibers from .22 to .44 Magnum, the Wesson system is best seen in their unique Pistol Pac, a package in which the basic revolver is supplied complete with four barrels, two sets of grips (service and target) plus a block of wood for carving a third set to your own specification, and a stripping tool for removing the jacket and barrel. All this is neatly packed into a hand case lined with sponge rubber. The barrels provided are 2, 4, 6 and 8 inches in length. In .357 Magnum chambering the Model 15-2 is standard and it is supplemented by the 15-2 VH which has heavier barrels and jackets with ventilated ribs.

Dan Wesson revolvers have a high reputation for accuracy and reliability. The Pistol-Pac idea allows the shooter to have the best of several choices at his fingertips at all times.

Detonics .45

Manufacturer Detonics .45 Associates, Seattle, WA 98101, U.S.A.
Type Locked breech semi-automatic
Caliber .45 ACP
Barrel 3.5in (89mm)
Weight 30oz (850gm)
Magazine capacity 6 rounds

We have observed elsewhere the interest in developing abbreviated automatic pistols capable of firing the .45 ACP cartridge and yet capable of concealment, and of these the Detonics is probably the best American example of the class. Though based generally on the Colt M1911A1 there are several differences, necessitated because of the reduction in size.

The frame, mainspring housing and butt have all been shortened, so that the magazine capacity is reduced to six shots; the standard M1911A1 magazine can still be inserted and used, but it will protrude about one inch from the bottom of the butt. While the 'swinging link' locking system is still used, and there are still two lugs on the barrel to lock into the slide, the barrel is shorter and flared-out towards the muzzle. There is no barrel bush, and the tapering section of the barrel allows it to be centered in the slide during counter-recoil. The return spring and guide have been considerably changed; there are two concentric return springs, and as the slide recoils so the spring guide protrudes from the front cap.

There is no grip safety and the hammer has been given a somewhat different shape to avoid it nipping the hand during recoil; the rear of the slide has been re-shaped so as to facilitate thumb-cocking with this hammer, which has led to the rear sight being moved forward. The sights are Patridge type, with square front blade and square rear notch; the rear leaf can be drifted sideways for windage corrections but there is no elevation adjustment. With such a weapon, though, 'instinctive' shooting is more the order of the day, and the sights will not be used all that often.

In use the Detonics is not unpleasant to shoot; the designers have been sensible in not paring the weight too far, so that there is still sufficient mass to assist resistance to recoil, and the short barrel reduces the velocity and energy. Accuracy is on the same order as that of any standard .45 ACP pistol in 'out of the box' condition, and in simulated combat conditions, firing two-handed, it proved to be convenient and capable of delivering shots on the target, which, in the last analysis, is what it is designed to do.

The Detonics .45 pistol, probably the ultimate in compact large-caliber semi-automatics.

Fabrique Nationale FN35DA Auto Pistol

Manufacturer Fabrique Nationale d'Armes de Guerre, Herstal, Belgium
Type Locked breech double-action, semi-automatic

	FN35DA & FA	Compact
Caliber	9mm Parabellum	9mm Parabellum
Barrel	4.64in (118mm)	3.78in (96mm)
Weight, unloaded	30oz (850gm)	25oz (708gm)
Magazine capacity	14	7

The Fabrique Nationale GP35 pistol has been in military use since 1935 and is now in service with some 55 countries; in many respects it is the standard against which other military pistols are measured. Fabrique Nationale know this, and they are aware that only by constant development will they maintain their position, and as a result they have now developed some new and improved models. These use the same basic design and parts, but all have special features which fit them into some particular aspect of service.

The Model 35DA is simply the old GP35 with the addition of a double-action lock and a safety lever which allows the hammer to be lowered safely on to the loaded chamber. It therefore operates in the usual manner of this class of pistol; the weapon is loaded and charged by operating the slide, the safety is set, lowering the hammer; and when necessary the safety is released and the trigger pulled to cock and drop the hammer.

This is satisfactory for most of the time, but there are occasions when a fraction of a second saved would mean the difference between success and failure; this is particularly the case in police actions against terrorists and criminals. For this situation the Model 35FA has been developed, the letters 'FA' meaning 'Fast Action'. The only change lies in the assembly of the hammer, which is now in two pieces, the hammer itself which is loosely pivoted about its axis pin, and an 'inertia ring' which is pivoted about the same axis but which is under the influence of the hammer spring and the trigger. When the slide is drawn back, either by hand or by firing, the hammer is rotated back and cocked in the usual way, but as the slide returns the hammer is free to move back with it, leaving only the inertia ring cocked. When the firer now draws the pistol and presses the

Unadorned and severe, the new FN double action service pistol in its basic form.

trigger, the action releases the inertia ring; this flies round and hits the hammer with a blow sufficient to drive it forward to depress the firing pin and fire the chambered cartridge. Due to the light action required to release the inertia ring, the trigger release is extremely fast and light, and trials have shown that the hit probability of the average firer is more than doubled in comparison with a normal double-action pistol.

The third model is the 'Compact', and the object here has been to provide a pistol which is small enough to go into a pocket but which still has the power of a full-calibre holster pistol. It consists of the standard mechanism, adapted to single-action, double-action or 'fast action' working, with the barrel and slide shortened by 27mm and the butt shortened by 37mm. There is a specially shortened magazine holding 7 shots. The standard 14-shot magazine can still be inserted into the butt and used, though it will, of course, extend well beyond the bottom of the butt and cancel out much of the compactness. The pistol contains 45 components of which 32 are standard, six are modified standard, and only seven are specially made for this model. So far as I am aware, this compact version has not yet been adopted by any military or police force, though it is understood that several are evaluating it.

Fabrique Nationale FN140DA Auto Pistol

Manufacturer Fabrique Nationale d'Armes de Guerre, Herstal, Belgium
Type Blowback, double-action, semi-automatic
Caliber .380 Auto/9mm Short; .32 ACP/7.65mm
Barrel 3.81in (97mm)
Weight 22.5oz (640gm)
Magazine capacity 13 rounds (9mm/.380) 12 rounds (7.65mm/.32)

This is a recent introduction by Fabrique Nationale and is intended as a general purpose defense weapon or for use by police and security forces. It uses a steel slide and alloy frame to keep the weight low and has a large magazine capacity, of the sort more commonly found in major-caliber military weapons. It has already been adopted by Belgian and several other European police forces.

The pistol is a simple fixed-barrel blowback in general form, though of extremely

The FN140DA, which resembles the Browning BDA and is yet another variation of the Beretta 81/84 design.

high-grade workmanship and reliability. It has a double-action lock and the trigger-guard is particularly large, permitting use in gloved hands. There is a complex safety system; the safety catch is mounted on the slide and has operating levers on both sides. On depressing the catch the firing pin is retracted into a 'neutral' position – with both ends concealed within its tunnel – and securely locked; the hammer is then dropped on to the rebound notch. To fire, the safety is released and the trigger pulled through to cock and release the hammer.

Any resemblance between this and the Beretta 84 is far from coincidence, since this is basically the Beretta 84 with some slight changes, notably the use of an all-enveloping slide instead of the open-topped slide which is virtually a Beretta trademark. There are also strong similarities between this and the Browning BDA sold in the U.S.A.

Hammerli 215 Target Auto Pistol

Manufacturer Hammerli SA, Lenzberg, Switzerland
Type Blowback semi-automatic target
Caliber .22 Long Rifle RF
Barrel Variable
Weight Variable
Magazine capacity 8 rounds

The Hammerli company have been in the target pistol business for many years and produce some of the world's finest competition weapons. Unfortunately, due to the strength of the Swiss franc they tend to be very expensive outside Switzerland, which did nothing for Hammerli's sales. As a result they decided to produce a weapon which, while remaining high quality, would be competitive in price.

The Model 214 resembles the older Model 208 in being a chunky semi-automatic using a heavy fixed barrel and a short recoiling slide moving in short frame rails. The trigger guard is a separate component and acts as a slide latch. The rear sight is held on a saddle unit which locks to the outside of the frame and straddles the recoiling slide. Since this would prevent gripping the slide in the normal way, it is made with extended sides which stretch forward, alongside the barrel, and have finger grips for cocking and unloading. The sight saddle unit has to be removed to strip the pistol, but the construction is such that it automatically returns to the pre-set zero when replaced. The pistol is hammer fired. The grips are of hard wood, anatomically shaped and have an adjustable palm rest.

The front sight blade can be easily changed, and blades of various widths are available; the rear sight can also be changed for different widths of slot and is fully adjustable. The trigger pull is smooth, with a consistent pull-off point. A balance weight is fitted beneath the muzzle; it can be adjusted or changed by use of an Allen key.

On the range this pistol performs as Hammerli products are expected to perform, firing with absolute accuracy and reliability. The only concession to price has been in the external finish which is not quite so luxurious as in previous products from this firm, but the performance is in no way diminished.

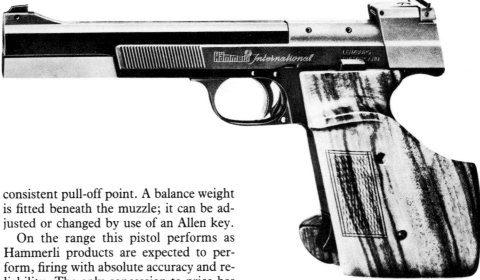

Above: The Hammerli target pistols have a world-wide reputation for accuracy and for winning international competitions.

Right: The Heckler & Koch P7 reduced to its basic components. Note the spring guide rod attached to the slide, which acts as a recoil buffer and delays breech opening.

Heckler & Koch Model P7 (PSP)

Manufacturer Heckler & Koch GmbH, D-7238 Oberndorf/Neckar, West Germany
Type Delayed blowback, semi-automatic
Caliber 9mm Parabellum
Barrel 4.13in (105mm)
Weight (empty) 27.7oz (785gm)
Magazine capacity 8 rounds

This unusual pistol was developed in response to a set of demands drawn up by the West German Federal Police authority. The principal demand was that the weapon should be rapid into action, without any delay necessitated by moving safety catches or cocking hammers, yet totally safe while being carried loaded or if accidentally dropped. These aims have been achieved in an unconventional way.

The P7 (originally called the PSP for 'Polizei Selbstlader Pistole) is a pocket or holster weapon, relatively small, but firing

a powerful cartridge. For this reason it demands some form of breech locking, and this is done by gas pressure. The slide has the usual recoil spring beneath it, with a guide rod inside the spring. But this guide rod is carefully machined and as the slide recoils it moves inside a close-fitting cylinder lying in the frame above the trigger. A port between this cylinder and the barrel allows high-pressure gas to flow in and fill the cylinder when the pistol is fired; this pressure resists the rearward movement of the recoil spring guide rod, so delaying the rearward movement of the slide. Once the bullet has left the barrel and the gas pressure drops, the rod can move back, forcing the gas out of the cylinder and into the barrel and thence out to atmosphere. Thereafter the action is that of any other blowback automatic pistol.

In order to carry the weapon safely in a loaded condition, the firing pin is not cocked during the recoil stroke as is usual; instead it is controlled by a grip forming the front edge of the butt. When the firer grasps the butt and squeezes this grip, the firing pin is cocked; there is no need for him to keep squeezing, since the grip engages in the cocked position. Once he releases his grip, however, the pistol is de-cocked. It

can thus be carried safely with a round in the chamber and brought into action with no delay; if, once cocked, the shooter drops it, it is uncocked before it hits the floor.

The sights are fixed, but the foresight can be changed and the rear sight moved sideways to zero the weapon. Both sights have inlaid white dots to assist in aligning in poor visibility and it is possible to have 'Betalight' luminous markers fitted for night firing. Disassembly is easy, though it requires the use of a special stripping tool.

Heckler & Koch P9S Auto Pistol

Manufacturer Heckler & Koch GmbH, D-7238 Oberndorf/Neckar, West Germany
Type Locked breech double-action semi-automatic
Caliber 9mm Parabellum
Barrel 4in (102mm)
Weight (empty) 30.8oz (875gm)
Magazine capacity 9 rounds

The Heckler & Koch P9S is a military and police pistol using an unusual breech locking system derived from the company's highly successful G3 rifle. The P9S has been adopted by West German armed

forces and police forces and has been widely sold throughout the world. Some have been manufactured in 7.65mm Parabellum chambering and also in .45 ACP chambering for export to the U.S.A., but the 9mm Parabellum version is by far the most common.

The roller locking system for the breech relies on a two-part breech block which is held closed by two small rollers which engage in recesses in the barrel extension. The rollers are carried on the forward, lightweight, portion of the block and are forced outwards into engagement by the action of the rear portion of the block which is actually part of the slide. When the pistol is fired, the light portion, impelled by the pressure on the cartridge case, attempts to move backwards, but the inertia of the slide keeps the rollers forced outwards and the block section locked to the barrel. As the inward pressure on the rollers, due to the pressure on the forward section of the block, gradually overcomes the inertia of the slide, so the bullet has sped up the barrel and left, allowing chamber pressure to drop to safe levels before the rollers move in and the slide and breech block assembly is free to move.

The pistol has an internal hammer, with a protruding indicator pin at the rear of the

The Heckler & Koch P9S, showing the decocking thumb lever just behind the trigger aperture.

frame which extends when the hammer is cocked. There is a thumb-operated hammer release and re-cocking lever on the left side, allowing the hammer to be lowered under control on to a loaded chamber or rapidly cocked from the 'down' position. The barrel has a 'polygonal bore' in which the four grooves (six in .45 ACP caliber) are merged into the rest of the bore so that the final result resembles a flattened circle. The manufacturers claim that this reduces friction and bullet deformation and promotes a somewhat higher velocity.

Two variant models exist; the P9, now discontinued, was the same pistol but with conventional single-action lock; the P9S 'Sport' Competition Model has a longer barrel with balance weight, adjustable trigger stop, fine-adjustment rear sight and an anatomical wooden grip. The barrel is 5.5in (140mm) long, leading to a slight increase in muzzle velocity; with barrel counterweight fitted and a full magazine it weighs 45.2oz (1290gm).

Heckler & Koch Model VP70 & VP70Z Auto Pistol

Manufacturer Heckler & Koch GmbH, D-7238 Oberndorf/Neckar, West Germany
Type Blowback semi-auto & machine pistol
Caliber 9mm Parabellum
Barrel 4.56in (116mm)
Weight (empty) 29oz (820gm)
Magazine capacity 18 rounds

The VP70 is another unusual design; firstly because it fires a heavy military cartridge in the blowback mode, and secondly because it can be turned into a machine pistol with three-round burst facility by simply attaching a shoulder stock. It has been purchased by military and police forces in several unnamed countries, and has also had considerable commercial success in Africa and the Middle East.

The VP70 manages to get 18 rounds in the magazine without being unduly bulky, and though the blowback action is quite conventional, the pistol is hammerless and is not cocked during the recoil stroke. Instead, the trigger has a somewhat long and slow pull and the firing pin is cocked during this movement, to be released at the end of the pull. The cocking movement gives a distinct 'first pressure' feel, followed by a positive check, after which there is a quite crisp let-off. As with the company's P7 model, the object behind this mechanism is to have a weapon which can be safely carried in the loaded condition but brought rapidly into action without having to operate safety devices or cock a hammer.

The holster-stock is a plastic structure which can be clipped into a slot in the back of the butt and snapped onto a clip at the

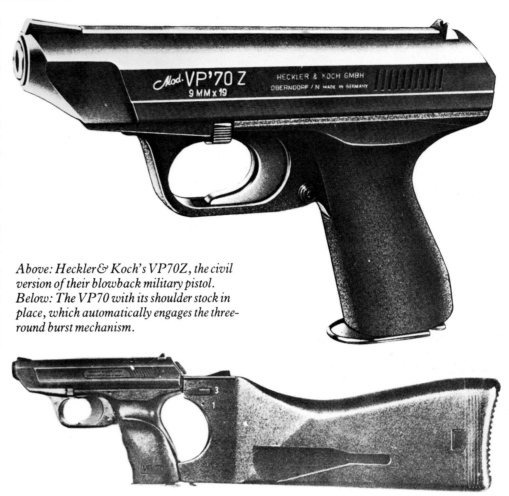

Above: Heckler & Koch's VP70Z, the civil version of their blowback military pistol. Below: The VP70 with its shoulder stock in place, which automatically engages the three-round burst mechanism.

rear of the frame. This automatically operates a catch which brings a three-round burst mechanism into a serviceable condition. A change lever on the stock selects single shots or bursts. With the stock attached the VP70 thus becomes a species of automatic carbine, while without it it is a straightforward single shot pistol.

Due to legal problems, Heckler & Koch found that exporting the VP70 to the U.S.A. was beset with difficulties, and so they developed the VP70Z. This is the same pistol but without the burst-fire facility and shoulder stock and with the addition of a cross-bolt safety catch in the bottom of the trigger guard.

High Standard Sentinel Mark I Revolver

Manufacturer High Standard Inc., East Hartford, CT 06108, U.S.A.
Type Nine-shot solid-frame double-action
Caliber .22 Long Rifle RF
Barrel 2, 4 or 6in (50, 102, 152mm)
Weight 23oz (652gm) with 4in barrel

The High Standard company made their reputation with their automatic pistols and turned to revolvers in the middle 1950s. Their first Sentinel of 1955 used an alloy frame, and in later years steel-framed designs were introduced. The current Sentinel Mark I uses investment cast steel

for the frame, checkered walnut stocks, and various barrel options to give a sound and practical result.

The various barrels can best be summarized as follows: a 2 inch with shroud for ejector rod and fixed sights; a 4 inch heavy barrel with shroud, adjustable sights; or a 6 inch barrel, no shroud and adjustable sights, this latter version being called the 'Camp Gun.' All are solid frame revolvers with swing-out cylinder, and in this new model the cylinder can be removed and replaced with an auxiliary cylinder chambered for .22 Winchester Magnum RF cartridges. The drill for removal is not something I would wish to attempt on a cold day in the middle of the mountains, but, in fairness, it is not something you

The High Standard 'Sentinel Mark III' revolver.

would often wish to do; I can visualize fitting the .22LR cylinder for some practise, then changing to the .22WMR cylinder before taking to the woods.

Without wishing to be accused of sexism, I would suggest that this would be a very good pistol for ladies; this is because of the shape and size of the frame, both well-suited to small hands. The trigger action is smooth in both single and double action, and the gun points well.

Accuracy is quite good with .22 Long Rifle, rather less good with the Magnum round; this is not the fault of the pistol but is the natural result of firing a basically rifle cartridge from a short barrel. Admittedly, the .22LR is also a rifle round, but the combustion characteristics of the propellant are somewhat different to the .22WMR, and I feel certain that this reflects on the accuracy. With .22LR though, the Sentinel performs well at 25 yards range, giving groups under three inches. .22WMR groups were around four inches; but it is probable that the 6in barrel model might improve on this. Altogether a good practical pistol.

High Standard 'Survival Pack' Auto Pistol

Manufacturer High Standard Sporting Firearms, 31 Prestige Park Circle, East Hartford, CT 06108, U.S.A.
Type Blowback, semi-automatic
Caliber .22 Long Rifle RF
Barrel 5.5in (114mm)
Weight 2lb 13.5oz (1290gm)
Magazine capacity 10 rounds

The High Standard company has been making variations on its basic automatic pistol for many years, and the 'Survival Pack' is a new version of their popular 'Sharpshooter' pistol which is, as the name implies, intended for the outdoorsman.

The basic High Standard weapon is a fixed-barrel semi-automatic using a short slide in the blowback mode, and it is a style perfected over long years to the point where

it is utterly reliable and predictable. In this version the barrel is a heavyweight 'bull' type, the grips are checkered walnut, and the entire pistol is finished in a corrosion-resistant electro-nickel finish which is attractive and which will demand the minimum of maintenance in use. The operating springs are of stainless steel, and the barrel latch mechanism has been strengthened, both in line with the robust use foreseen for the pistol.

The foresight is a fixed blade and the rear sight is adjustable for elevation and windage and has a Patridge-type square notch. The trigger has a smooth pull and crisp let-off at about 2lbs weight. Although not a target weapon, the Survival Pack is as accurate as many rifles over median ranges, due to its barrel length and weight, is well-balanced, and appears to be a sensible instrument for its designated role. With suitable ammunition two inch groups from rest at 25 yards should not be difficult.

Korth .357 Magnum

Manufacturer Willi Korth Sportwaffen-Herst, D-2418 Ratzeburg, West Germany
Type Six-shot, double-action, solid-frame
Caliber .357 Magnum
Barrel 3in (76mm); 6in (152mm)
Weight 35oz (992gm) with 3in barrel

The firm of Willi Korth is little known outside Germany; it is a subsidiary of the Dynamit-Nobel group and has produced limited numbers of sporting weapons in the past. It is now exporting a revolver which, at well over $1000, must qualify as the most expensive handgun in existence.

The Korth .357 Magnum is a conventional solid frame pistol with swing-out cylinder with some likeness to the Colt Python. Under the skin, however, there are some interesting differences. The barrel, for example, is a separate component shrouded within a steel jacket which also

Above: Another Model of the Korth .357, together with a 'ghost' view of the mechanism.

Below: The High Standard 'Survival pack'.

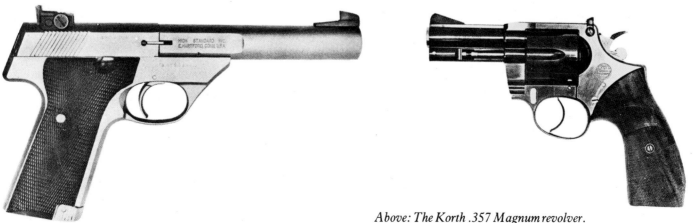

Above: The Korth .357 Magnum revolver.

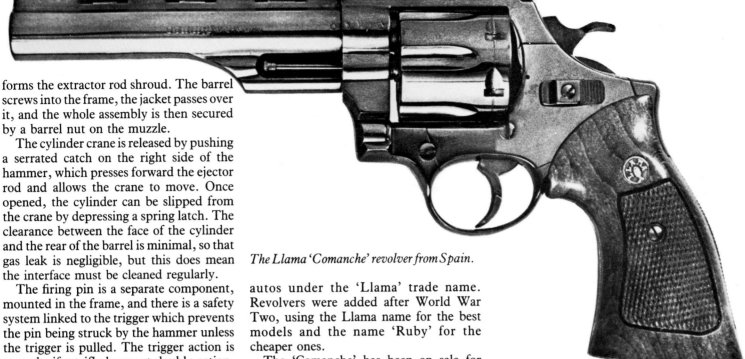

The Llama 'Comanche' revolver from Spain.

forms the extractor rod shroud. The barrel screws into the frame, the jacket passes over it, and the whole assembly is then secured by a barrel nut on the muzzle.

The cylinder crane is released by pushing a serrated catch on the right side of the hammer, which presses forward the ejector rod and allows the crane to move. Once opened, the cylinder can be slipped from the crane by depressing a spring latch. The clearance between the face of the cylinder and the rear of the barrel is minimal, so that gas leak is negligible, but this does mean the interface must be cleaned regularly.

The firing pin is a separate component, mounted in the frame, and there is a safety system linked to the trigger which prevents the pin being struck by the hammer unless the trigger is pulled. The trigger action is smooth, if a trifle heavy at double action, but the let-off point is clean and crisp. The trigger is adjustable for travel.

The foresight is a conventional ramp blade, while the rear sight is a notch, adjustable for windage and elevation. The grip fills the hand well and gives good control of the pistol when firing. Finish is excellent, the metal being well blued and the grips being high-grade walnut, while hammer, trigger and barrel lock nut are chromium-plated.

In use the Korth is pleasant to shoot and as accurate as might be expected, capable of delivering tight groups in single-action mode, slightly larger in double-action. So far as performance goes, I would say that it is on a par with other high-quality revolvers; the finish, inside and out is excellent, the design good; but I cannot honestly see where the high price is justified in any concrete manner. But then again, one could perhaps make the same sort of observation about some breeds of cameras and automobiles which carry a high price tag but still sell all they can make.

Llama 'Comanche' Revolver

Manufacturer Gabilondo y Cia, Vitoria, Spain
Type Six-shot, solid frame, double-action
Caliber .357 Magnum
Barrel 4in (102mm) or 6in (152mm)
Weight 31oz (880gm)

The Gabilondo company began business in 1904 making cheap pocket revolvers; during World War One it moved to cheap automatic pistols, and then in the early 1930s began making a line of good quality autos under the 'Llama' trade name. Revolvers were added after World War Two, using the Llama name for the best models and the name 'Ruby' for the cheaper ones.

The 'Comanche' has been on sale for some time, but deserves mention as the top pistol in the line-up. It is a conventional solid frame double-action revolver bearing more than a passing resemblance to the Smith & Wesson pattern. The finish is excellent, a smooth and lustrous blue with well-checkered walnut grips of good hand-filling shape. Both single- and double-action trigger pulls are smooth, with crisp let-off. There is a ramp front sight with a square-notch rear sight which is adjustable for both elevation and windage.

The interior of the pistol is to the same standard as the exterior, and the double-action trigger is smooth and not of excessive tension, while the single-action let-off is crisp and consistent. Accuracy is good, and in practical use will group as closely as the skill of the owner allows.

Llama Omni Auto Pistol

Manufacturer Gabilondo y Cia, Vitoria, Spain
Type Locked breech semi-automatic, double-action
Caliber .45 ACP or 9mm Parabellum
Barrel 4.31in (110mm)
Weight 40.5oz (1148gm)
Magazine capacity 7 rounds (.45); 12 rounds (9mm)

The Llama 'Omni' doubtless takes its name from being available in either .45 ACP or 9mm calibers, so as to satisfy almost all the pistol fraternity with one or other model. The 9mm has a very slightly shorter barrel, weighs two ounces less and carries more ammunition than the .45, but mechanically they are the same.

The company claim that they have made new and important design improvements aimed at curing certain well-known defects in automatic pistols. In the first place they have used two sear bars instead of one; one acts in the single-action mode, the other in the double action mode, so that either mode has a sear bar designed for optimum performance. The second change has been to surround the hammer spring plunger with twenty ball bearings which reduce friction during the cocking movement of the hammer and thus make cycling the slide much easier; they also ensure that the hammer mechanism is consistent from shot to shot. Next is a change in the firing pin; most firing pins break sooner or later, but the Omni has a two-piece pin with the parts linked by a ball-joint; the makers are so confident of this that they unconditionally guarantee the firing pin for life.

Other improvements include a much larger-than-normal bearing surface where the barrel lugs and slide lock together; improved rifling, with the trailing edge bevelled to reduce friction and redundant engraving of the bullet; and a new type of magazine for the 9mm version which tapers at the upper end to cut down the likelihood of feed jams.

The remainder of the Omni is fairly conventional; it is a double-action pistol using the familiar Browning type of breech lock in which the barrel is withdrawn from the slide by a cam under the breech end. There is a safety catch on the slide which shields the firing pin and drops the hammer when applied, and the firing pin also has a locking pin which prevents forward movement unless the trigger is pressed. The trigger-guard is shaped at the front for two-handed grasping, but the grip shape and angle makes for a very comfortable single-handed hold, and the pistol is comfortable to shoot and accurate when used in either manner. Quality of workmanship and finish is excellent. The Omni is new on the market, but I expect that it will prove a popular weapon.

Mab Model PA-15 Auto Pistol

Manufacturer Manufacture d'Armes Automatiques, Lotissement Industriel des Pontots, F-64100 Bayonne, France
Type Delayed blowback semi-automatic
Caliber 9mm Parabellum
Barrel 4.5in (114mm)
Weight (empty) 38.4oz (1090gm)
Magazine capacity 15 rounds

The Manufacture d'Armes of Bayonne has been in business since 1921, concentrating on the manufacture of automatic pistols. In about 1950 they produced a 'Model R' in 7.65mm Longue caliber which featured an external hammer, and some time afterwards they modified this to fire 9mm Parabellum ammunition, calling it the 'Model R Para'. This was then further modified and was adopted in the late 1970s by the French Army to replace their ageing MAS 1950 pistol.

In order to cope with powerful 9mm cartridges the original blowback design of the Model R had to be considerably modified, and breech locking in the P-15 is done by a rotating barrel which gives a delayed blowback effect. The barrel has a lug on the top which engages in a recess in the slide; it has another lug at the bottom which engages in a curved cam groove cut in a seating block held into the frame by the slide stop pin. In the closed position, the lower lug is rotated sideways by the curved track, forcing the barrel to turn and thus turning the top lug into a recess which prevents the slide moving backwards. On firing, the slide attempts to move back on recoil and pulls on the barrel via the top lug; the force is transferred to the bottom lug which must first follow the curved track and thus rotate the barrel until the top lug is disengaged

The French Army have recently standardized on this MAB PA-15 pistol, made in Bayonne.

and the slide is free to move backwards, leaving the barrel where it is. The delay is enough to permit the bullet to exit the barrel and the chamber pressure to drop to a safe level before the breech opens.

The lockwork is conventional single action, the rearward movement of the slide cocking the external hammer after each shot. There is a manual safety and there is also a magazine safety which prevents the pistol being fired if the magazine is removed. The sights are standard military type, the rearsight being capable of lateral movement for zeroing. There is also a competition version of the pistol used by French Army pistol teams; this is known as the 'PAPF-1' and has the barrel and slide lengthened and adjustable sights fitted.

Mamba Auto Pistol

Manufacturer Navy Arms, Ridgefield, NJ 07657, U.S.A.
Type Locked breech semi-automatic, double-action
Caliber 9mm Parabellum
Barrel 5in (127mm)
Weight 42oz (1190gm)
Magazine capacity 15 rounds

The Mamba automatic pistol has had a very mixed history, though it now appears to have settled down with a manufacturer who can actually produce them. It first appeared in Rhodesia in 1977 and was taken up in South Africa; plans were laid for production there, so as to ensure a locally-manufactured alternative to the day when the U.N. arms embargo began to bite and there would be no Browning, Colt, Llama, Beretta or other large auto pistols available. Somehow, though, this doesn't seem to have happened, and so the urgency for producing the Mamba died down. A number were produced in South Africa,

sufficient for people to realize that this was a very good pistol, and some were imported into the U.S.A. by Navy Arms. Since then they have been licensed to manufacture the pistol. It is said that a large overseas contract has been filled by them, and now the Mamba is once more beginning to appear in the civil market.

It will have been worth waiting for. The Mamba was billed, on first appearance, as 'the world's first stainless steel double-action 9mm automatic' and that description still holds good. It resembles the Smith & Wesson Model 39 to some degree, but its all stainless-steel construction is a factor which makes for an immensely strong weapon as well as one which can survive the worst possible conditions without corrosion. The breech is locked by a variation of the Browning 'swinging link' – in this case a shaped ramp beneath the barrel which guides the breech down to detach it from the slide. In addition, slide and frame are positively locked together at the instant of firing, a patented Mamba design feature. There is a double-action trigger, but the weapon can also be 'cocked and locked' in the single action mode and carried that way if preferred.

The original design incorporated a two- or three-round burst-fire facility, available only on those weapons destined for security forces, but less of this has been heard in recent years and I suspect that it has been abandoned. In my experience such a device is worthless unless the pistol has some form of shoulder-stock to aid control, and no stock was ever advertised for the Mamba. Another early promise was a version in .45 ACP caliber, but this, too, seems to have evaporated.

Other features of the Mamba include an ambidextrous safety, a magazine catch operable by the shooting hand, an adjustable hammer spring, micro-groove rifling, and a trigger guard shaped to fit the two-handed combat style of holding. Reports on this pistol indicate good accuracy – two-inch groups at 25 yards are regularly spoken of – and extremely high reliability and ruggedness.

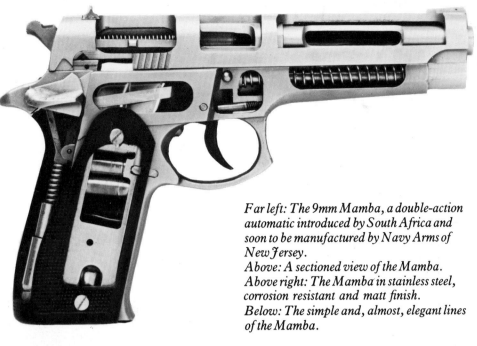

Far left: The 9mm Mamba, a double-action automatic introduced by South Africa and soon to be manufactured by Navy Arms of New Jersey.
Above: A sectioned view of the Mamba.
Above right: The Mamba in stainless steel, corrosion resistant and matt finish.
Below: The simple and, almost, elegant lines of the Mamba.

Manurhin Model MR73 Revolver

Manufacturer Manufacture de Machines du Haut-Rhin (Manurhin), F-68060 Mulhouse-Bourtzwiller, France
Type 6-shot solid-frame double-action revolver
Caliber .357 Magnum or 9mm Parabellum
Barrel 2.5in (63.5mm); 3in (76.2mm); 4in (102mm); 5.25in (134mm); 6in (152mm) and 8in (203mm)
Weight (empty) 31.4oz (890gm) (3in barrel)

This is a compact revolver basically intended for police use, though the longer-barrel-ed versions can also be bought in competition form. They are currently used by French police and security agencies and are commercially sold.

The MR73 is a conventional solid-frame revolver with swing-out cylinder. In 'combat' form (ie with 2.5, 3 or 4in barrels) it has the usual fixed blade and notch sights. In competition form (ie with 4, 5.25, 6 and 8in barrels) an adjustable rear sight is provided. The cylinder is removeable and can be replaced by a special cylinder which chambers the 9mm Parabellum rimless cartridge; in this case the cartridges must be loaded with a special spring clip in order to position them correctly and also to ensure that the empty cases are ejected properly. The standard cylinder is designed for use with rimmed .357 Magnum or .38 Special cartridges.

The lockwork is fairly conventional and there is a safety bar which prevents the firing pin striking a cartridge unless the trigger is pulled. The linkage between trigger and hammer spring, via the rebound slide, is engineered so that the load felt by the trigger finger remains almost constant throughout the double-action pull.

The Manurhin MR73 revolver has been adopted as a military arm by a number of African states, and also makes a good target pistol.

Merrill Single Shot Pistol

Manufacturer Merrill Co., Fullerton, CA 92631, U.S.A.
Type Single shot
Caliber Various
Barrel 9in (228mm) or 12in (305mm)
Weight ca. 68oz (1920gm)

Single shot pistols are less common today than in years gone by, when 'saloon' and 'parlor' pistols firing low-power ammunition were a popular source of amusement. Today the single shot survives for two principal purposes; specialized target shooting and hunting, and the Merrill will perform either of these very well indeed.

The Merrill uses a stainless steel frame and standing breech, to which is hinged the barrel, fixed so that it drops down to expose the chamber for loading. As the barrel is opened, so it automatically cocks the striker, and as it is closed so an automatic safety comes into play, locking the trigger and firing pin. This safety can only be re-leased by pressing the safety lever at the top of the left hand grip plate with the thumb. To cater for left-handed shooters, a left-handed model is available which has the safety on the other side.

The barrel unit can be in carbon or stainless steel, and is easily interchanged since the hinge-bolt is an Allen-type socket screw. Barrels in over a dozen calibers, from .22RF upwards, can be obtained, and they can be in either smooth 'bull' contour or with ventilated ribs. Two standard lengths are used, nine or 12 inches.

The front sight is a blade, the rear a Patridge-type notch, fully adjustable. The sight normally provided is of Micro manufacture, but other makes can be supplied to order. Trigger pull is adjustable by a set-screw at the rear of the frame.

The accuracy of the Merrill is beyond reproach; in virtually any caliber it should be possible to make one-inch groups at 25 yards and in the larger calibers this makes an excellent hunting or silhouette-shooting weapon.

Renato Gamba Trident Super Revolver

Manufacturer Armi Renato Gamba SpA, Post Box 48, I-25063 Gardone Val Trompia, Italy
Type 6-shot double-action solid frame revolver
Caliber .38 Special
Barrel 4in (102mm)
Weight (empty) 25.4oz (720gm)

This is a conventional design of solid frame revolver with swing out cylinder and rod ejection. The grip is well-proportioned to fill the hand and the barrel is slab-sided to lighten it, which results in a particularly well-balanced weapon. The foresight is mounted on a ventilated rib and the back-sight is fully adjustable for elevation and windage. The finish is in bright blueing, with well-checkered walnut grips, and the workmanship is good.

The Merrill single-shot pistol.

Renato Gamba HSc80 Auto Pistol

Manufacturer Armi Renato Gamba SpA, Post Box 48, I-25063 Gardone Val Trompia, Italy
Type Blowback, double-action, semi-automatic
Caliber 7.65mm ACP, 9mm Short or 9mm Police
Barrel 3.34in (85mm)
Weight (unloaded) 24.7oz (700gm)
Magazine capacity 13 rounds

Armi Renato Gamba of Gardone Val Trompia, Italy, are a relatively new company in the firearms field. They obtained a license from Mauser to manufacture the Mauser HSc automatic pistol, a prewar design, and have done this for some time. They have now made some improvements to the design. The butt has been lengthened, allowing the magazine capacity to be increased to 13 rounds, and the frame has been altered to give the trigger guard a recessed curve on its forward edge so as to make it suitable for a two-handed grip. The pistol can be obtained chambered for 7.65mm ACP, 9mm Short or 9mm Police cartridges. It retains the double-action feature of the original HSc, is a simple blowback, and in 9mm Police caliber would appear to be a sound pistol for use by police or security forces or for home defense.

Ruger Redhawk Revolver

Manufacturer Sturm, Ruger & Co., Southport, CT 06490, U.S.A.
Type Solid frame double-action 6-shot revolver
Caliber .44 Magnum
Barrel 7.5in (190mm)
Weight 52oz (1474gm)

Sturm Ruger have acquired a fine reputation for their heavy revolvers, and this is one of their masterpieces. It is a big gun by any standards, it fires a heavy cartridge, and

Above: Renato Gamba's HSc Super automatic is the Mauser HSc, improved, and license-built in Italy.
Below: The Ruger Redhawk revolver in .44 Magnum caliber.

takes some controlling, but the effort is worthwhile.

The Redhawk is a conventional double-action solid frame revolver made of stainless steel, with the cylinder swinging out on a crane for loading and ejection. The cylinder has ample metal on the outside of the chambers and is securely locked by an additional lug in the crane which engages into the frame, as well as the usual ejector rod locking points. A small but important detail is that the cylinder locking notches are located off the axis of the chambers so that they are not liable to weaken the chamber walls. The barrel is ribbed and both the rib and the ejector rod shroud are forged in one piece with the barrel. The foresight is of blued steel with a red insert, and the backsight, also of blued steel, is a Patridge type notch with a white line around it and is capable of adjustment for both windage and elevation.

The lockwork has been redesigned and is extremely simple, robust and reliable. Moreover it can be easily dismantled for cleaning; the grips are removed, after which the hammer can be removed by inserting a pin (provided, and kept inside the grip) into the mainspring so that when the hammer is cocked, tension is taken off it and the pivot can be removed and the hammer slipped free. The mainspring can now be removed, and by pulling on a stud behind the trigger guard the entire trigger guard and trigger mechanism can be taken from the frame. As with all Ruger revolvers, there is a rising transfer bar which acts as an intermediary between the hammer and the firing pin only when the trigger is correctly pressed, so that the pistol cannot be accidentally discharged.

On the range, this elegant pistol performs well; like any .44 Magnum it is a handful, but the weight and size allow good control and it is capable of close groups at all ranges. For day-to-day practise .44 Special can be used, the sights requiring altering, and with this loading one can shoot all day without discomfort.

Ruger Mark II Auto Pistol

Manufacturer Sturm, Ruger & Co., Southport, CT 06490, U.S.A.
Type Blowback semi-automatic
Caliber .22 Long Rifle RF
Barrel 4.75in (120mm)
Weight (empty) 36oz (1019gm)
Magazine capacity 10 rounds

The Sturm Ruger company virtually made its name with its 'Standard' .22 automatic pistol which was first introduced in 1949 and has been the firm's anchor ever since. At the end of 1981, with over one million of this and its target version the 'Mark One' sold, it was announced that an improved version, the 'Mark II', would be marketed during 1982; at the time of writing we have not yet been able to obtain one, and the

following information is based upon published data.

The Mark II maintains the same basic form and appearance as its predecessor, a blowback pistol using a fixed barrel and a bolt which reciprocates within a tubular receiver; several component parts will, if fact, be interchangeable between old and new models. The changes are minor in form but add up to significant improvements; the trigger has been changed in material and shape, and its pivot system has been redesigned; the safety catch has been redesigned so that it is now possible to retract the bolt to unload or examine the chamber while the safety is applied and with the sear firmly locked; the magazine has been reworked and now accepts 10 rounds instead of the former nine; the rear of the receiver has been cut away on each side so that it is now easier to grasp the bolt retraction ears; and a new bolt hold-open device has been adopted. The old model used the safety catch as a hold-open device, but the Mark II has a small catch above the left grip which, when depressed, allows the bolt to close after it has been held open by the magazine follower after the last shot has gone.

The Mark II Ruger will be available in Standard models with fixed sights and with 4.75in or 6in barrel lengths, a Target model with fully adjustable sights and a 6in barrel, and a 'Bull Barrel' model with adjustable sights and a heavy 5in barrel. It has been hinted that further variations may be expected to follow when the initial demand for these basic models has been satisfied.

Semmerling LM-4 Pistol

Manufacturer Semmerling Corp., Newton, MA 02160, U.S.A.
Type Manual repeating pistol
Caliber .45 ACP
Barrel 3.656in (92.8mm)
Weight (empty) 26.5oz (751gm)
Magazine capacity 4 rounds

This is one of the most unusual pistols in existence, a pistol designed solely as a defensive weapon and using a unique mechanical action. It is also one of the strongest pistols in existence, and probably the most expensive .45 – the most recent quoted price was $748.

The Semmerling looks like an automatic but is actually hand-operated. The frame carries a heavy standing breech and the four-round magazine and trigger mechanism; on the forward section of the frame is the barrel unit which can slide forward, exposing the chamber. When it is manually pushed forward and pulled back, the chamber slides over the top round in the magazine and the breech is closed. Pulling the trigger now brings up a lock to hold the barrel in place during firing and then cocks and releases the hammer to fire the cartridge. The firer then pushes and pulls once more on the barrel, first ejecting the fired case and then reloading the fresh round.

This all sounds very difficult, but with practice it all works very well; the light weight and small size of the LM-4 demand a two-handed grip, and thus the free hand is

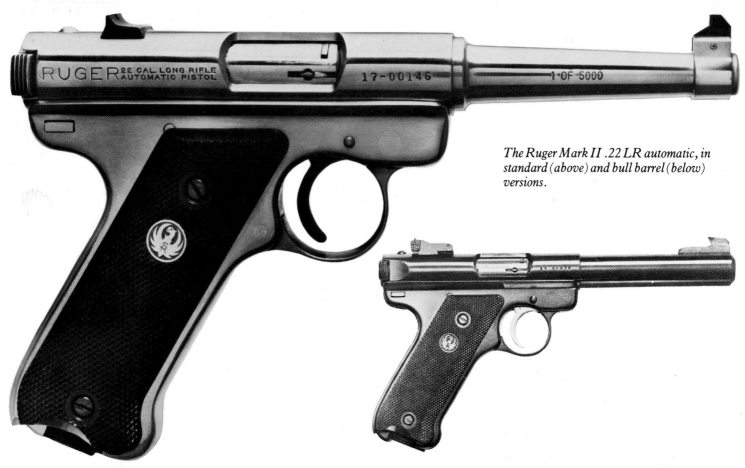

The Ruger Mark II .22 LR automatic, in standard (above) and bull barrel (below) versions.

The Semmerling LM-4 pistol, a hand-actuated repeater.

ready to perform the reloading movement. This can be done by thumb pressure on the serrated area on top of the barrel, or by grasping the side serrations. The firer must remember to release the trigger, however, since as long as the trigger is pressed, the barrel is securely locked to the breech; conversely, if the breech is not properly closed, then the trigger cannot move and the pistol cannot be fired.

There is no manual safety; however, there is a slight possibility that in drawing the pistol from a holster the barrel could be pulled forward, and to guard against this there is a 'holster lock' lever on the right side which can be set to hold the barrel firmly closed. It is automatically disengaged as the trigger is pulled to fire the first shot. The sights comprise a fixed blade front and square notch rear and are not adjustable.

As might be expected, the recoil is quite violent, but accurate shooting in combat is well within the pistol's capability. It should only be used with standard military or jacketed commercial .45 ACP ammunition, and handloading should be done carefully so as not to exceed standard pressure levels.

The SIG-Hammerli P240 target automatic pistol.

Sig-Hammerli Model 240 Pistol

Manufacturer Collaboration between Schweizerische Industrie Gesellschaft, Neuhausen-Am-Rheinfalls, Switzerland and Hammerli SA, Lenzburg, Switzerland
Type Target, locked-breech, semi-automatic
Caliber .38 Special
Barrel 5.81in (148mm)
Weight (empty) 43.5oz (1233gm)
Magazine capacity 5 rounds

This is a highly-specialized pistol intended for one purpose only, making holes in targets with supreme accuracy, and that only in international-class formal contests. It is not intended for combat shooting, either real or simulated, or casual plinking at vermin.

The P-240 might be said to be a SIG P-210 which has been worked over by the Hammerli people to give it the accuracy desired. SIG are without peers for producing well-built and fitted automatic pistols, while Hammerli, as we have pointed out elsewhere, have a long history of producing prize-winning match pistols, and the combination is unbeatable.

The 240 uses the now-standard Browning cam breech lock system in which the barrel is withdrawn from engagement with the slide by a shaped cam beneath the breech. Having said that, one has to add that in this case the machining and fit is to the finest tolerances and the muzzle is shaped to fit closely into the slide. The slide itself, in SIG fashion, rides inside the frame, a method which gives good support to the moving parts. The barrel is rifled to very close tolerances, which is part of the secret of its accuracy, and the loading ramp is particularly carefully contoured since this pistol fires only one type of ammunition, the .38 Special Wadcutter, a most unusual cartridge to find in an automatic but one with enormous potential for accuracy.

The grip is large, plain wood, and with a palm rest, giving an excellent grip, and the whole pistol is large and muzzle-heavy, promoting a firm and steady aim. The wide trigger is fully adjustable for tension, slack and over-travel, with a clean and consistent let-off. The foresight is a blade, the rear sight a square notch adjustable for elevation and windage.

The accuracy of this gun is beyond question; to put it plainly, it is capable of whatever accuracy the shooter can bring to it, and quoting figures would be meaningless.

Sig-Sauer Model P225 Auto Pistol

Manufacturer J.P. Sauer & Son, Eckenford, West Germany, SIG, Neuhausen-Rheinfalls, Switzerland
Type Locked breech, double-action, semi-automatic
Caliber 9mm Parabellum
Barrel 3.85in (98mm)
Weight (empty) 26.1oz (740gm)
Magazine capacity 8 rounds

This pistol was designed by SIG (Schweizer Industrie Gesellschaft) of Neuhausen-Rheinfalls, Switzerland and was first announced in 1978. Due to the restrictions placed on arms sales by the Swiss Government, SIG have entered into agreements with J.P. Sauer & Son of West Germany so that the SIG designs can be manufactured by Sauer, thus giving them an export market since the West German Government's regulations are much less restrictive. The Swiss-manufactured pistols have been adopted by the Swiss police, while those made in Germany have been adopted by the West German Border Police, Customs Administration, and six regional police forces. In West Germany it is known as the 'Pistole 6.'

The P225 is a slightly smaller and slightly modified version of the earlier P220. It uses the well-known Browning link method of breech locking, using a shaped cam to withdraw the barrel from engagement with the slide. Its principal feature is the incorporation of improved safety devices, and there is no applied safety, so that the weapon can be brought into action very rapidly. Once the pistol has been loaded by operating the slide, the hammer can be safely lowered by pressing on the de-cocking lever on the left side of the frame. The firing pin is securely locked by a spring-loaded pin which passes through it, but the hammer is stopped short of striking the pin. To fire, the trigger is pulled through to raise the hammer and then release it; as the hammer reaches the full-cocked position, a safety lever is rotated by the trigger bar. This rises beneath the firing pin and pushes the locking pin up and clear of the hole, so that as the hammer drops the firing pin is

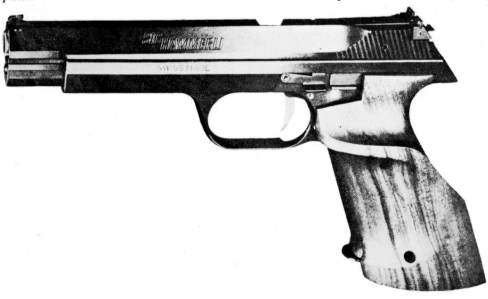

The SIG-Sauer P220 combat pistol, adopted by the Swiss Army as the 'Pistole 75', and also by the French and Japanese armies.

free to move when struck. As soon as the slide moves on recoil, the disconnector allows the firing pin safety pin to drop back into place and the pin is again securely locked.

The design has been careful to obtain the best possible balance, and the P225 performs well on the range. Like all SIG products the finish is immaculate, and quality control is such that parts from Swiss or West German pistols are freely interchangeable.

The SIG-Sauer P230, adopted by Swiss and other European police forces.

SIG-Sauer P230 Auto Pistol

Manufacturer J.P. Sauer & Son, Eckenford, West Germany
Type Blowback semi-automatic
Caliber 7.65mm/.32 ACP; 9mm Short/.380; 9mm Police
Barrel 3.62in (92mm)
Weight (empty) 16.2oz (460gm) in 9mm Short
Magazine capacity 8 rounds (7.65mm); 9 rounds (9mm calibers)

This is another Swiss-designed, German-manufactured fruit of the cooperation between SIG and J.P. Sauer & Son. It is used by a number of European police forces and enjoys a wide commercial sale.

The P230 is a simple blowback weapon with double-action lockwork and is provided with a de-cocking lever on the left side, by means of which the hammer can be lowered on a loaded chamber. As with the P225 the firing pin is securely locked at all times except for the instant that the hammer is released by the trigger. There is no manual safety catch.

The various caliber types are identical in appearance and major dimensions but there are differences in weight; the 7.65mm and 9mm Short versions have an alloy frame and there is only 5 grammes difference between them. But the 9mm Police version, firing a more powerful cartridge, uses a steel frame which adds 170gm, and also has a heavier slide so as to reduce the recoil force, adding another 70gm to make the total weight 690gm or 24.3oz.

The 9mm Police (9×18mm) cartridge is a special round developed in Germany in order to obtain the maximum possible performance from an unlocked-breech weapon. It is not yet commercially manufactured in the U.S.A.

Star Model BKM Auto Pistol

Manufacturer 'Star', B. Echeverria, Eibar, Spain
Type Locked breech, semi-automatic
Caliber 9mm Parabellum
Barrel 3.9in (100mm)
Weight 26oz (737gm)
Magazine capacity 8 rounds

The Star line of 9mm automatic pistols has generally been developed along military lines, but in the late 1970s, with the 9mm Parabellum cartridge beginning to become popular in the U.S.A., they were prevailed upon to produce a smaller weapon, one more suited to concealment for personal defence. Their answer was the BKM.

With an overall length of just over seven inches and weighing less than two pounds when loaded, this meets the specification, but the result is something of a handful. A

light alloy frame helps to keep the weight down, but the combination of short barrel, light weight and the 9mm Parabellum cartridge means recoil and muzzle blast both heavier than average; this is particularly noticeable when firing some types of European military 9mm ammunition. It is rather more acceptable when using commercial 'Luger' loadings.

The finish is excellent, with blued slide, anodized black frame, and well-checkered walnut grips. The foresight is the usual blade and the rear a square notch which is rather too narrow for easy alinement in a hurry. The rear sight may be drifted sideways in its notch for zeroing but there is no other adjustment. The breech locking is by the traditional Browning-Colt swinging link, though there is only one locking lug on top of the barrel to engage with the slide. It is worth noting that the firing pin is not an inertia type, and this pistol should never have the hammer lowered on to a loaded chamber.

In practical use the BKM delivers good accuracy for such a short barrel, giving two to three inch groups at 25 yards quite regularly. Like many autos it tends to be fussy over its ammunition, and several brands should be checked for their compatibility before deciding which to use. Once the recoil and noise are mastered, the BKM becomes an extension of the hand, and is well-suited to the defensive role.

Star Model FR Target Pistol

Manufacturer 'Star', B. Echeverria SA, Eibar, Spain
Type Blowback, semi-automatic
Caliber .22 Long Rifle RF
Barrel 7in (178mm)
Weight (empty) 29oz (820gm)
Magazine capacity 10 rounds

The number of target shooters who cut their teeth on the Star Model F target pistol in years gone by must be astronomical; it was cheap, reliable and sufficiently accurate to satisfy the beginner at target work and it also made a very satisfactory 'fun gun'. Un-

fortunately Echeverria found more lucrative things to do in the early 1960s and stopped making it. They have now returned to this field with the new 'Model FR' which is simply the old Model F revived and somewhat better made.

This is a basic blowback pistol, having a heavy barrel fixed into the frame and a slide which has a front arms frame which traps the recoil spring beneath the barrel. It is simple to dismantle; one merely pulls the slide slightly back, presses the dismantling button above the left grip, lifts the slide and slips it off forward, over the barrel. End of dismantling; nothing further is needed.

There is an external hammer and a safety catch which locks the slide while disconnecting the trigger. A hold-open catch ensures that the slide stays to the rear after firing the last shot in the magazine; with a new magazine in, the slide can be closed by pressing this catch or by simply pulling it back and releasing it. The foresight is on a ramp and is adjustable for elevation; the rear sight, a square notch, is adjustable for windage. Balance weights are available, which can be attached to the barrel to adjust the point of balance for the individual shooter.

Altogether the FR is a good beginner's pistol which will provide accuracy enough to satisfy many shooters for their entire career. But what a sign of the times: price in 1961 – $54.50; price in 1982 – $315 or thereabouts.

Star Model PD

Manufacturer 'Star', Echeverria SA, Eibar, Spain
Type Locked breech semi-automatic
Caliber .45 ACP
Barrel 3.94in (100mm)
Weight 25oz (710gm)
Magazine capacity 6 rounds

The venerable U.S. Government Colt M1911A1 pistol is a splendid weapon for stopping malefactors, but it is rather bulky and heavy; as a result there has long been a tendency to develop lighter and smaller pistols firing the .45 ACP cartridge. Many

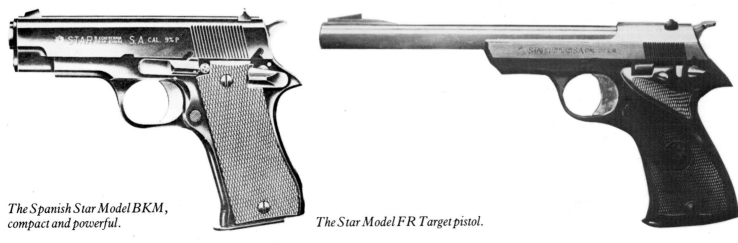

The Spanish Star Model BKM, compact and powerful.

The Star Model FR Target pistol.

The Star Model PD, one of the most compact production .45 pistols yet made.

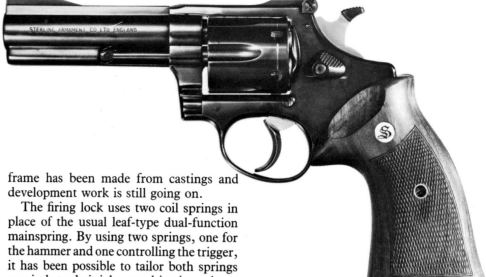

The Sterling .357 Magnum revolver, a new departure for the company and the first new revolver in Britain for almost sixty years.

have been short-lived hack-and-chop jobs done on the basic Colt, but some have been designed from the ground up, as it were, and have been more successful.

The Star PD is one of the earliest of this group and probably the most long-lived. In order to bring the size down there have been some changes from the basic Colt-Browning swinging link breech locking system; there is only one interlocking lug and notch holding slide and barrel together, and the recoil spring and guide rod are an assembled unit instead of separate components. The frame is of alloy, and there is no grip safety. The foresight is a blade and the rear sight a fully adjustable leaf with open notch.

The PD is much lighter than the Colt M1911A1 and, consequently, rather more difficult to control, though it is not uncomfortable to shoot. Due to the short barrel the velocity and muzzle energy is less than in full-sized pistols but there is still ample stopping power, and the PD is a sensible gun for those who need a potent but concealable pistol.

Sterling Revolver

Manufacturer Sterling Armament Company, Dagenham, Essex, UK
Type Six-shot solid frame double-action revolver
Caliber .38 Special
Barrel 2in (51mm); 4in (102mm)

The Sterling Armament Company are well-known for their submachine gun, and in 1980 they announced their entry into the revolver field, the first British company to design and produce a revolver for almost 60 years. The company aim to sell it to police and security forces and it is also expected to have military applications.

The Sterling revolver is a conventional solid frame type with swing-out cylinder, ribbed barrel and shrouded ejector rod. It is fitted with an adjustable rear sight or with fixed sights at the customer's requirement. In order to keep the cost of manufacture within limits, much use has been made of die and investment casting. Much of the

frame has been made from castings and development work is still going on.

The firing lock uses two coil springs in place of the usual leaf-type dual-function mainspring. By using two springs, one for the hammer and one controlling the trigger, it has been possible to tailor both springs precisely to their jobs, resulting in a trigger action which is undoubtedly among the smoothest ever experienced.

Sterling Mark II Auto

Manufacturer Sterling Arms Corp., Lockport, NY 14094, U.S.A.
Type Blowback, double-action, semi-automatic
Caliber .380 Auto/9mm Short
Barrel 3.56in (90.5mm)
Weight 25.5oz (723gm)
Magazine capacity 8 rounds

The .380 Auto, or 9mm Short as it is known in Europe, is a somewhat under-rated cartridge. It has served as a police cartridge through Europe for several decades and as a military cartridge too. The bullet will deliver something in the order of 165 foot-pounds of energy at the muzzle, which is sufficient to make most people stop and think, and it is also less likely to ricochet than higher powered cartridges such as the 9mm Parabellum. For many years it was just about the most powerful cartridge which could be managed in a blowback action without going to design extremes, another point which counted in its favor.

The Sterling is one of the few .380 automatic pistols made in the U.S.A.; it is an inexpensive pistol and the standard of finish

Sterling Arms' .380 automatic.

reflects its price, but there is nothing wrong with its quality of construction and it is surprisingly accurate. The action is a straightforward blowback with an external hammer, and with double-action trigger. There is a slide-mounted safety which, when operated, moves a steel barrier behind the firing pin, so that should the hammer fall it cannot discharge a cartridge. Once the safety is on, the hammer may be lowered by controlling it with the thumb while pressing the trigger; thereafter the pistol can be fired by releasing the safety and pulling the trigger to cock and drop the hammer. Once the first shot has been fired, subsequent shots are in single-action mode, the recoiling slide cocking the hammer.

The foresight is a fixed blade, the rear-sight, a square notch adjustable for elevation and windage. The Sterling is comfortable to fire and can deliver consistent three- to four-inch groups at 25 yards range.

Steyr Model GB Auto Pistol

Manufacturer Steyr-Daimler-Puch AG, Postbox 1000, A-4400 Steyr, Austria
Type Delayed blowback double action semi-automatic
Caliber 9mm Parabellum
Barrel 5.35in (136mm)
Weight (empty) 29.8oz (845gm)
Magazine capacity 18

The Steyr GB is the latest version of a design which appeared some years ago as the 'Pi 18' model. This incorporated a three-round burst facility, with a special 36-round magazine and a shoulder stock, and the semi-automatic pistol alone was also sold in a stainless steel version in the

The Steyr GB pistol, entirely of steel – even the grip plates.

U.S.A. as the P-18. However, it did not prosper and was withdrawn. The GB has now been announced and there appears to be considerable interest in it in Europe, though no official adoption has yet been disclosed.

The GB has been designed for military, police or civil use and it incorporates an unusual gas-actuated delayed blowback mechanism. The barrel is fixed in the frame, with the slide free to move over it in the conventional way, but the recoil spring, mounted around the barrel, is retained in place by a barrel bushing which extends inside the slide and surrounds the barrel. About half-way down the barrel it is externally shaped into a tight-fitting piston head which rides inside the barrel bush cylinder, and in front of this 'piston head' is a small port connecting the inside of the barrel with the annular space formed inside the bush cylinder. When the pistol is fired, gas passes through this port and fills the space at high pressure; the normal recoil action tends to blow the slide back, forcing the barrel bush over the piston head formed by the barrel, but the high pressure of gas inside resists this action and thus the movement of the slide is delayed until the bullet is well clear of the barrel.

On the left rear of the slide is a safety and de-cocking lever; turning this down first moves the firing pin out of line with the hammer, then lowers the hammer and locks the firing pin safely. The pistol can be fired in single-action mode, by thumb-cocking the hammer, or in double-action mode by simply pulling-through on the trigger.

Smith & Wesson Distinguished Combat Magnum

Manufacturer Smith & Wesson, 2100 Roosevelt Avenue, Springfield, MA, 01101, U.S.A.
Type Six-shot, solid frame, double-action revolver
Caliber .357 Magnum/.38 Special
Barrel 4⅜in (110mm); 5⅞in (149mm)
Weight (empty) 4in barrel: 42oz (1190gm) 6in barrel: 46oz (1304gm)

This is the latest offering from Smith & Wesson and like all their products is beautifully finished and absolutely reliable. It is a conventional enough double-action revolver of the type they have been producing since before the start of the century, but it incorporates one new feature, their 'L' frame. Smith & Wesson have long categorized their pistols according to the size of the frame, the smaller and lighter weapons using the 'K' and the very large revolvers the 'N'; the 'L' falls between these, giving additional strength and size to cope with today's magnum ammunition but not increasing the size to an incommensurate amount.

There are, in fact, four distinct models in this range; the Model 586 comes in steel with a blued finish and has 4in or 6in (nominal – the actual lengths are as quoted above) barrel lengths. The Model 686 is similar but in stainless steel with a satin finish. Both models have adjustable rear sights. Model 581 is steel, blued, with a 4in barrel and fixed frame notch rear sight, while the Model 681 is the same but in stainless steel with satin finish.

There are certain refinements; revolvers with 4in barrels and 'target accessories' and all revolvers with 6in barrels are furnished with a trigger stop; the 'standard' 4in barrel models – ie the 581 and 681 – will not have a trigger stop. The 586 and 686 are fitted with

The Smith & Wesson Distinguished Combat Magnum revolver.

Goncalo Alves checkered target grips cut away for use with a speed loader, while the 581 and 681 have straightforward checkered walnut grips.

Smith & Wesson have said that they developed these revolvers from lessons learned in Police Combat Competitions, and on the range this appears to be borne out in practice. The trigger is wide and smooth and with a good double-action movement and a crisp let-off in the single-action mode. The pistol balances well, comes quickly to the aim and is as accurate as anyone could wish. There is sufficient weight and good balance to prevent excessive throw-off after firing, so that the shooter can quickly regain his point of aim. For practical shooting contests, or for service, it would be hard to fault this weapon.

Smith & Wesson Model 547 Revolver

Manufacturer Smith & Wesson, 2100 Roosevelt Ave., Springfield, MA 01101, U.S.A.
Type Solid frame, double-action revolver
Caliber 9mm Parabellum
Barrel 3in (76mm); 4in (102mm)
Weight 3in – 32oz (907gm)
4in – 34oz (964gm)

This revolver is something of a milestone in that it is designed solely for use with rimless 9mm Parabellum cartridges. There are other revolvers which will fire 9mm rimless, but they all demand some form of spring clip with which to prevent the cases from slipping too far into the chamber and also to give the extractor something to push against when removing the empty cases. The Smith & Wesson design is the result of careful thought and design work and requires no clips or other devices; you put the

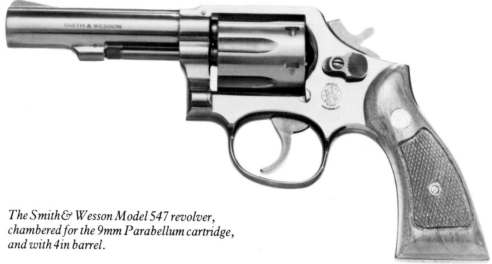

The Smith & Wesson Model 547 revolver, chambered for the 9mm Parabellum cartridge, and with 4in barrel.

cartridges into the cylinder in the usual way, fire them, and then eject them in the usual way. It sounds simple, but it took some very clever engineering to do it.

The Model 547 is a conventional solid frame revolver, double action, with a swing-out cylinder and a rod ejector. In order to work with rimless cases, the ejector is a totally new concept. Instead of the usual 'star' plate at the rear end, to lift the rims of cases, the central rod has six splined recesses which correspond to the chambers. Inside these recesses are six sprung ejectors. At rest, the notched heads of these ejectors protrude into the chambers; as the cartridge is inserted, the bullet and case body force this notch inward, against its spring. As soon as the notch reaches the sloped forward edge of the extraction rim on the case it can spring out, into the groove, and rest there. When the ejection rod is pushed back, so the notch catches on the flat face of the ejection groove and forces the case out of the chamber.

Should one case be missed, there is none of the nonsense which occurs with rimmed

cases, with the rim lodging under the extractor star; one merely releases the ejection rod, allowing the rod to return and the ejector notch to snap into the case groove, and then you try again, and it works.

The second practical difficulty with rimless cases is that they are slightly tapered, and therefore tend to set back from the chamber during firing. Thus there is no certainty about the amount the firing pin must travel to make a fair strike on the cap. One could design for the worst case, with ample travel, and have the danger of piercing the occasional cap; or design for the best case, with minimum travel, and have the occasional failure to strike. Neither would be considered very satisfactory by users. Moreover, 9mm Parabellum issued to military and police forces is usually designed with submachine guns in mind and has hard caps demanding a good firm strike. This problem has been solved by the use of a 'limit pin'. The firing pin is a floating pin, set in the frame; above this is a second pin, the limit pin which is calculated on the precise distance between the face of the hammer and the cap of a correctly-loaded cartridge. The falling hammer strikes the firing pin first, then contacts the limit pin and drives it through the frame to touch the base of the cartridge case. Once this contact is made the limit pin stops and this also stops the hammer's travel, so that it cannot go further and force the firing pin to pierce the cap. Should the case set back on firing, as often happens, the limit pin will go back with it, forcing the hammer back and so allowing the firing pin to ride freely back, avoiding impaling the case cap on the firing pin.

The sights are fixed 'combat' type, and the grip is a most comfortable rounded pattern. The hammer spur is unusually short, and it has been suggested that this has been done deliberately in order to prevent injury to the hand when firing some of the 'hotter' types of military ammunition which tend to make the gun jump rather more than normal. In practical use, however, using some European service military loadings, I found

The Smith & Wesson Model 547 revolver with 3in barrel.

the pistol eminently practical and controllable, even though some of the shots went off with a sharper report than is usual in revolvers of this size. This is, of course, basically a service weapon, for military or police use, but even so the accuracy is excellent. I would, though, qualify that and say 'with some ammunition.' Military 9mm is, as we have said, primarily made with SMGs in mind and not all types perform well in a revolver; it is worth doing some experimenting before committing oneself.

Smith & Wesson Model 459 & 559 Auto Pistols

Manufacturer Smith & Wesson Inc., 2100 Roosevelt Avenue, Springfield, MA 01101, U.S.A.
Type Locked breech, double-action semi-automatic
Caliber 9mm Parabellum
Barrel 4in (102mm)
Weight 30.5oz (865gm) (M459); 40.5oz (1148gm) (M559)
Magazine capacity 14 rounds

These two pistols are almost identical in specification, the difference being that the Model 459 has an alloy frame while the Model 559 has a steel frame. The basic model is the 39, first produced in 1954; this had a single-column magazine holding eight rounds, and in 1971 the Model 59, holding 14 rounds, appeared. The new models have added several new safety features.

The pistol is a locked breech type relying upon the well-tried Browning swinging link method of locking, in which a cam cut in a lump beneath the breech bears against a cross-pin to withdraw the barrel downwards during recoil and disconnect it from engagement with the slide. There is an external hammer and an inertia firing pin, which requires a sharp blow to send it forward far enough to strike the cartridge cap. The pin is securely locked in its rearward position by a spring-loaded plunger at all times except at the instant of hammer release, when a trigger-actuated linkage forces the plunger clear to allow the firing pin to move. When the pin rebounds, assisted by a spring, the plunger reconnects and the pin is once again locked.

There is a safety catch at the rear of the slide which, when operated, rotates a solid block of steel into place behind the firing pin and then releases the hammer to drop on to this block. At the same time the shaft of the safety catch engages in a slot in the firing pin, providing an additional lock. To fire, the safety catch is released and either the hammer thumbed back to full cock or the trigger pulled through to cock and release it.

The trigger pull is somewhat heavy at about 6lbs for single action and almost

Smith & Wesson Model 459 pistol, a double-action design, is in use by some military forces in South America and Africa.

15lbs for double action, but these pistols are intended for practical applications rather than target shooting, so this is of little consequence; although heavy the pull is precise in both models, with a crisp let-off in single action and a very even pull during double action. The sights are excellent, a square blade front and a fully adjustable notch at the rear, shielded by protective 'ears' on both sides.

Super Titan II

Manufacturer G. Tanfoglio, Mogno, Gardone Val Trompia, Italy
Type Blowback, semi-automatic
Caliber .380/9mm Short: .32 ACP/7.65mm
Barrel 3.9in (99mm)
Weight 28oz (794gm)
Magazine capacity 11 rounds (.380); 12 rounds (.32)

Under the name Tanfoglio & Sabotti this company exported large numbers of in-

The Tanfoglio Super Titan II, a workmanlike pistol from Italy.

expensive auto pistols to the U.S.A. in the 1950s, one of them being a .25 auto called the 'Titan'. The 1968 Gun Control Act stopped this trade and shortly afterwards there was news of an American company being set up to import component parts and assemble them in the U.S. This does not seem to have prospered particularly well, and now Tanfoglio (Sabotti having left the concern) have completely rebuilt the Titan into the 'Super Titan II' and are marketing it in the U.S.A. via the F.I.E. Corporation of Hialeah, Florida.

The new pistol follows the current fashion in having a magazine larger than was previously considered normal, during its first production run but apart from that it is of conventional design, somewhat resembling Beretta from its use of an open-topped slide. It is rather unusual in having two manually-operated safety catches; the catch on the left rear of the slide simply locks the firing pin, while the one on the left side of the frame, above the trigger, locks the trigger. In addition to these there is a magazine safety and a half-cock notch on the hammer. The frame safety catch also doubles as a stripping catch; when turned to the 'safe' position the slide can be pulled back and lifted off the frame at its rear end, then slid forward to clear the barrel. With the catch in the 'fire' position dismantling is impossible.

The sights are roughly what one might expect in this sort of pistol; a blade at the front and a fixed notch at the rear, mounted in a block which can be knocked sideways for windage correction when zeroing. Accuracy is likewise average for the class, about four-inch groups at 25 yards. On the whole the Super Titan is a reliable and robust workaday pistol.

Taurus PT-92 and PT-99 Auto Pistols

Manufacturer Forjas Taurus SA,
Estrada do Forte 511, CP44, Porto Alegre
RS, Brazil
Type Locked breech, double-action semi-automatic
Caliber 9mm Parabellum
Barrel 4.9in (125mm)
Weight (empty) 34oz (964gm)
Magazine capacity 15 rounds

These two pistols bear a considerable resemblance to two Beretta designs, and it would appear that they are based on Beretta models but with slight modifications, and made under license in Brazil. They are currently being offered on the commercial market in the Americas and there is strong probability of their adoption by Brazilian military and security forces.

The PT-92 and PT-99 are virtually identical, the difference being that the 92 uses fixed sights and is intended as a service or combat weapon, while the 99 has wooden grips and adjustable rear sights and is intended for target shooting. The general form is that of the Beretta Model 92, a locked breech pistol using a variation of the Walther P-38 dropping block to lock barrel and receiver together during firing. The principal change is in the trigger guard, the front edge of which has a reverse curve which is serrated to provide a good grip for the popular two-handed grasp. The magazine is slightly different from the Beretta design, having a number of small holes in the rear face through which the cartridge contents can be counted.

The workmanship and finish of the

The Taurus PT-92 (top) and PT-99 pistols are based on Beretta designs; the PT-92 is now being issued to the Brazilian Army.

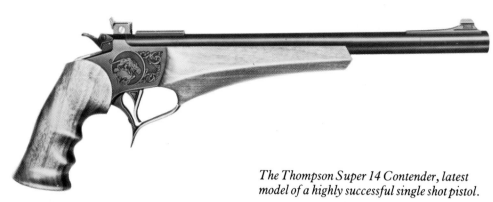

The Thompson Super 14 Contender, latest model of a highly successful single shot pistol.

Taurus pistols is very good, and they are of above-average accuracy for basic military pistols. The adjustable-sight model, once zeroed, is very good, being capable of off-hand two-inch groups at 25 yards in the hands of moderately-practised shooters.

Thompson-Center Super 14 Contender

Manufacturer Thompson-Center Arms Ltd., Rochester, NH 03867, U.S.A.
Type Single shot pistol
Caliber Various
Barrel 14in (355mm)
Weight ca 46oz (1315gm)

The Thompson-Center single shot pistol has been in existence since the late 1960s and has proved a very successful design. It has been made available in almost every possible caliber at various times; the company is a small one and staffed by practical men who, if they see a trend, can rapidly produce barrels to suit. Thus in the days when .17 caliber was all the rage, they produced several .17 chamberings, and when the fashion died away they abandoned them. It would profit us little to tabulate all the variations that have existed. The latest model, the Super 14, is intended principally for silhouette shooting, though it is likely to appeal also to hunters who prefer to use handguns.

The Super 14 would appear to have gained its name from the combination of several powerful chamberings and a 14in barrel; it is available in .30 Herrett, .357 Herrett, .30-30, .35 Remington, .41 Magnum and .44 Magnum, all of which qualify as 'super' loadings.

The basic design has changed little over the years. The Contender is still an elegant single-shot with a standing breech and a barrel which hinges down for loading. The Super 14 has a new grip, designed to provide a more firm anchorage when firing heavy loads, and a nicely-shaped fore end which is designed for a two-handed hold.

The foresight is a blade, while the rear sight can be had in two forms, open notch or aperture, both fully adjustable for elevation and windage. The long and heavy barrel gives good balance and a long sight

base, so that the pistol is certainly capable of as much accuracy as the shooter is likely to bring to it. Fired from a rest at 50 yards, groups between three and four inches are easily obtainable, though some care should be taken in selecting the ammunition.

Uberti Single Action Revolver

Manufacturer Aldo Uberti SpA, Brescia, Italy
Type Six shot, solid frame, single-action
Caliber .45 Colt
Barrel 7.5in (190mm)
Weight 40oz (1134gm)

This is not exactly new, though it reappears under a new name every few months. In the 1960s the 'spaghetti western' movies and the quick-draw craze appear to have hit Italy and several companies began making cheap and cheerful copies of the Colt 1873 'Frontier' to meet the demand. One or two of them realized that there could be something better in this, and seeing that there was a large demand for good single action revolvers (since Colt had stopped making theirs) began making good quality pistols and exporting them. Uberti are one of the best, and their products have appeared under their own name, under the names of various importers in the U.S. (eg Mitchell Arms Corp, Costa Mesa, CA.; Western Arms, Santa Fe, NM; Iver Johnson, Middlesex, NJ; and many more), and under various brand names – Cattleman, Buckhorn, Trailblazer and so forth.

The Uberti standard .45 uses a 7.5in barrel on a nicely color-hardened frame with brass trigger guard and solid walnut grip. The foresight is a serrated blade on a

One of several 'Western' designs from Uberti of Italy.

ramp, the backsight a square notch with adjustment for elevation and windage. The finish, both in appearance and in fit of the cylinder, is excellent, and the single-action trigger 'breaks' very cleanly with a consistent feel. It is capable of very good accuracy, provided some care is taken over selecting compatible ammunition; groups of under two inches at 25 yards are possible when rest-fired.

The Uberti design can be had in a wide variety of caliber and barrel length options; .44 Magnum and .357 Magnum chamberings are offered, and barrel lengths of 4.75, 5.5, 7.5, 10, 12 and 18 inches are possible; with the latter a shoulder stock is available.

Unique DES-69 Target Auto Pistol

Manufacturer Manufacture d'Armes de Pyrenees Francaises, Hendaye, France
Type Blowback, semi-automatic
Caliber .22 Long Rifle RF
Barrel 6in (152mm)
Weight 37oz (1050gm) (without weights)
Magazine capacity 5 rounds

This is another specialized weapon, specifically tailored to suit the requirements of the European 'Standard Pistol' match, which is based on the U.S. National Match rules. The dimensions of the weapon and such parameters as sight radius, trigger pull and weight are all closely regulated, so that the manufacturer's job is to produce the most accurate machine within those tolerances that he can.

The Unique DES-69 is one of the best-known stock European pistols for this type of contest and it is made by a company who have been in the pistol business since 1923. It has a long record of successes and will be seen on almost every pistol range.

The DES-69 is a simple blowback using a heavy fixed barrel and a short breech-block/slide with long 'wings' which run alongside the barrel and are serrated to provide finger grips for retracting the slide. The wooden grip is anatomically shaped, with palm rest, and frame and grip run

back, over the web of the thumb, to form a support for the rear sight, so as to take advantage of the maximum limits for sight radius of 8.6 inches (220mm). The construction is such that the barrel 'sits' low in the hand, and since all mechanical movement is confined to a short space above the grip, there is minimal disturbance of aim with each shot. Balance weights of 150, 260 or 350gm are provided and can be secured to the barrel, forward of the slide.

The pistol is hammer fired, the hammer operating in a well between the breech and the sight unit, though it is possible to reach it for thumb-cocking. The five-round magazines are loaded through the bottom of the butt in the usual way, and there is a magazine release button low on the left grip. The trigger is fully adjustable for reach, pull weight, slack and backlash, and the sear spring is also capable of adjustment, so that the shooter can tune the pull-off to his exact requirements.

On the range the DES-69 is capable of ultimate accuracy, but most shooters agree that it should be tested with various brands of ammunition in order to find one which is ballistically suited. Once this is determined, half-inch groups at 25 yards should be within most shooters' ability with some application.

Walther Model P5 Auto Pistol

Manufacturer Carl Walther GmbH, Post Box 4325, D-7900 Ulm, West Germany
Type Locked breech double-action semi-automatic
Caliber 9mm Parabellum
Barrel 3.5in (90mm)
Weight (empty) 28oz (795gm)
Magazine capacity 8 rounds

This is virtually an updated version of the well-known Walther P-38, used by the German Army from 1938 to 1945 and afterwards, as the P-1, adopted by the Bundeswehr. Like the Heckler & Koch P7 it was designed in response to demands from the West German police for a pistol which

combined rapid response with total safety. Walther took the well-proven locking system of the P-38 and wrapped a completely new configuration of pistol round it, incorporating several new safety features.

The P5 has an enveloping slide, but the barrel is semi-fixed and breech locking uses the familiar dropping block of the P-38, in which a locking plate holds slide and barrel together during a short recoil after which the plate descends and the slide is free to move backwards. An external hammer is cocked during this movement. However, the double action now incorporates a large thumb-lever which in one movement activates all the safety devices and drops the hammer safely on a loaded chamber. From this position the firer needs only to pull the trigger to fire the pistol; there is no manual safety catch to be operated.

Safety relies on the fact that until the very moment of firing the firing pin is held aligned with a recess on the face of the hammer; thus if the hammer should accidentally fall it will surround the firing pin head without touching it. In addition, the firing pin is never aligned with the solid part of the hammer except at the instant the hammer is released by the action of the trigger. There is also a disconnector which ensures that the trigger cannot affect the hammer unless the slide is closed and the breech securely locked.

When the trigger is pulled it begins to cock the hammer, and as the hammer reaches full cock so a trip lever is extended upwards and forces the firing pin into alignment with the hammer's solid face just as the hammer is released. If the hammer is thumb-cocked, or cocked by the action of the slide, then the releasing action of the trigger will still cause the trip lever to rise and align the firing pin.

The P5 has been adopted by the Netherlands Police and by the police forces of Baden-Wurttemburg and Rheinland-Pfalz in West Germany.

Walther PP Super Auto Pistol

Manufacturer Carl Walther Sportwaffenfabrik, Ulm 79, West Germany
Type Blowback, double-action, semi-automatic
Caliber 9mm Police
Barrel 3.62in (92mm)
Weight (empty) 30oz (850gm)
Magazine capacity 7 rounds

The Walther PP (Polizei Pistole) is well-known around the world and has been the source of inspiration for a number of copyists for many years, and in spite of its age it still sets the standard for the rest and sells as fast as Walther can make it. It is an elegant design, reliable and accurate, and it pioneered a double-action lock which has

The Unique DES-69 target pistol, showing the various balance weights and their application around the barrel.

PISTOLS

The Walther PP Super, another revision of a well-known model, chambered for the 'Police' cartridge.

rarely been surpassed for smoothness of operation. In the mid-1970s Walther decided to give it a face-lift and a new caliber in order to keep up with the changing demands of police authorities in Europe; though not exactly new, this pistol is so little-known outside Germany that we feel it is worth bringing into sharper focus.

The PP Super uses the same basic mechanism as the older PP but has an entirely new frame and slide assembly and is chambered for the 9mm Police (or 9mm × 18mm) cartridge, a round devised in Germany in order to obtain the maximum power from a blowback pistol, combined with good stopping power and a low risk of ricochet for use by police in urban areas. The frame is slightly longer, the slide longer and more 'squared-off' at its front end. The grips are carefully molded to a hand-filling shape and provided with a thumb-rest; wooden grips of similar contour can be had as an alternative. The trigger guard has been made slightly larger and with a vertical front edge to facilitate a two-handed grip of the pistol. The front sight blade has a night-aiming luminous spot in its rear face, while the rear sight is a square notch adjustable for windage and with a central luminous patch which can be aligned with the front spot in poor light.

The most significant change has been in the safety arrangements. In the old PP the safety catch on the slide dropped the hammer, locked the firing pin, and locked the trigger. With the pistol loaded, pressing the safety dropped the hammer and left everything locked; to fire, it was necessary to push the safety up and then pull the trigger to double-action the hammer to cock and drop. In the PP Super the safety locking function has been omitted; the safety catch is now only a decocking lever, and once the pistol is loaded this lever is pressed down; this rotates a block in front of a shoulder on the firing pin and releases the hammer. The firing pin is capable of vertical movement, and at this time is forced down in its housing by a spring, so that its end is aligned with a recess on the face of the hammer. Thus when the hammer falls, the face strikes the rear of the

slide while the recess surrounds the firing pin but does not touch it. If the trigger is now pulled, the hammer begins to rise to the cocked position, while a linkage forces the firing pin upwards in its housing, against the spring. This lifts it clear of the safety block and lines the end of the pin up with the solid face of the hammer, so that when the hammer falls, the pin goes forward to fire the cartridge. It is thus unnecessary to move the safety catch when firing in a hurry. This arrangement may sound somewhat unsafe, but it should be remembered that this is a weapon intended for use by police and similar well-trained people, so that some degree of short-cutting is acceptable.

Walther Model GSP-C Target Pistol

Manufacturer Carl Walther Sportwaffenfabrik, Ulm, West Germany
Type Blowback, semi-automatic
Caliber .32 S&W Long
Barrel 4.2in (107mm)
Weight 2.875lbs (1305gm)
Magazine capacity 5 rounds

This is the latest of a series of pistols developed by Walther for various types of pistol competition. The International Shooting Union (UIT) standard pistol contest has .32 as the minimum caliber, and since it is obviously advantageous to use the lowest caliber so as to have the least recoil and disturbance of aim, the .32 Smith & Wesson long cartridge became popular in Europe as a competition round. Walther had developed their GSP pistol for .22 Long Rifle rimfire, and seeing the rise of interest in .32 S&W they modified the design to centerfire and produced the GSP-C.

The pistol has a fixed barrel and a reciprocating bolt which works inside the square receiver. A box magazine fits ahead of the trigger guard, which helps, with the heavy barrel block, to keep the weight forward and thus arrive at the balance preferred by contestants. The rimmed cartridge might be expected to give problems in feeding from the magazine, but this has been overcome by raking the magazine rather sharply so that the rounds are loaded with the rims ahead of each other; feeding is thus

The Walther GSP-C target pistol, firing the .32 Long Wadcutter cartridge.

smooth and feed jams are unknown.

The wooden grips are angular in appearance but fit the hand well and there is a palm rest on the right side. The foresight is a blade, interchangeable for others of different height and thickness, while the rear sight is a leaf with square notch, fully adjustable for elevation and windage. The trigger assembly is in an interchangeable unit; there are adjustments for slack, trigger position, travel and weight of pull within certain limits; if these limits do not suit the firer he can change the unit for one with a different range of pull tension and begin adjusting again. The trigger unit can also be replaced by a special training unit which has a ratchet device and gives five 'dry shots' for every winding.

Accuracy is what one would expect from a pistol of this type and quality; groups fractionally over one inch at 25 yards when fired from a rest. Certainly the pistol will be capable of as much accuracy as the firer will be able to put into it.

Wichita Mark 40 Target Pistol

Manufacturer Wichita Arms, 333 Lulu, PO Box 11371, Wichita, KS 67211, U.S.A.
Type Bolt action single shot target pistol
Caliber .308 Winchester (7.62mm NATO)
Barrel 13in (330mm)
Weight (empty) 4.5lbs (2.04kg)

This is a highly specialized pistol known more specifically as a 'Silhouette Pistol' since it is primarily designed for the competitions organized under the rules of the International Handgun Metallic Silhouette Association. Briefly, these involve shooting high velocity ammunition against life-like animal silhouettes at long ranges; there is, though, no reason why this pistol should not make a good hunting weapon, fitted with suitable sights.

The Mark 40 pistol uses an aluminium receiver which has a steel insert for attachment of the barrel; within the receiver slides a breech bolt using three lugs to lock into the breech, giving an extremely secure lock. The bolt handle is on the left side of the pistol, and has a flattened and turned-down handle which can be operated by the shooter's left hand while he retains his hold on the pistol with his right. There are three holes in the bolt which will allow a safe venting of gas should a primer be punctured.

The stock of the pistol is of glass fiber-reinforced plastic and is shaped into a comfortable pistol grip with thumb rest. The trigger is fully adjustable for travel and weight of pull and is smooth in action with a crisp let-off point.

The sights consist of a tubular front with post insert and an open rear with arcuate

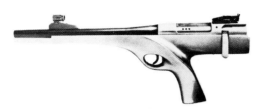

The Wichita Mark 40 long range bolt action pistol.

notch; the two combine to form the 'Wichita Multi-Quick' system in which the front sight can be adjusted in elevation and the rear sight for both elevation and windage. The rear sight has a knurled adjusting knob which can be used to set predetermined values once these have been established by zeroing and the sight settings recorded by tightening specified screws in the rear sight unit. The front sight can be used for making corrections on the day to compensate for minor meteorological and other changes.

In practical use the pistol is heavy, but necessarily so when one considers that this is firing a full-sized rifle cartridge. The sights are clear and the pistol is extremely accurate; indeed, some observers have said that it really needs a telescope sight to bring out its full potential, though this, of course, is going beyond what the designer set out to do. For its specified purpose the Mark 40 sets a very high standard and reaches it admirably. Like most target weapons it needs to be fired with various types of ammunition to decide which suits it (and the shooter) best, but with this question settled, two-inch groups at 100 yards are well within its capability. We should also note that it can be obtained chambered for a specialized 'wildcat' cartridge, the 7mm IHMSA, a round developed for silhouette shooting and based on the .308 Winchester case.

Wildey .45 Auto Pistol

Manufacturer Wildey Firearms Co. Inc., Cold Spring, NY 10516, U.S.A.
Type Locked breech, gas-operated, semi-automatic
Caliber .45 Winchester Magnum or 9mm Winchester Magnum
Barrel 6in (152mm)
Weight 51oz (1445gm)
Magazine capacity 8 rounds (.45); 15 rounds (9mm)

This pistol has been the better part of seven years in development and now appears to be entering commercial production. It stems from a basic idea which was briefly explored by Husqvarna, the Swedish gunmakers, before they got out of the firearms business several years ago. The Swedes saw little point in the complication of gas operation with the standard military

calibers, but the Wildey company saw that this system could sustain extremely high pressures and in conjunction with Winchester developed the idea of the pistol and the idea of specially powerful pistol cartridges in parallel. The result is a pistol which will handle two unique cartridges in safety and comparative comfort.

The Wildey relies upon a rotating breech block which locks into a series of lugs in a barrel extension which overhangs behind the chamber. The block is carried in the slide, which resembles the slide of any other auto pistol in external appearance and function. The block is capable of limited rotation, controlled by a cam pin and cam track in the slide. In front of the slide, and surrounding the barrel is an annular gas piston, and in front of that is a vent leading to the interior of the barrel. This vent is interrupted by a regulator which permits more or less gas to be admitted from the barrel to the piston, or which can shut off the gas altogether to permit the pistol to be used as a hand-loader.

On firing, a proportion of the gas passes through the vent and impinges on the piston, driving it back for a short distance; the rear face of the piston is in contact with the slide front, so that the slide is thus driven back. As it moves, so the bolt cam pin rides down a straight section of track, thus permitting the bolt to remain closed and locked until the bullet has left the muzzle and the gas pressure has dropped, after which the pin is made to move sideways by the cam track; this causes the bolt to rotate through an angle, unlocking its lugs from the recesses in the barrel extension. Once this unlocking has taken place the slide and bolt are free to recoil, against twin recoil springs, cocking the hammer; at the end of the recoil stroke the slide is driven forward, chambering a cartridge, and the bolt is rotated into the locked position.

The two special cartridges developed for use with the Wildey are the .45 Winchester Magnum and the 9mm Winchester Magnum. These have been developed from scratch and are not merely modifications of existing cases; the cases are particularly strong so as to withstand the high pressures. In broad terms they resemble the .45

The Wildey .45 gas-operated automatic pistol.

ACP and 9mm Parabellum except that they are considerably longer, and they develop much higher velocities – about 1450ft/sec for the .45 and about 1500ft/sec with the 9mm. As might be imagined, these give rise to considerable recoil in the pistol, but due to the weight and the absorbent qualities of the gas locking system, it is not excessive.

It is early days yet to say how the Wildey will catch on, but it certainly gives every appearance of being a practical hunting pistol and it has also been suggested as a possible for metal silhouette shooting.

Zastava Model 70 Auto Pistol

Manufacturer Zavodi Crvena Zastava, Beograd, Jugoslavia
Type Blowback, semi-automatic
Caliber 7.65mm (.32) or 9mm Short (.380 Auto)
Barrel 3.7in (94mm)
Weight 26.1oz (740gm)
Magazine capacity 8 rounds

This well-finished pistol is the standard side-arm of the Yugoslav Army in .380 caliber and is commercially available in many parts of Europe and under various trade-names in 7.65mm caliber. It may also be met in the U.S.A. under different names. A point to note is that the company monogram of ZCZ on the grips is very similar to the CZ of Ceskoslovenska Zbrojovka, leading the unwary to believe they are acquiring a Czechoslovakian product.

The Zastava, in either caliber, is a robust and simple blowback pistol of conventional pattern. The design is, in fact, a scale-down of the Soviet Tokarev, in some respects, though the locked breech has been abandoned. There is a manual safety on the left side of the frame which locks the slide and the trigger mechanism when applied, and there is also a magazine safety which locks the sear when the magazine is removed. The frame is well-shaped for a firm grip, and the distribution of weight has been carefully controlled so that the weapon tends to stay on target when firing and thus deliver better accuracy and quicker response.

The Jugoslavian Zastava pistol.

The Great American Pistol Test

For many years the US military were reluctant to part with the well-tried Colt .45 M1911A1 pistol, even though none of their NATO partners used .45 ammunition. Old habits die hard, and the arguments advanced in 1908 to justify selection of the .45 bullet were still being advanced sixty years later to justify its retention, even though the NATO standard 9mm Parabellum bullet has killed far more people than the .45 ever has.

Eventually, in 1979, the US Army decided that it was time to consider replacing the aged warrior with a modern 9mm pistol. This decision was forced on them since the supply of M1911A1s was beginning to dry up. None had been made to Government contracts for many years, most of the military stock has been reconditioned at least once, and the guns in service were gradually succumbing to old age, wear and tear. Morover a long series of experiments at Edgewood Arsenal had finally shown that the 9mm bullet was just as lethal as the .45 model.

Once the decision to test was taken, the next question was to lay down some sort of guide-lines as to what was wanted, largely in order to screen out designs which were obviously useless and which could waste valuable testing time. The general specification asked for a pistol with double-action trigger, a minimum of 13 rounds in the magazine, and capable of being used by either left- or right-handed shooters. in order to conduct a meaningful test it is, of course, necessary to establish some basic standards, so two existing service pistols were selected as 'control' models, their performance being the acceptable standard which the test pistols had to reach or exceed. The two controls were the .45 M1911A1 and the Smith & Wesson Model 15 .38 Special revolver with 4-inch barrel, as used by the Air Force.

The pistols eventually selected for test were, by any reckoning, among the world's best military handguns. Heckler & Koch of Germany submitted their VP-70 and P9S models; Star of Spain their M28DA; FN of Belgium their well-known GP-35 Hi-Power model, the FNDA which is a double-action variation of the GP-35, and their new FNFA or 'Fast Action', an FNDA with a new hammer mechanism. Beretta of Italy offered their Model 92S, Smith & Wesson their well-known M549, and Colt produced the 'SSP' or 'Stainless Steel Pistol', a new design based on the M1911 mechanism but with double action and various other improvements.

Since the US Army has very few 9mm weapons in its inventory, it has paid very little attention to development of a 9mm cartridge, and the service 9mm M1 round is not exactly at the leading edge of ballistic technology. So much so that when testing began it was found that nothing of any significance could be determined because the ammunition itself was inaccurate and inconsistent in its performance. So it was necessary to purchase commercial hollow-point cartridges in order to carry out the first test, which consisted of accuracy firings.

In order to set a standard, test barrels were used to evaluate the ammunition. These are heavy barrels, devoid of any furniture or other mechanism, simply a tube by which the bullet is directed at the target. They are so heavy that there is no weapon jump or other effect worth considering, so that what happens at the target is entirely due to the ammunition.

Left: Pistol testing in Britain, using the Smith & Wesson revolver as the control weapon, just as in the U.S.A.
Below: The Beretta Model 92, the basic model of the series, showing the double-column magazine.

By these firings it was possible to specify the size of 10-shot group which the cartridge were capable of producing, after which the pistols could be fired to see what size of group *they* produced.

The pistols were first fired from a machine rest, firmly clamped so that there could be no movement of the weapon as happens when held by a human firer. Ten 10-shot groups were fired from each pistol. The pistols had to deliver a 10-shot group not more than 1.4 times the size of the group delivered by the test barrel with the same ammunition. In practice this meant that a pistol delivering a group measuring between six and seven inches in diameter was graded as 'marginal'; anything greater than seven inches was out, anything less than six inches was in.

Winner of this phase of the event was the Heckler & Koch P9S, all of whose shots were covered by a 3.5 inch circle. Runners-up were the Smith & Wesson revolver and the Beretta M92S. Also within the 'acceptable' category were the Smith & Wesson M459 and the FNFA. 'Marginal' classification went to the Star M28DA and the FN GP—35. The remainder – H&K VP-70, FNDA, Colt SSP and M1911A1 were all rejected as inaccurate, having exceeded the seven-inch circle; indeed, the M1911A1 needed a 15-inch circle to contain its average 10-shot group.

Having shown what the pistols could do alone, the next test was to put them in the hands of some actual people and see what difference that made. Practical accuracy tests are always a bone of contention with testers; if you put up a team of crack-shots, you are immediately criticized because in real life half the people using the weapon won't be that good; if you put up a team of 'average' shots, the argument then starts about how average is average? And if you put up a team of absolute tyros, then nobody gives the results any credence anyway. The testing panel decided to try and solve this one by using three teams; the first was composed of highly skilled shots, the second of 'above average' shots, and the third were female security police, so that the final figures ought to be an acceptable average, not unduly weighted either to the expert or to the tyro.

Each tester fired ten 10-shot groups from each weapon; not straight off the string, but spread over a period of time; they might fire 20 shots from Weapon A today, 10 from Weapon C tomorrow, 30 from weapon F the day after. This ensured averaging-out such things as weather conditions, the 'Monday morning feeling,' 'off days' and all the notional ills which tend to plague the human race.

The results were examined in relationship to the person doing the shooting; an expert shot, it was felt, should be capable of consistently firing five-inch groups at 25 yards, while the 'above average' group should be capable of making seven-inch groups. Unfortunately the records do not tell us what was expected of the novices; their results were discarded from the test since several of them missed the target entirely.

Left: Old Faithful; the colt M1911 (top); M1911A1 (center) and 9mm Commander (bottom), showing the gradual evolution of John Browning's classic design.
Right: The Beretta 92SB, a special version of the Beretta 92 developed for the U.S. trials, showing the ambidextrous safety catch on the slide and the relocated magazine catch.

A Spanish contender, the Star 28DA, a very modern design which did not do well in the trials.

Rated 'acceptable' from the hand-firing test were the Smith & Wesson M15 revolver, the Beretta M92S and the Heckler & Koch P9S. The Star M28DA, FN FA, Colt SSP and Smith & Wesson M459 rated 'marginal', and the FN HP and the M1911A1 were beyond the limits.

The hand-fired accuracy test was solely concerned with accuracy, and the firers had complete freedom as to how they held the pistol, how they stood, how long they took. And in those conditions accuracy can be expected. But as anyone with experience will tell you, what comes out of that sort of accuracy test does not necessarily bear any relationship to what happens when the pistol is used 'for real,' when the shooter is confronted with multiple targets and is pressed for time. So the next test was for effectiveness in a simulated combat situation.

The shooters were confronted with a number of targets between 25 and 50 yards away, and stood facing the target with the pistol drawn and loaded and with the hammer down. On command, two shot were fired at each target in succession, with various time limits imposed. Once again each shooter fired each competing pistol at least twice, but at this stage of the trial the inevitable organizational hiccups began to make themselves felt. There were changes in personnel, delays due to various reasons, and as a result it became impossible to quantify the results as to the ability of three groups of shooters.

Nevertheless, the results were impressive. No matter who

Modern techniques in use; a trial is recorded by video camera for subsequent analysis. Here a technical expert explains the pistol and ammunition about to be fired.

fired the Beretta M92 they showed an averge of over 50 percent better results than they could achieve with either of the two 'control' pistols. Similarly, the FN GP-25 showed a 45 percent improvement, and the Heckler & Koch P9S a 37 percent improvement. The Smith & Wesson M459 gave a 33 percent gain, the Colt SSP a 32 percent gain, the FNFA 16 percent and the Star M28DA one percent. So all the test pistols proved that they were better in combat than either of the existing service weapons.

Having thus sorted out the contestants for their accuracy, the next question was to grade them for their reliability. Indeed, for military use reliability is sometime considered to be more important than accuracy, and there are several instances of reliable but less accurate weapons being selected for service over accurate but less reliable designs. The only way to test reliability is to fire the weapon until something goes wrong, and a 10,000 round program was, therefore, organized for each pistol. If any pistol developed an obvious design fault at the commencement of the test, then the manufacturer would be allowed to modify it, but this had to be a genuine re-design. No patching up, or running repairs were permitted, and once the trial had gotten fairly under way, then no further modification would be allowed.

The Colt M1911A1 has often been held up to be a model of reliability, and it was, therefore, surprising to find that of the four pistols used in the 10,000 round test, only two survived. One pistol suffered a cracked frame at 8,000 rounds, while the other had a cracked slide at 6,400 rounds. The magazines also gave trouble, lips deforming and cracking so as to prevent feeding. In some repects, however, it has to be said that this was an unfair test for the 'controls,' since the M1911A1s must have been at least thirty years old and there is no telling how many thousnds of rounds they had already fired. Take this factor into account and the Colt record doesn't look quite as bad.

Surprisingly, the worst performer in the reliability test was the Heckler & Koch VP-70, a weapon which most Europen tests have indicated to be simple and rugged. In this case the four test guns fired 771 rounds between them, suffered 109 failures to fire, 22 failures to feed, one failure to chamber, four failures to eject and one other, unspecified, failure, giving an average of five shots between malfunctions.

Equally bad was the Star M28DA. For a total of 5526 rounds fired there were 1142 malfunctions, again giving a mean time between failure of five rounds.

Next came the FNFA, with 8585 rounds fired, 305 malfunctions, 28 rounds between failures. It is interesting to note that although the FNFA gave several failures to feed, chamber and eject, it never once failed to fire once the cartridge was in the chamber, a record unequalled by any other competing weapon.

The Heckler & Koch P9S fired 18,697 rounds, suffered 357 malfunctions to give a mean of 52 rounds between failures. The P9S gave no failures to eject, but managed 113 failures to fire.

FN's GP-35, another well-tried weapon, fired 18,796 rounds, suffered 254 malfunctions and gave a failure rate of

The Beretta SB Compact, a further refinement of the original Model 92 which emerged as a direct result of the US Army specifications.

72 rounds. Its principal defect appears to have been a reluctance to extract or eject the fired case.

Colt's SSP fired only 7636 rounds before being retired from the test. It produced 63 malfunctions for a mean figure of 121 rounds between failures. Unfortunately some of the malfunctions were pretty basic – front sights kept falling off, for example – which rather spoiled the good effect.

FN's DA model came in with 33,600 rounds to its credit and 81 malfunctions, giving an average of 415 rounds between failure. Even so, this performance fell below the cut-off point of 500 rounds between failure, so the DA, and all the others so far mentioned, were graded 'Unacceptable' for reliability.

Which left just three weapons; the Colt M1911A1, in spite of its cracked frame and slide problems, managed to fire 34,400 rounds – in other words, two of the four test pistols managed the full 10,000 rounds without major problems. Malfunctions totalled 46, giving 748 rounds between failure. Then came the Smith & Wesson M549, the only contestant whose four pistols all fired their allotted 10,000 rounds. This produced 42 failures, giving an average of 952 rounds between malfunctions.

And top of the list was the Beretta M92S. For a variety of reasons these four pistols were unable to complete the full

10,000 round test and were only able to fire 28,000 rounds between them. But those 28,000 rounds produced only three failures to feed, two failures to chamber, two failures to fire, six failures to extract or eject, and one 'miscellaneous' failure, a total of 14 failures to give a remarkable 2000 rounds between malfunctions.

Mathematical analysis of reliability is one thing; making sense of the figures is another. It is incredible, for example, that the Heckler & Koch VP-70, which has been on the market now for ten years, could only manage five rounds between failures. The Star is another astonishing perform-

The Heckler & Koch P7 in its original '9mm Police' caliber; a special version in 9mm Parabellum featured in the U.S. Trials.

The SIG-Maremont P226, devoloped by SIG of Switzerland and marketed in the U.S.A. by the Maremont Corporation.

ance, since this pistol is used by the Spanish Army and also by the South Africans, without complaint. And considering that something like 50 armies have the FN GP-35 as their standard, and that it has been in production and service for almost fifty years, one begins to wonder how the 'unacceptable' rating fits in with such distinguished service. As any practical shooter knows, auto pistols tend to be somewhat choosy about ammunition, and we rather think that a different make of 9mm brass might have given a very different answer. Admittedly, a military pistol *shouldn't* be choosy; it should cheerfully swallow anything and everything which it come across, so perhaps the test would have had more meaning if the ammunition had been a randomly-mixed pile of 9mm Parabellum garnered from all over the world.

The test then went on the grade 'maintainability' which, to most eyes, is a somewhat subjective criterion. In this case it was assessed by considering the record of failure with the amount of effort required to bring the pistol back into firing order and the speed at which the repair could be completed. There were only two complete failures among the test pistols, the Star and the Colt SSP, both of which were rated 'Unacceptable'. The Beretta 92S rated 'Excellent', the FN DA 'Marginal' and the rest were 'Acceptable'. Of the two 'control' pistols, the M1911A1 rated 'Acceptable' while the Smith & Wesson Model 15 revolver failed.

Finally there were to be comprehensive environmental tests; the pistols were to be frozen in −65°F cold stores and baked in 125°F hot boxes before being fired for reliability, but this program had to be cancelled after it was found that (again) the ammunition was incapable of functioning reliably in these extremes of temperature. After this came the test routine which normally segregates the sheep from the goats in any weapons test program – the dust, sand and mud tests.

In these tests the weapons were loaded and cocked and the hammer lowered; they were then thrown into a container filled with the selected medium, swished around, left to stand for a while, and then removed. The firer was then permitted to shake the weapon and brush it with his hands so as to remove whatever he could, after which he attempted to fire it. The result was graded according to how much additional effort was then needed to make the pistol function. 'Without Assistance' meant just that; the firer raised the pistol, pressed the trigger, and it fired. 'With Minor Manipulation' meant that pushing the slide forward, giving the pistol a sharp blow with the hand, nudging the cylinder round, allowed the weapon to be fired. 'With Significant Manipulation' indicated that the firer had to take several seconds of time and go through some involved routine to get the weapon to work.

Now, in the field, of course, the firer might rescue his pistol from the sand or mud and, having time and being an intelligent man, would eject the magazine or empty the cylinder and reload. So after the initial firing attempt, successful or not, this was the next test. The gun went back

The Smith & Wesson M459, second place winner in the U.S. trials.

into the container, was swished around again, removed, the magazine removed and the chamber cleared, a new magazine inserted, the slide operated and an attempt made to fire. And finally a loaded magazine was flung into the medium, removed, hand-cleansed, loaded and another attempt to fire was made.

The results of this series of tests makes complicated reading, but the outcome was that the Smith & Wesson revolver came out tops in both the sand and mud tests, carrying its original load of ammunition. In the sand test it was seconded by the M1911A1 and then by the FN DA, the Beretta 92S and the Smith & Wesson M459. In the mud test the Beretta 92S came second. Permitted to reload, the Beretta came first in the sand test, the S&W revolver in the mud test with the Beretta second.

And with that the test came to a close – and although it may sound like a fairly simple set of routines it in fact took about a year to complete – and the Joint Services Small Arms Panel sat down to look at the results and make some reports and recommendations. The first conclusion was that of all the pistols tested the only ones sufficiently reliable for military use were the Beretta 92S and the Smith & Wesson M459. Then came a string of conclusions regarding relative accuracy and reliability of the various test pistols and the controls. Then the final conclusion, that the Beretta 92S was superior to all of the other 9mm pistols and to the two controls. Finally came the recommendation: That the Beretta M92S pistol should be adopted to fulfil all military requirements for a standard sidearm.

And that, you might have thought, would be that; a somewhat shaming result for some manufacturers, but at least a clear-cut statement of what was considered, on all the evidence, to be the best available handgun for adoption by the US services. Moreover, it had been a condition of entry into the tests that any foreign manufacturer had to agree to manufacturing this pistol, should it be selected, in the USA. So on the face of it there was no reason why the recommendation should not have been followed up by some sort of action. But nothing whatever came of it.

Some time after the results of the trial had been determined, the US Army decided to conduct another trial of its own. Again it circularized the world's manufacturers, but this time only four were interested enough to submit pistols. Beretta came along with their Model 92SB, a slight modification of the successful M92S which had a safety locking device on the firing pin; Smith & Wesson came back with their M459A, again, a slight modification to the safety system; Heckler & Koch put forward their P7A13, an improved version of their standard P7 which had a 13-round magazine; and a new entrant, the Maremont Corporation, put forward the SIG-Maremont P226 which is, in fact, the Sig-Sauer P226 used in Europe.

The Army test followed much the same lines as had the JSSP test, except that the requirement that every pistol fire 5000 rounds between the breaking of any components in order to be rated 'Acceptable' was cut out and no limiting figure was quoted. The reliability test specified that the gun could not jam more than once in 800 shots, whereas the previous test had specified once in 1500 shots. Whether these changes were made in order to arrive at a figure somebody

felt was more realistic, or whether, as some critics have suggested, they were changed simply to make the test easier, is open to discussion, but don't expect the US Army to join in. They resolutely refuse to discuss any aspect of this test. The only thing they have said is that the test was not designed to suggest that the earlier tests were bad; the earlier tests were conducted merely to allow some figures to be arrived at so that the Army could establish guidelines for a Request For Proposals for the second test.

The results of the Army tests have never become public; all that was announced, on February 19th 1982, was that

Pistol testing involves hours of hard work; boredom cannot be allowed to creep in, since the testers must ensure that every pistol is given an even chance.

'The Army, today, in it role as the Defense Department executive agent for 9mm handgun procurement, has cancelled the procurement. It was not possible to make an award because the submitted weapon samples of all offerors had substantially failed to meet the essential requirements contained in the procurement solicitation. The Department of Defense intends to re-examine its requirements for a new handgun.'

Heckler & Koch's VP70 proved a disappointment in the trials, with a very high malfunction rate.

After much questioning, the Army made another statement, this time in mid-April; 'All candidates failed to meet test criteria in three areas; reliable operation in low temperature conditions; reliable operation in sand; and reliable operation in mud. No information on candidate weapons outlining specific shortfalls will be released. Since the Army is re-evaluating its requirements, the possibility of renewed competition exists, and such information is considered to be competition sensitive,'

As an example of how to lose friends and influence people adversely, this is in a class of its own. Three of the competitors threatened to take legal action for defamation, averring that the Army's announcement condemned their products for failure without specifying what the requirements had been nor how they failed. In both trials the manufacturers had gone to considerable trouble and expense to develop pistols tailored very closely to what the army wanted – Beretta, for example, moved their magazine release from the butt heel, the normal European location, to the butt front edge, the normal American location, and all the manufacturers had to develop ambidextrous safety catches. Modifications of this sort are not made cheaply nor easily. To

produce ten pistols each for trial must have involved the manufacture and testing of many more than that number, and, of course, as with all speculative military trials, the entire expense of development and supply was on the manufacturer's shoulders.

And there, for the time being, the matter rests. the Army and the JSSAP have retired behind the barricades and are remaining silent; the only official indication has been that the search for a new pistol has been postponed indefinitely. Meanwhile the M1911A1s continue to grow older; they are the oldest military weapon in service with any major armed force in the world, and they look like becoming the first centenarians.

The Colt SSP (Stainless Steel Pistol) is the latest derivation from the M1911 line of descent.

Ammunition Developments

Although the shape of the average round of small arms ammunition has not changed very much in the last 80 or so years, it would be wrong to think that there has been no advance at all in design. Indeed, it is probably only the shape which displays anything in common between today's ammunition and that of the earlier generations.

At the heart of the matter is the simple desire of the shooter to have a cartridge which will fire a bullet on a perfectly flat trajectory and, having reached the target, kill the game stone dead without damaging it. The fact that this is a physical impossibility does nothing to stop him wanting it. The designer, for his part, is anxious to provide the shooter with the closest approximation to what he wants, but at the same time do it without wearing out the rifling of the weapon or subjecting the shooter to a recoil force which will break his shoulder. And it is the various ideas which appear in the hope of solving these problems which account for the changing inner design of ammunition.

If we get away from the game-shooting field and into the military and security fields, the desires are somewhat different. The military want a bullet which, much the same as the game shooter, will go straight to the target and kill, but they are constrained by sundry international conventions which prevent them using anything other than a jacketed solid-point bullet. Morover, if, by some means or other, they manage to step up the lethality of the bullet without contravening the conventions, then the humanitarian lobby will soon be condemning them. Fifty years of 'B' pictures has conditioned people to think of bullets as killing neatly and with minimum damage to the recipient; which, I suppose, is why we never hear the humanitarian lobby having much to

Above: The basic bullet types; left, a non-streamlined bullet, best for use at supersonic velocities; right, a boat-tailed bullet, best for use where much of the flight is at subsonic velocities.
Opposite: What the sub-projectile can do; a depleted uranium sub-projectile from an experimental discarding sabot shot, together with the hole it makes in two inches of armour plate.
Below: Spark photograph of a .308 Winchester bullet in flight shows the sonic wave springing from the tip, the air flow over the surface, and the turbulent drag area behind the base. The boat-tailing of the rear section of the bullet allows a smoother air flower and reduces the drag turbulence.

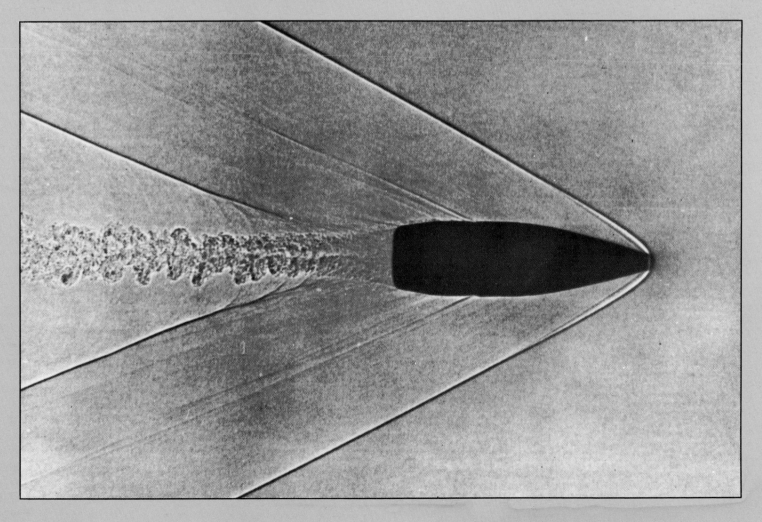

say about landmines or artillery shell fragments. It is perfectly acceptable to have your head taken off by a flying shard of steel, but unacceptable to have the back of it removed by a .223 bullet.

Police and security men have another set of problems. Here they need to stop a felon in his tracks at one hundred yards range, but should the bullet miss, then it must be completely harmless to innocent bystanders and not ricochet. If the designer despairs of this, he can turn to the other request, for a bullet capable of dropping a hi-jacker but not of ripping through the pressure fuselage of the airplane should it miss.

Exaggerated? Well, perhaps so, but there remains an element of truth in all of it. So let us look at how the designers are getting to grips with the problems.

Velocity lies at the root of most ammunition problems and their solution. If you fire it fast enough a plain ball of lead will penetrate armor plate, but here we are talking about 6-7000 feet a second, something which can be achieved in ballistic experimental ranges with special equipment but which is out of the question for practical application. But the higher the velocity which can be achieved, the more accurate the shooting will be, other things being equal. This is simply because of the flatter trajectory to be obtained with a rise in velocity; and the flatter the trajectory, the easier the sighting problem and the more likely the bullet is to hit where it is aimed.

So long as we are talking about standard commercial cartridges, whose dimensions are long settled and may even be governed by international standards, it must be obvious that there is a limit to the velocity to be achieved, a limit which is reached when the cartridge case is as full of powder as it can be. This is not to say completely full; it is vital to leave a small air space in the case to permit proper ignition and burning, but the net result is the same. Once you have reached the capacity limit of the case, with the best propellant you can find, then you have reached the limit of velocity for that particular charge and bullet combination. Improvements can be obtained by using a lighter bullet, but for a given caliber and twist of rifling there isn't all that much latitude in bullet weight.

One must, of course, retain a sense of proportion when filling the cartridge case, since there is a limit to what the rifle itself will stand in the way of internal pressure, and it is this safety limit which, in some cases, governs the maximum charge possible. We feel sure, though, that if some ammunition designer was to produce a round which would develop 5000ft/sec at 75,000lbs pressure, it would not be long before a rifle capable of accepting it would appear.

More important than velocity, though, is consistency. It is of little use to have a cartridge which pokes out the first shot at 3500ft/sec, the second one at 3200, the third at 3400 and so on; more than one highly-touted cartridge of high velocity has quietly settled down to a slower figure in later life once it has become apparent that the top figure is reached but rarely and the inconsistencies mean a variety of trajectories with which the sights cannot cope. This is, perhaps, less important in pistol ammunition than in rifle ammunition, for in the latter case we are dealing in longer ranges in which the changes in trajectory can have a considerable effect. Pistol rounds, used over short ranges, are less sensitive, though

target shooters would probably disagree with that remark. Some years ago I ran several batches of 9mm Parabellum through a chronograph test and discovered some astonishing things. The hottest loading was German, dating from 1944 and delivering over 1225ft/sec; ten rounds of this gave a spread of 41ft/sec round-to-round variation. Modern NATO standard rounds from a British factory, less than two years old, averaged 1155ft/sec with a spread of 44ft/sec. A batch of five rounds made in Erfurt in 1914 gave 1067 with a spread of only 5ft/sec, while another German batch, made in Durlach in 1940 delivered 1127 and had a scarcely-believable spread of 1ft/sec from round-to-round. It is doubtful whether the recipient could tell the difference between 1225ft/sec and 1127ft/sec, but the consistency and accuracy of that last batch was well worth the loss in velocity.

The late Major Frank Hobart used to claim that the superior accuracy of some types of German military ammunition was due to the fact that it was designed to produce a higher chamber pressure and lower muzzle pressure than the equivalent British or American ammunition which, in general, developed lower chamber pressures and high muzzle pressures. Unfortunately he died and I retired before we could put together a test rig to pursue this theory, but anyone with the equipment and time to follow it up might make some interesting discoveries. One of the fundamental truths in artillery ballistics is that the all-burnt posi-

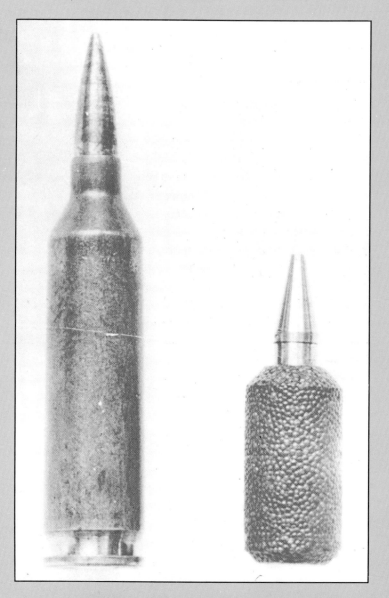

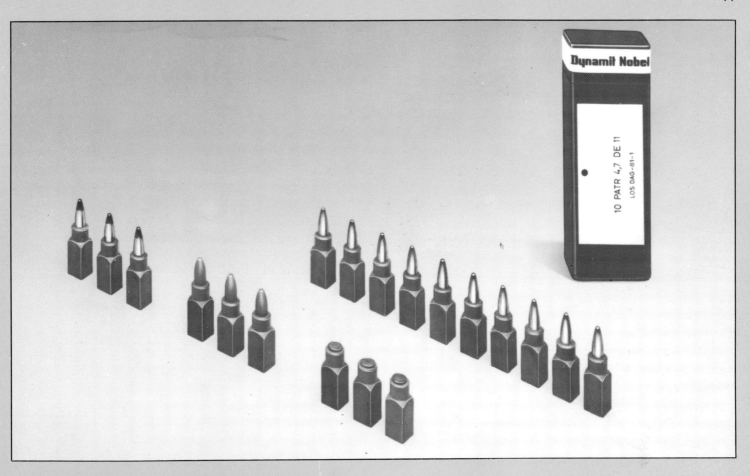

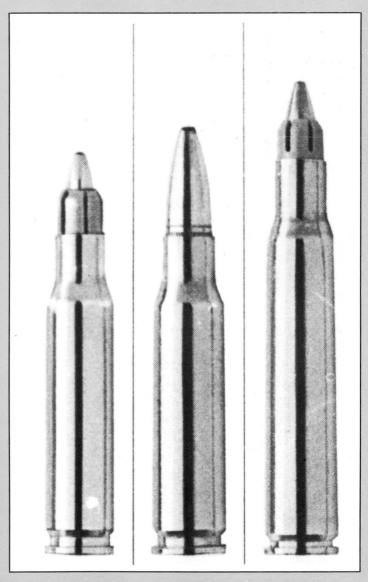

Above: Range of caseless cartridges developed for the Heckler & Koch G11 rifle; ball; tracer; practice (plastic bullet); and blank.
Left: An early type of caseless cartridge compared with a conventional round of the same caliber and performance. Notice that the propelling charge is normal ball powder held together by a plastic binder.
Right: Two Remington Accelerator cartridges with a conventional cartridge; left to right, Accelerator .308 WIn.; normal .308 WIn.; Accelerator .30-06.

tion – the location of the projectile at the instant all the propellant powder is consumed – needs to be about one-third the bore length back from the muzzle, so that the shell can settle down and attain a consistent velocity before leaving the muzzle. This rarely seems to obtain in small arms design, since many hot loadings are still burning the powder as the bullet makes its exit, and what this must do to consistency I hate to think.

So the optimum design involves velocity and consistency, but the existing cartridge cases are just about full of powder and there is very little room for further improvement along the basic lines of adding more powder or lightening the conventional bullet. There are two possible lines of attack, and both are currently being explored. One is to change the nature of the propellant powder, and the other is to change the nature of the bullet.

As mentioned elsewhere in these pages, Heckler & Koch of Germany have developed a rifle firing a caseless cartridge, and they have, more recently, been awarded a substantial contract from the US Army to lay the foundations of a caseless rifle program to meet American requirements. Their most pressing demand in the ammunition area was to develop a propellant which had sufficient mechanical strength to hold the bullet and primer and withstand the rough and tumble of travel through the magazine and into the chamber

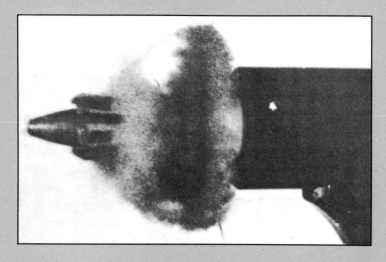

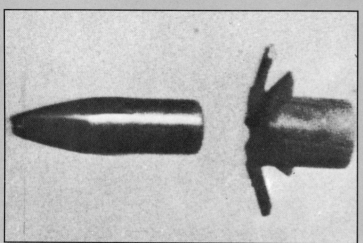

at a high rate of fire. Previous attempts at caseless cartridges used standard nitro-cellulose powder bound together with a synthetic resin, but this solution gave temperature problems. After several rounds had been fired, the heat transfer from the burning propellant to the rifle's chamber left the chamber so hot that an unfired caseless round would 'cook off' in a few seconds. To cure this, Heckler & Koch, in conjunction with Dynamit Nobel, the long-established German ammunition and explosives manufacturers, developed a totally new propellant which was not based on the traditional type of powder at all.

This new High Ignition Temperature Propellant (HITP) is derived from the hexogen (RDX) family of high explosives. Normally, the use of high explosive in a propelling cartridge would be fatal; instead of controlled burning you would get a detonation, a sudden molecular disruption, which would simply blow the weapon's chamber to pieces. But by 'moderating' the explosive with various types of additive, it becomes possible to dilute the action until it is no longer a detonation but, once again, a controlled burning.

Above left: A Remington Accelerator bullet leaving the muzzle of a rifle; the sabot is already beginning to separate from the sub-projectile.
Left: A Remington Accelerator bullet, clear of the muzzle, and with the sub-projectile cleanly separated from the sabot. Notice how the leaves of the sabot have been flung outward by centrifugal force while air drag has caused the whole sabot to fall behind the speeding sub-projectile.
Below: A collection of oddities; military experimental ammunition from the early 1970s. Left to right – two types of caseless cartridge, a discarding sabot round, a conventional bullet; a long-nosed bullet; and a cartridge with long bullet.

Once this stage is reached, you have a propellant, but because high explosives are more thermally efficient than standard propellants, you have a cartridge powder which will deliver much more power than simple nitro-cellulose. What this new propellant promises, therefore, is greater power for a given bulk, and therefore more velocity from a loading which will still fit into a standard cartridge.

We are still, however, faced with the question of maximum safe pressures, and here I have to admit that we are in unknown territory, since the pressures generated in the H&K G11 rifle have not been divulged and are unlikely to be for some time. But it does seem probable that this new propellant technology is capable of generating its energy in such a way as to keep the chamber pressure within limits but sustain a higher average pressure throughout shot travel – which comes back to Major Hobart's contention mentioned previously.

The HITP lifted the cook-off temperature by some 100°C, into the bargain, which solved Heckler & Koch's problem very nicely. So far as we are concerned, this additional attribute is also useful, since one of the prime defects of hot loadings is that they are, literally, hot – so hot that they melt away the steel of the chamber throat and gradually destroy the rifle's accuracy. A hot propellant which has a lower flame temperature and does not, therefore, wear out barrels, is something well worth thinking about. At the moment none of the world's ammunition manufacturers has yet offered a new propellant of this type, and we doubt whether we shall see one on the commercial market for perhaps three or four years, not until long trials and experiments have been performed and equivalent loadings worked out. But come it will.

So far as the bullet is concerned, the only feasible step in the direction of higher velocities is the discarding sabot bullet, currently marketed by Remington as their 'Accelerator'. In this, the bullet is one or two calibers smaller than the bore of the rifle, and the difference is made up by a plastic shoe or sabot which fills the bore. Obviously the smaller bullet plus the sabot weigh less than the standard bullet for the parent caliber, so that the sabot combination steps off up the barrel at a higher velocity. Once outside the muzzle, centrifugal force and air pressure strip away the plastic sabot and leave the bullet to travel to the target at a higher velocity than could be achieved by a full-size bullet from the same rifle.

So far, so good; but the bullet – or, to use the proper technical term, the 'sub-projectile' – is, doubtless for the same manufacturing convenience, the standard .223 (5.56mm) bullet, and, therefore, its flight characteristics outside the weapon are identical with those of a .223 bullet fired from a .223 rifle. In fact, if you plot the remaining velocity against range, you will obtain a graph which suggests that beyond 300 yards range the sub-projectile will lose velocity faster than a standard .30 full-caliber bullet.

But these are early days yet in the discarding sabot small arms field; it took the developers of discarding sabot

Right: Not small arms by any means, but an example of where the discarding sabot principle is at its best; this is a French fin-stabilized discarding sabot shot for a 105mm tank cannon.

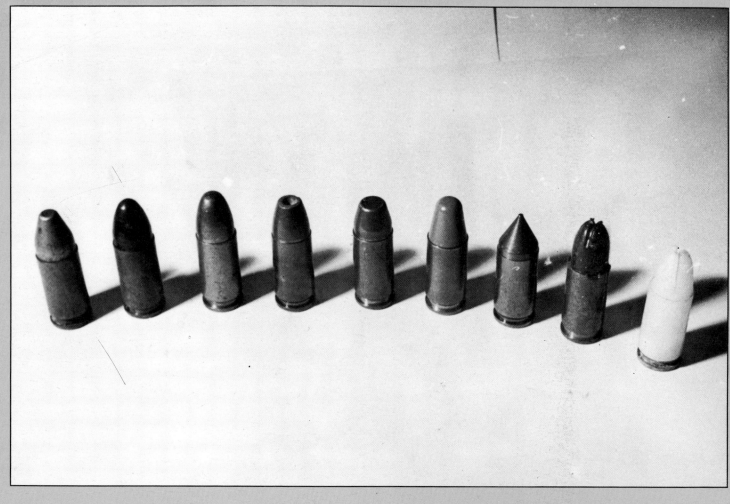

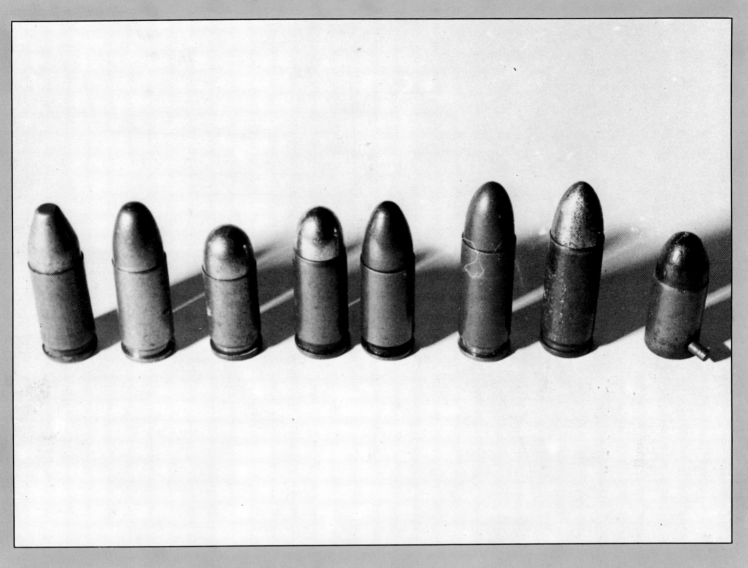

Above left: Left to right – the .62 × 39mm Soviet cartridge complete and separated, the .223 Armalite round; and the 7.92mm German 'Kurz' cartridge.
Below left: Left to right: original German Luger; German sintered-iron bullet; NATO standard; hollow-point commercial; explosive bullet; KTW metal-piercing; French metal-piercing spire-point bullet; plastic-bullet blank; completely plastic blank.
Above: Left to right; 9mm Luger; NATO standard 9mm Parabellum; 9mm Short; 9mm Browning Long; 9mm Makarov; 9mm Bergmann-Bayard; 9mm Steyr; and 9mm pinfire.

ammunition for artillery several years to perfect their design, and we can expect it to take even longer for commercial sabot ammunition to reach its optimum, if only because it is commercial and doesn't have the same resources as might a military development program. The first thing which will need to be looked at is the shape of the sub-projectile. It is often overlooked by commentators, but one of the greatest benefits promised by the sabot system is that it frees the designer of the sub-projectile from any shape restraints which are normally imposed by the peculiar conditions of use. For example, any conventional bullet must have a parallel-sided portion so that it has a bearing surface which can engage with the rifle's barrel, be engraved for spinning and also stabilize the bullet so that it exits spinning around its axis and not wobbling to any great degree. But in a sabot design, this task of collecting spin and riding on the rifle's bore is done by the sabot, and since this is going to be thrown away as soon as it leaves the muzzle, it can be designed for optimum performance inside the bore without having to

worry about its flight characteristics. The sub-projectile, on the other hand, can now be designed for the best possible flight characteristics without having to conform to any rules for inside the gun bore. This means that the tiny bullet need not have a straight line anywhere; it can be a perfectly-curved shape with a long nose and hemispherical base to cleave its way through the air and develop a smooth airflow over the body and minimal base drag behind it. Or, for that matter, any other shape which the designer calculates will give the flight characteristics – velocity, consistency, low drag, no yaw and so forth – that he desires.

The seond point about sabot ammunition is the fact that the best rifling twist for a sabot projectile is not the best for a conventional bullet, and it is not an ideal solution to ally a sabot design of cartridge to a standard rifle. To get the best possible accuracy and consistency from a sabot round it is generally necessary to steepen the twist of rifling to give a faster spin. This would, of course, mean over-spinning a conventional bullet from the rifle, but this is much the lesser of two evils. We might expect, therefore, that if sabot ammunition gathers momentum in the market-place, rifles designed to make the best use of it will soon appear.

The final point is that since the sabot-cum-sub-projectile weighs much less than the conventional bullet, it will be possible to step up the propellant loading without raising the chamber pressure to danger levels, and this will increase the velocity yet again. Unfortunately the normal pressure/time/space curve which depicts the performance inside the rifle as

the bullet departs is somewhat distorted in the case of sabot ammunition, due to the very high acceleration rate of the bullet. This means little to the bolt- or lever-action rifle, but it can play hob with a gas-actuated automatic, and Remington have pointed out that the Accelerator cartridge will not always work faultlessly in automatic rifles of different types.

At the present time the advantage of the discarding sabot cartridge is that it produces a muzzle velocity some 25-35 percent better than a conventional bullet in either the sub-projectile caliber or the parent caliber. This advantage dwindles as the bullet goes uprange but is still substantial; at 300 yards, for example, a .303 Win. bullet will be travelling at about 1950ft/sec, while a .308/.223 sabot sub-projectile will be moving at about 2250ft/sec. It is this retention of velocity which promises better performance at the target – cleaner kills against game – and which is drawing the attention of the military to this type of ammunition.

The most attractive area is in the development of an armor-piercing bullet. The standard .223 bullet is not the best vehicle in the world for tracer or armor-piercing roles, due to the relatively small space available in the bullet for the special fillers. Sabot design can do nothing for tracers, but by providing greater terminal velocity it could result in a more effective AP bullet. Moreover the freedom of design, mentioned earlier, could mean that a more effective AP core could be developed. At present, the steel-piercing element of the AP bullet has to fit inside the envelope and still leave sufficient jacket around it to allow the rifling to engrave and crush the envelope before it meets the resistance of the core. The core is, therefore, restricted in its dimensions and shape. But sabot design, as already explained, means that the sub-projectile is no longer governed by in-bore considerations; it is not too much to suggest that it might be possible to dispense with the jacket altogether and simply make the AP sub-projectile of nothing but hard steel, since there is no longer any need for a soft jacket of any kind when it is being carried in a sabot.

Turning now to the civil security and police aspect, the problem here is to develop a bullet which will stop the desperado but which will not richochet nor fly to extreme ranges should the firer miss. The military-style high velocity jacketed bullet is of little use in the close-quarter, usually urban, environments in which police generally operate. Fired at short range, these cartridges will most certainly stop the opposition, but they will pass through him and continue, to strike an innocent bystander or ricochet off the first hard surface. The most usual solution is to adopt soft-point or even hollow-point semi-jacketed or lead bullets. These meet most of the demands, but they have attracted a good deal of noise from the civil rights movements, who have lumped them under the general (and totally erroneous) term 'Dum-Dum Bullets,' and such a highly emotive name has given them some powerful lobby support. More seriously, the fact remains that hollow-points and the like cannot be guaranteed to perform in a predictable fashion. The same bullet might

One way of hitting the target is to double up on the bullets; the US Army's 'Duplex' .223 cartridge, in which the first bullet has the base slightly angled so that it veers off-axis as it leaves the muzzle. The second bullet stays on the bore axis, and the result is that the two strike within about one yard of each other at 300 yards range.

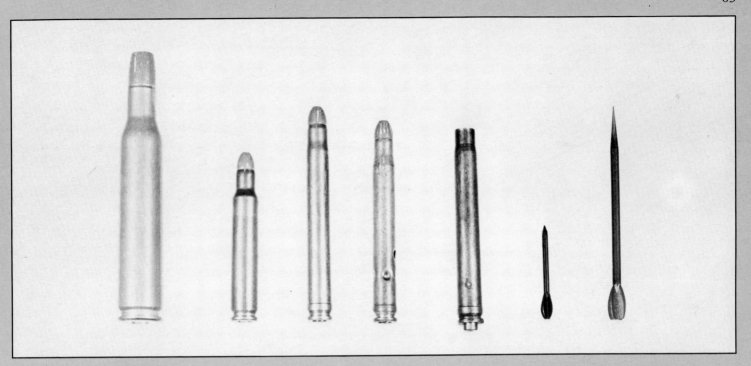

mushroom and make an effective stopping agent today, yet pass clean through the same type of target tomorrow without taking effect. Tiny differences in bullet construction, angle of incidence, velocity, and the precise point on the human body at which the bullet impacts can all make a surprising difference in performance. There is also the point that the velocities advertized by manufacturers are frequently not attained in actual use; a series of tests performed some years ago by the National Institute of Law Enforcement and Criminal Justice (NILECJ) showed that a .357 Magnum round with a nominal velocity of 1800ft/sec actually deliverd 1226ft/sec, while another which claimed 1900ft/sec could only produce 1161ft/sec. Police officers and others might like to bear this in mind when objectors cite 'advertized' velocities and extrapolate them into potentially fearful wounding powers.

In Europe, where police rarely use revolvers and rely more upon small-caliber automatic pistols, the use of hollow-point bullets is rare, simply because they tend to give feed problems in small automatics. As a result there is a good deal of work going on in Europe aimed at developing a bullet which will feed satisfactorily in automatics but which will produce stopping power as, or better than, a hollow-point revolver bullet. Metalwerke Elisenhutte have developed a 'Deformation Bullet' which outwardly resembles a standard 9mm Parabellum round-nosed bullet but which has most of the forward section of the bullet core hollowed out, with the curved jacket metal concealing the cavity. The jacket nose is sufficiently strong to allow the bullet to feed without hesitation, but on impact it deforms and, in effect, converts the bullet into a sort of hollow-point.

Dynamit-Nobel have developed what they call the 'Action Safety' bullet, a light copper alloy bullet with a hollow point filled with a plastic plug. The tip of the plug is shaped to the usual round-nose contour and allows for smooth feeding from the magazine into the chamber, and behind the plug, passing through the bullet, is a tiny vent or channel. When fired, the gas pressure behind the bullet passes through this vent and forces the plastic plug out of its seat, and because of

Flechettes and their cartridges; a selection of flechette designs tried out in the U.S.A. in the 1960s.

its low weight and consequent high acceleration the plug leaves the muzzle in front of the bullet. The design of the plug is such as to ensure a slight imbalance, so that once clear of the muzzle it yaws to one side and out of the path of the following bullet, which is now a hollow-point. The bullet's shape ensures a good stopping power, while its low sectional density, since it is made from low-weight alloy, leads to a rapid fall-off in velocity and striking energy and a low risk of ricochet.

Usually-reliable sources, as they say, indicate that other manufacturers are working along similar lines, but these are the only two which have seen any public description. It should be borne in mind that Europe has no equivalent of the Freedom of Information Act, nor is it ever likely to, and police activities fall under a similar blanket of security as military matters. Moreover the whole question of police armament is so set about by sociological, political and similar considerations, that it is hardly surprising that both the security forces and the manufacturers prefer to keep quiet about what they are doing until they can present a *fait accompli*.

Modern assault rifle ammunition: left to right – Soviet 5.45mm; British 4.85mm; .223; Soviet 7.62mm; NATO 7.62mm.

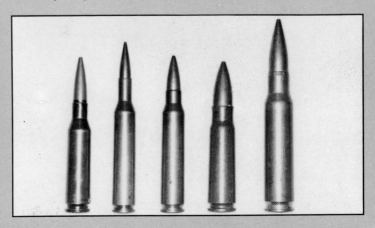

A U.S. Marine Corp sergeant on exercise with
his M-16 assault rifle. The M-16 is standard
U.S. issue.

RIFLES

The Anschutz Model 64 target rifle.

Anschutz Model 64 Silhouette Rifle

Manufacturer J.G. Anschutz GmbH, Ulm, West Germany
Type Bolt action, single shot
Caliber .22 Long Rifle RF
Barrel 21.63in (550mm)
Weight 7.93lbs (3.59kg)

The Anschutz Model 64 rimfire target rifle has been in production for some time, but this is a specially developed model intended to suit the growing sport of 'silhouette shooting' in which metal silhouettes of various animals are engaged at long range from the standing position, the idea being to approximate to hunting conditions. In smallbore silhouette shooting the targets are scaled down and the ranges are shorter than those used in full-bore contests, but the basic features remain the same.

The principal difference between this and 'prone' target rifles lies in the shape of the stock, which has a deep pistol grip and a high Monte Carlo comb so that the sights fall to the eye with minimum neck-twisting and the shooter can get a really firm grip on the rifle. The stock material is walnut, well finished and liberally stippled wherever the hand is likely to need to grip.

The bolt is substantial, and the trigger can be adjusted for first pressure and tension. The muzzle is counterbored to protect the edges of the rifling, and no sights are provided. The receiver is grooved to accept telescope mounts, which are the standard means of sighting in this type of shooting and the reason for the high comb of the stock.

The barrel is almost an inch in external diameter and heavy, and as might be expected the accuracy of this rifle is beyond reproach. Fired from a rest at 50 yards it should give groups well under an inch in diameter with almost any brand of ammunition, and if care is taken to match ammunition to rifle, then successive shots will practically go through the same hole.

Beretta BM-62

Manufacturer P. Beretta SpA, Gardone Val Trompia, Italy
Type Gas-operated semi-automatic
Caliber .308 Winchester (7.62mm NATO)
Barrel 17.6in (448mm)
Weight 8.72lbs (3.95kg)
Magazine capacity 20 rounds

After World War Two the Italian Army re-equipped and adopted the U.S. M1 Garand rifle. Shortly afterwards Beretta obtained a license to manufacture Garands and produced them first for the Italian Army and then for export, supplying the Indonesian and Danish Armies. When the NATO countries began seeking a replacement weapon in the 1950s Beretta took the Garand as a basis and modified it, fitting a detachable 20-round magazine, a fire selector, grenade launcher and flash suppressor. This became the BM-59 and has equipped the Italian Army since 1962. Now in response to those who like shooting military rifles but who cannot, for various reasons, join the Italian Army, Beretta have civilianized the BM-59 into the BM-62.

The principal change, of course, has been to remove the facility for full automatic fire; in addition the complex service flash hider-cum-grenade launcher and its associated special sight has been removed and a simple flash hider fitted. For the rest, it is still BM-59, and the mechanism is obviously Garand. The great advantage over the Garand, of course, is the 20-round box magazine which can be removed and replaced with a full one or topped up by loading from clips through the open action. But the operating handle, gas mechanism, sights and general feel are all as per the Garand and anyone familiar with the M1 would have no difficulty in coming to terms with this rifle.

In practical use one should bear in mind that it is a military rifle firing a military cartridge, and make certain allowances; not in the accuracy field, for this is probably of the same measure of accuracy as any contemporary military rifle, giving three to four inch groups at 100 yards. But muzzle blast and noise are rather higher than sporting shooters are perhaps accustomed to, due to the short barrel and the ballistics of the 7.62mm NATO round. Some observers have pointed out that the flash hider appears to do little good, but it should be remembered that the object of the hider is to hide the flash from the firer so as not to blind him at night, not to hide it from casual observers standing alongside him. On balance this is a good conversion and for those who prefer military rifles it makes a good working weapon. But at just under a thousand dollars it isn't a cheap one.

Top: The Beretta Model 62, the civilianized version of a military rifle.

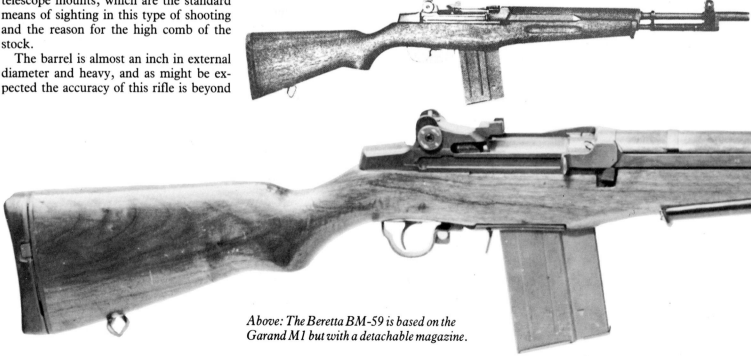

Above: The Beretta BM-59 is based on the Garand M1 but with a detachable magazine.

The variant models are the SC-70 – Special Carbine with folding metal butt, otherwise as for the AR70; the SC-70 Short, with folding metal butt and 320mm barrel; and the Light Machine Gun 70-78 which has a heavy 450mm interchangeable barrel, a stronger bipod, and the 40-round magazine as standard.

The various rifle models have been taken into service by the Italian Special Forces and by the Jordanian, Malaysian and other armies; the machine gun is undergoing evaluation by several armies but has not yet been formally accepted.

Browning BBR Rifle

Manufacturer Miroku Firearms Mfg. Co., Kochi, Japan
Type Bolt action, center-fire, magazine
Caliber Various
Barrel 24in (610mm)
Weight 8lbs (3.63kg)
Magazine capacity 4 rounds

The Browning Company of Morgan, Utah, the spiritual successors of John Moses Browning, imported Belgian Browning rifles from Fabrique Nationale's Liege factory for many years, discontinuing in 1974. In 1978 they re-entered the bolt-action field with this rifle (BBR means Browning Bolt-action Rifle) made for them in Japan by one of the more respected Japanese companies.

The BBR is a handsome weapon, with a walnut stock with Monte Carlo butt and cheekpiece, a good pistol grip with thumbrest, and a somewhat angular fore end. The finish is lustrous and the checkering well done. The fore end has a strip of aluminum channel let into the woodwork in order to resist warping.

The bolt action is robust, the bolt locking on nine forward lugs. The action is cocked as the bolt handle is raised, and the tail of the firing pin sear protrudes from beneath the end of the bolt sleeve as a visual indicator. The handle has a short lift, in order not to interfere with any low-mounted telescope which may be fitted.

Three versions of the Beretta Model 70 5.56mm assault rifle.

Beretta 70-223 Rifle

Manufacturer P. Beretta SpA, Gardone Val Trompia, Italy
Type Gas-operated, selective fire
Caliber 5.56mm (.223)
Barrel 17.7in (450mm)
Weight 8.4lbs (3.8kg)
Magazine capacity 30 or 40 rounds
Cyclic rate of fire 650 rounds/minute

This is a good example of the modern technique of developing a basic mechanism and then configuring it into a variety of weapons to suit varied requirements, an approach first seen in the 'Stoner 63' system in the U.S.A. some twenty years ago.

In its basic form the Beretta 70-223 is an assault rifle – the AR70 – of the usual gas-operated type; there is a gas cylinder above the barrel, containing a piston which drives back on the bolt carrier through the inter-mediary of the cocking handle. There is a rotating bolt which is locked to the barrel by twin front lugs and is opened and closed by a cam track in the carrier. Butt and fore-end are plastic, there is a box magazine, and a selector allows single shots or automatic fire. The aperture rear sight is a two-position flip-over unit for 150m and 300m range and is adjustable for windage; the foresight is a post, adjustable for elevation when zeroing.

The barrel terminates in a flash-hider which doubles as a grenade launcher, and there are special grenade launching sights which can be folded up when required; folding up the front sight also shuts off the gas flow to the piston so that blank cartridges can be used. A light bipod is available, and the receiver is prepared for NATO standard sight mounting bases which will accept telescopes or night vision sights.

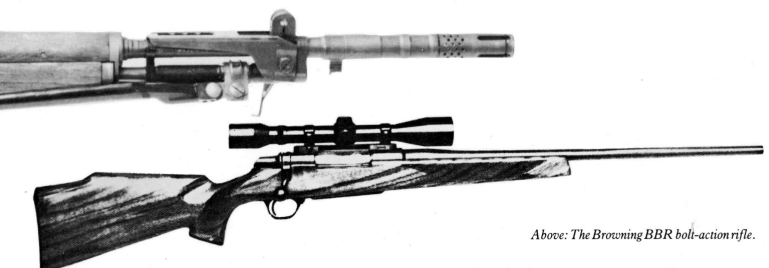

Above: The Browning BBR bolt-action rifle.

The magazine is attached to its floor plate, which in turn is hinged at its front end, so that the whole lot can be swung down by depressing a release catch. The magazine can be loaded in this position, or it can be detached from the floor plate, loaded, and re-attached, the plate then being swung up and the magazine brought into position below the bolt. Alternatively, of course, the bolt can be opened and the magazine loaded through the action, but this is not always feasible when a telescope is in use. The trigger is adjustable for pull.

No sights are furnished with the rifle but the receiver is drilled and tapped for a telescope mount.

Accuracy is good, with groups of one to one-and-a-half inches possible at 100 yards range. The rifle is available in calibers from .25-06 Remington to .300 Winchester Magnum.

Browning BPR Rifle

Manufacturer Miroku Firearms Mfg. Co., Kochi, Japan
Type Slide action, rimfire
Caliber .22 Long Rifle RF
Barrel 20.125in (511mm)
Weight 6.5lbs (2.95kg)
Magazine capacity 15 rounds

Fabrique Nationale of Belgium used to make a .22 pump-action rifle for many years prior to the Second World War, rifles which became extremely popular as vermin guns as well as being the mainstay of in-

numerable European shooting galleries and funfairs. After several years absence, this rifle has reappeared, in modern form, but now made in Japan to be marketed in the U.S.A. by the Browning Firearms Company.

The BPR (Browning Pump Rifle) is a handsome weapon, with glossy stock and fore-end and well-blued metalwork. Indeed, the fore-end is so substantial that it does not immediately suggest a slide action. The operation is smooth and short, performing without fail with a wide variety of ammunition. The magazine is tubular, beneath the barrel, and is charged by slid-

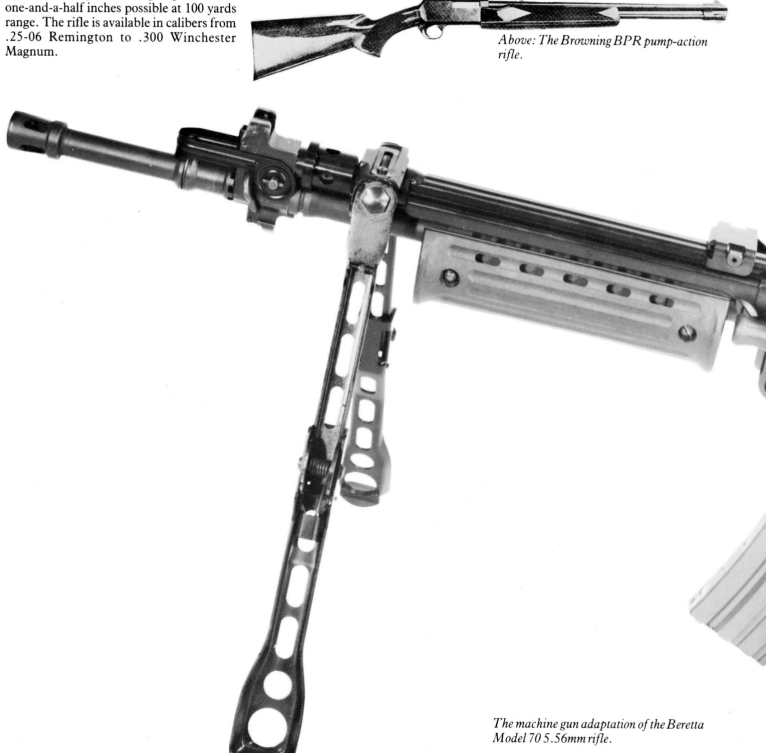

Above: The Browning BPR pump-action rifle.

The machine gun adaptation of the Beretta Model 70 5.56mm rifle.

ing the inner tube out, forwards, after depressing a small latch, so that rounds can be individually loaded through a slot in the outer tube.

The foresight is a gold bead, the rear sight a folding leaf, and the receiver is grooved for telescope mounts. Accuracy is very good, the rifle producing two-inch groups at 50 yards without difficulty when fired from a rest.

The breech is positively locked during firing; this may be felt to be superfluous in this caliber, but there are plans to introduce a version in .22 Winchester Magnum RF chambering, in which case the locked breech will be needed.

Browning Model 92 Carbine

Manufacturer Miroku Firearms Mfg Co., Kochi, Japan
Type Lever action, magazine
Caliber .44 Remington Magnum
Barrel 20in (508mm)
Weight 5.72lbs (2.59kg)
Magazine capacity 11 rounds

The classic lines of the Winchester Model 92 carbine still have a considerable appeal and there have been innumerable near-copies over the years. This one, however, is

The Browning Model 92, a traditional saddle-gun carbine.

an almost precise replica and it is fitting that it should be sold under the Browning name in the U.S.A. since the original was, of course, designed by John Browning for Winchester.

The breech mechanism, operated by the under-lever, uses vertical locking bolts which interconnect the block to the receiver. As the lever is lowered, so the bolts are withdrawn and the breech block retracted to extract the fired case and operate the cartridge lifter. On the return stroke the cartridge is chambered and the bolts move vertically to lock the breech closed. The external hammer is cocked during the opening stroke of the block. The tubular magazine is loaded by means of the usual side trap.

The foresight is a simple blade, while the rearsight is a 'buck-horn' notch, adjustable for elevation and windage. There is no safety other than the existence of a half-cock notch on the hammer.

The carbine is extremely well finished, with blued metal, gold-plated trigger and walnut stock with silky luster finish.

Accuracy is acceptable, within the capabilities of the .44 Magnum bullet, giving groups between two and three inches at 50 yards range. Light and handy, this is a good hunting gun for close country against small to medium game animals.

BSA CF2 Stutzen Rifle

Manufacturer Birmingham Small Arms Co., Birmingham, England
Type Bolt action, magazine
Caliber Various

'Stutzen' means 'to cut, clip, dock' so a 'Stutzen' rifle is a shortened rifle; older German dictionaries go further and give 'stutzen' as meaning 'carbine', from which you may make what you will. What it means in practice is a short full-stocked rifle or carbine, often called 'Mannlicher-style', a type of weapon popular among mountains and forests for its convenience in carrying and using in close country.

The BSA Stutzen rifle is a full-stocked weapon with high quality wood and with rosewood tips to fore end and pistol grip. The bolt mechanism is amply strong, and the rifle can be had in any of nine different calibers from .222 to .30-06. The bolt head is located well inside the receiver when

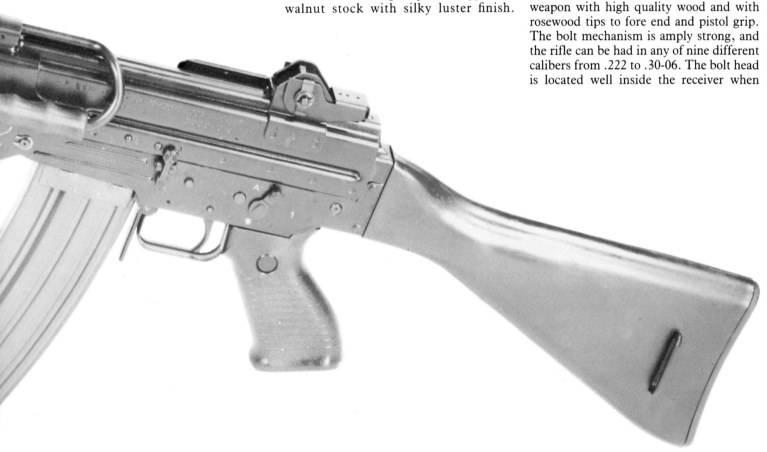

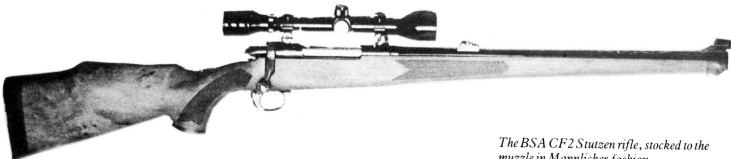

The BSA CF2 Stutzen rifle, stocked to the muzzle in Mannlicher fashion.

closed and locks by two front lugs, while the handle is slender and well-shaped for rapid operation. The magazine is concealed within the stock and has a hinged floor plate.

The foresight is a hooded blade, and the rear sight is an open notch mounted ahead of the chamber; there are dovetails for a telescope and the iron sights can be removed when such a sight is fitted. The trigger pull is adjustable, and leads to a crisp let-off; a double set trigger can be supplied if required.

The Stuzen handles extremely well, coming into the shoulder rapidly and naturally. Its accuracy is more than adequate; the manufacturers claim two-inch groups at 100 yards and this is easily achieved.

BSA CFT Target Rifle

Manufacturer Birmingham Small Arms Co., Birmingham, England
Type Bolt action, center fire, single shot
Caliber 7.62mm NATO (.308 Winchester)
Barrel 26.5in (673mm)
Weight 10.8lbs (4.9kg)

Many European shooting contests are based on military calibers and since the 7.62×51mm cartridge has become NATO standard it has also begun to appear in competitive shooting. At first, converted military rifles were the norm, but then single-shot and magazine weapons began to appear, and in 1981 the BSA company decided to develop a single shot rifle for this cartridge.

There is no short cut to excellence, and this rifle goes to prove it; the receiver is milled from a solid block of steel and the only aperture is the feed and ejection slot, just big enough for its task, and the entry for the bolt. As a result it is stiff and holds the bolt absolutely rigidly, locked by two front lugs. The barrel screws into the front

with an imperceptible join, and the chamber has been extremely carefully dimensioned to the minimum acceptable tolerance and contoured specifically to the NATO bullet.

The trigger is adjustable for weight of pull and for depth of engagement, and the let-off is crisp; it is a single-stage trigger, which takes some time to become familiar if the shooter has been using military or converted military rifles with their usual double pull.

The stock is fairly severe, though with cheek-rest and a good pistol grip, and is of beech or walnut to choice. There is a rail inletted beneath the fore-end to take a sling swivel and a hand stop is fitted. The barrel is fully floating in the stock.

The foresight is interchangeable and mounted in a dovetail; the rear sight is a fully adjustable aperture fitted on a bracket so that various positions for eye relief are possible. The rear sight can be removed and there are tapped holes for telescope mounting.

Accuracy is all that could be expected, the finish is excellent, and it looks as if BSA have produced a rifle which will be seen more and more on the firing line in the future.

CETME Model L Assault Rifle

Manufacturer Centro de Estudios Tecnicas de Materiales Especiale (CETME), Madrid 46, Spain
Type Delayed blowback, selective fire
Caliber 5.56mm (.223)
Barrel 15.75in (400mm)
Weight 7.49lbs (3.4kg)
Magazine capacity 20 rounds
Cyclic rate of fire 750 rounds/minute

CETME is the Spanish government research and development establishment, and in the early 1950s a Herr Vorgrimmler went to work there. Vorgrimmler worked

for Mauser during World War Two, particularly on their Sturmgewehr 45 project which was never completed, and he adapted the Mauser design to produce the first CETME rifle. Several countries showed interest in this, and eventually the Germans obtained a license, and with some working over by Heckler & Koch it became the G3. Meanwhile CETME continued development and their 7.62mm 'Model C' was adopted by the Spanish Army. In conformity with the general move to smaller calibers they have now developed a 5.56mm rifle, the Model L, and this is now being evaluated by the Spanish Army and may well become their next service rifle.

As might have been inferred from the reference to the G3 above, the CETME relies upon the same divided bolt and roller locking system as the Heckler & Koch rifles. CETME have made one important addition, though, in the form of a spring-loaded locking lever in the bolt assembly which adds resistance to the initial opening movement of the bolt. No reason has been

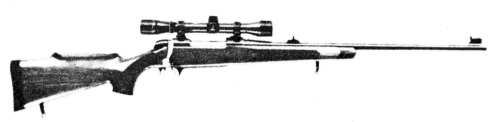

Left: The BSA CFT Target Rifle, fitted with telescope sight.
Above: The Czechoslovakian CZ58 assault rifle, now appearing in other parts of the world.

given for this, but it is likely that the increased unit pressure on the smaller base of the 5.56mm case led to too-fast initial opening and stretched or blown cases.

The structure of the rifle is largely plastic, with a sheet metal receiver. There is a selector on the left side which gives single shots, three-round burst fire or full automatic fire. The standard magazine is a 20-round model, but 10- and 30-round alternatives are available. The foresight is an adjustable post, between protective wings, and the rear sight is a rotating disc with a notch for 100m and apertures for 200, 300 and 400 meters. A mount base is incorporated and may be used for optical or electro-optical sights.

In addition to the standard rifle there is a short model which has a 12.6in (320mm) barrel and a telescoping metal butt.

Czech CZ58 Assault Rifle

Manufacturer Czeskoslovenska Zbrojovka, Uhersky Brod, Czechoslovakia
Type Gas-operated, selective fire
Caliber 7.62×39mm Soviet
Barrel 15.78in (401mm)
Weight 6.92lbs (3.14kg)
Magazine capacity 30 rounds
Cyclic rate of fire 800 rounds/minute

This weapon is not really new, having been issued to the Czech Army for some years, but it is now beginning to appear outside Czechoslovakia; we understand that its cost is low in comparison to western rifles of comparable specification, and that a concerted export drive has been launched. As a

The CETME Model L semi-automatic rifle has distinct affinities with the Heckler & Koch designs; notice the cocking lever at the forward end of the gas piston.

result we can expect to see this weapon becoming more prominent in Africa and the Far East in future.

Although there is a superficial resemblance to the Kalashnikov AK47, this is a totally different weapon, designed and built in Czechoslovakia and owing nothing to Russian design. In its original form it was even of a different caliber to the rest of the Warsaw Pact countries, but this was thought too much of a deviationist measure, and it was re-chambered to fire the standard Communist 7.62mm short cartridge.

The rifle is gas-operated, using a chrome-plated short-stroke piston; this strikes the bolt carrier a sharp blow, sufficient to send it backwards. After a short free travel the breech lock is freed from engagement with the receiver and the bolt is withdrawn from the chamber by the movement of the carrier. The locking of the breech is done by a hinged plate beneath the carrier which closely resembles the locking system used on the Walther P-38 automatic pistol. Firing is done by a hollow hammer tube which lies in the bolt and is propelled by a spring; when released by the sear, the hammer flies forward and strikes a floating

firing pin. It is cocked by being caught by the sear during the recoil movement; indeed, if the firing pin was attached, the whole assembly would be called a striker.

The stock and fore end of the rifle are of wood-powder-reinforced plastic material, with a polished finish, and the metalwork is blued or phosphated. The receiver is machined from the solid, and has a sheet steel cover. The rear sight is a tangent V-notch mounted on a steel block welded to the receiver and acting as a gas piston rod guide. The foresight is a post with protective ears, set well above the muzzle.

The CZ58 is light and robust, with a degree of internal finish which is sufficient for the job in hand but without excessive frills. It is a highly satisfactory military rifle, and the folding-butt variation appears to be used in place of submachine guns in the Czech Army.

Enfield L70 Individual Weapon

Manufacturer Royal Small Arms Factory, Enfield Lock, Middlesex, England.
Type Gas operated, selective fire
Caliber 5.56mm (.223)
Barrel 20.4in (518mm)
Weight 8.20lbs (3.72kg)
Magazine capacity 20 rounds
Cyclic rate of fire 800 rounds/minute

The British Army began looking for an automatic rifle in about 1910, but the research program was interrupted several times and it was not until 1950 that a design was finally approved. Just as it was about to go into production, though, the politicians got into the act and the design was dropped in favour of the Belgian FN-FAL and the

RIFLES

The British Enfield Individual Weapon L70E3 in 5.56mm caliber, now in production for the British Army.

The Enfield Light Support Weapon L72E2, the light machine gun version of the rifle, with bipod and longer barrel.

7.62mm NATO cartridge. When this rifle began to be outdated, Enfield began designing once more, this time with a new cartridge of 4.85mm caliber, ready for the 1978 NATO small arms trials. Their 1950 model, the EM1, had been dropped because it could not be reworked into 7.62mm caliber (from .280) when the need arose, so the designers of the new rifle were wise enough to build it so that it could be re-calibered if necessary. When the NATO trial decided on 5.56mm as the next standard caliber their foresight paid off; the Enfield design was rejigged to 5.56mm and has now been approved for service. It is believed that a number of pre-production models were evaluated in combat during the recent Falkland Islands campaign.

The Enfield 'Individual Weapon' is a conventional gas-piston-operated design, using a rotating bolt in a carrier which rides on two guide rods. It is of 'bullpup' layout, the magazine being well behind the trigger and the action lying under the firer's cheek. The receiver is a pressed-steel component which requires little machining since the

guide rods control the bolt's movement. The furniture is of plastic, and the gas system has a three-position regulator giving normal, extra power for fouled actions, and closed for grenade launching.

The standard sight is the 'SUIT' or 'Sight Unit, Infantry, Trilux,' a short optical telescope containing an illuminating source for shooting in bad light. This is a sealed unit and adjustments for elevation and windage are carried out on its supporting bracket. On top of the SUIT unit there are emergency iron sights; there are no sights on the body of the rifle, though a foresight blade and a two-aperture backsight can be fitted if desired.

The Enfield rifle is extremely easy to shoot and very accurate; in spite of its compactness, the bullpup layout ensures a good barrel length, and the latest models will be rifled to suit the new SS109 NATO standard 5.56mm bullet. There is also a heavy-barrelled version with a bipod which is intended as the squad automatic weapon; this rejoices in the name 'L73 Light Support Weapon'.

Erma EM1 and EGM1 Carbines

Manufacturer Ermawerke, Dachau, West Germany
Type Blowback, semi-automatic
Caliber .22 Long Rifle RF
Barrel 18in (457mm)
Weight 5.5lbs (2.49kg)
Magazine capacity 10 rounds

The U.S. Army's M1 Carbine of World War Two had some mysterious charisma which made people lust after it, even though it was a pretty dismal combat weapon at anything over 50 yards range. As a result there have been numerous look-alikes over the years, and the German Erma company, renowned for military weapons in days gone by, have now produced a pair of .22 rimfire carbines which look almost like carbon copies of the 'real thing'.

There are two models which are mechanically identical; the EM1 is the 'standard' and is almost indistinguishable from an M1; the EGM1 is the 'de luxe' version fitted

Top, the Erma EM1, bottom the EGM1 – differing in the shape of the front sight and in having only a five-shot magazine.

with a sporterized walnut stock. The receiver is of alloy, blackened to match the finish of the steel barrel, and the cocking handle operating rod vanishes forward into the woodwork just as did that of the M1, but has nothing on the forward end except the return spring and its guide rod; the bolt is a straightforward blowback action. Since there is thus no need to revolve the bolt, the connection between cocking handle and bolt is not so complex as that of the M1. Firing is performed by a spring-driven firing pin which has a bent protruding below the bolt to be caught by the sear on the reloading stroke.

The carbines are equipped with replicas of the original sights; a front blade between protective ears, and a rear aperture 'battle' sight. They are efficient within their capabilities, and on the range the carbine showed itself to be capable of sufficient accuracy for its purpose in life, which is eminently that of a 'fun gun' for casual plinking or vermin shooting at moderate ranges. It is light, handy, reliable if cleaned regularly of the grease and fouling which 'shooting' .22 ammunition generates, and good value for money.

Erma EG73 Carbine

Manufacturer Ermawerke GmbH, D-8080 Dachau, West Germany
Type Lever-action, rimfire, magazine
Caliber .22 Winchester Magnum RF
Barrel 19.5in (495mm)
Weight 5.5lbs (2.49kg)
Magazine capacity 12 rounds

Although the experts are fond of telling us that lever-action carbines are inherently inaccurate, up until now nobody has told the carbines anything of the sort and they still go on shooting straight. There is no doubt that there is a great visual appeal in the classic saddle-gun lines of straight stock and short fore-end, with the barrel and tubular magazine in front, and as long as this appeal remains, gunmakers are going to produce them and sell them.

The Ermawerke of Germany have had considerable experience in weapon design and construction, and one of their latest offerings is this Magnum carbine. Its lines follow the classic Winchester, though the action is entirely their own, with a solid-topped receiver. The bolt is unlocked and retracted by a full 90° swing of the under-lever, and in doing so it cocks the external hammer and lifts a fresh cartridge from the magazine. Pulling the lever back chambers the round and locks the bolt, ready to fire. The action is exceptionally smooth, being made to fine tolerances and well fitted, and the quietness will be appreciated by hunters.

The magazine is of steel, unlikely to be accidentally dented, and holds 12 cartridges, after which a 13th can be loaded into the breech. The foresight is a post concealed in a hood, while the rear sight is a notch on a step-adjustable leaf. There is no windage adjustment as such, though the sight can be moved sideways in its mounting for zeroing. The only safety device is the usual half-cock notch on the hammer.

The stock is of walnut and well finished, the steel of the barrel, magazine and action, is blued and polished, and the whole weapon makes an attractive and functional package.

Fabrique Nationale FNC Rifle

Manufacturer Fabrique Nationale d'Armes de Guerre, Herstal, Belgium
Type Gas operated, selective fire
Caliber 5.56mm (.223)
Barrel 17.7in (450mm)
Weight (empty) 8.37lbs (3.80kg)
Magazine capacity 30 rounds
Cyclic rate of fire 650 rounds/minute

Some years ago the FN company developed a 5.56mm rifle which they called the 'CAL' (Carabine Automatique Legere), anticipating that 5.56mm would become popular as a military caliber; they were right, but it took longer than they thought and the CAL was rather in advance of its time. Several armies bought small quantities for evaluation, and their reports, together with FN's own expertise, suggested that it should be possible to develop a cheaper and better design; this FN did, the result being the FNC. It is now undergoing extensive military trials in Sweden and in some NATO armies, and the Indonesian Army has adopted it for service.

The FNC makes extensive use of pressed steel and plastic components; it follows the general pattern of FN automatic rifles and the body opens on a front hinge pin to allow the working parts to be withdrawn to the rear. Operation is by gas tapped from the barrel and fed to a conventional gas cylinder above the barrel. The gas piston is driven back to strike a bolt carrier which contains the usual type of two-lug rotating bolt. The bolt and carrier are among the few components in the FNC which demand precision machining. The gas cylinder has a two-port regulator which can be switched from the normal position to admit more gas when operating under adverse conditions.

The trigger mechanism allows selection of single shots, three-round bursts, or full automatic fire, controlled by a selector switch on the left side. The box magazine is interchangeable with that of the U.S. M16A1 rifle, and both can also be used on the FN 'Minimi' light machine gun. The tubular steel butt can be folded alongside the receiver either for transport or to make the weapon more compact for use in the submachine gun role.

The barrel is rifled one turn in 32 cali-

The Erma EG73 carbine, a European version of the Western saddle gun.

bers, much tighter than previous 5.56mm weapons, and is optimized for use with the Belgian SS109 bullet, which has now been selected as NATO standard. With this ammunition the three-round burst will deliver shots dispersed by 70cm at 500m range, and will penetrate the standard U.S. Army steel helmet at over 1000 yards. The standard sights consist of a front post and a flip aperture rear sight set for 250m and 400m, but the rifle can accept all types of telescope, image intensifying and thermal imaging sights for sniping or night operations.

Fabrique Nationale Sniper Rifle

Manufacturer Fabrique Nationale d'Armes de Guerre, Herstal, Belgium
Type Bolt action, magazine
Caliber 7.62mm NATO
Barrel 19.76in (502mm)
Weight 11.02lbs (5.0kg)
Magazine capacity 5 rounds

Fabrique Nationale have a long tradition of building sporting rifles and they have applied much of their knowledge in this field to the development of a rifle suitable for use either as a game weapon or as a sniping weapon for police or military use.

The basic action is FN's well-tried Mauser bolt, with front and rear locking lugs for maximum rigidity and accuracy. The barrel is particularly massive, one inch in diameter for most of its length, and fitted with a flash hider. There is a recessed track beneath the fore end which accommodates the sling and which can also fit a hand-stop and the optional bipod. The stock is a no-nonsense walnut design but with an inge-

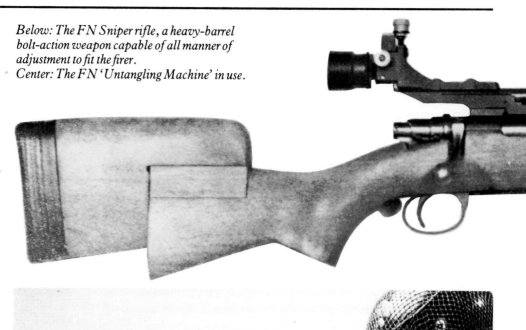

Below: The FN Sniper rifle, a heavy-barrel bolt-action weapon capable of all manner of adjustment to fit the firer.
Center: The FN 'Untangling Machine' in use.

Fabrique Nationale's FNC-Standard Model, optimized for the new NATO standard SS109 5.56mm bullet.

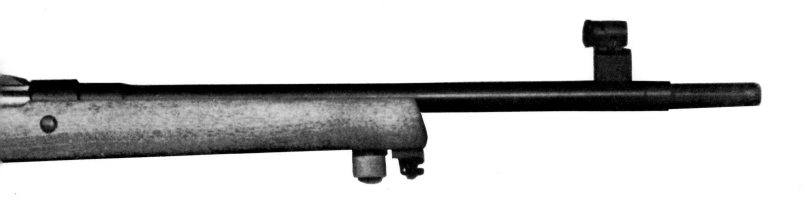

nious butt which can, by the insertion of a variety of spacers, be adjusted for height of comb and for length.

There are several sighting options. The basic rifle has no sights but is fitted with a special mount on the receiver bridge. There is also a mount which attaches to the front end of the barrel and on to which an Anschutz foresight unit can be mounted. This goes with an Anschutz rear sight which slides on the rear mount and provides a diopter aperture with full adjustment for elevation, windage and eye relief. The foresight is a hooded unit with a replaceable diaphragm with varying designs of post or spot to suit the individual shooter. Alternatively, the foresight is dispensed with and the rear mount occupied by an FN telescope of 4× magnification, graduated from 100 to 600 meters and fully adjustable. Or, for night shooting, various types of image-intensifying or thermal imaging sights can be fitted, since the mounting is compatible with the

NATO standard mount for these types of sight.

FN call this rifle 'The untangling machine' in their publicity brochures, and it will do just that, out to 600 meters without fail.

Feinwerkbau 2000 Match Rifle

Manufacturer Feinwerkbau GmbH, West Germany
Type Bolt action, single shot
Caliber .22 Long Rifle RF
Barrel 26in (660mm)

Feinwerkbau have built up a considerable reputation for their air rifles, which consistently march off with most of the top prizes in international competition. They have now taken a logical step and progressed to a rimfire target rifle; logical because many match rifle shooters use air rifles to keep their eye in, and by building a

rimfire rifle which is closely comparable to their air rifle Feinwerkbau have made the transition a very smooth one.

The Model 2000 is a conventional bolt action weapon, but its appearance is somewhat unconventional since, as we have indicated, it owes more to air rifle practice than to sporting rifle design. The trigger guard, for example is peculiarly square, the butt deep and short, the fore end similarly deep, but it all hangs together and with time taken over making sure every aspect is properly adjusted for the individual shooter, the result is comfortable and functional. The stock is of high quality walnut, oil finished, and deeply checkered in areas of grip.

The bolt is massive, comparatively speaking, over five inches long and almost an inch in diameter, which suggests the utmost rigidity when closed. It locks on the bolt handle, the forward section being constrained in its movement by a rib which rides in the cartridge feed channel beneath

*The Feinwerkbau 2000 Match Rifle,
intended to smooth the transition from air rifle
to rimfire competition.*

it. There are twin extractors, and the bolt cocks on opening, revealing the red tip of the cocking piece as a reminder.

The trigger is capable of every imaginable adjustment; weight, angle of pull, slack, travel, release point, all are capable of a wide range of adjustments and it should be possible to obtain precisely what any particular shooter demands.

The foresight is hooded and has a replaceable diaphragm with a selection of rings; the rear sight is an aperture with full adjustment for elevation and windage and also for eye relief, being carried on a slide which allows adjustment to cater for individual tastes.

It scarcely needs to be said that this rifle is capable of more accuracy than the majority of shooters; it performs equally well in any position, being comfortable in prone, standing or sitting attitudes, and looks bound to reach the same position of eminence that the company's air rifles have achieved.

FFV Assault Rifle 890C

Manufacturer Forsvarets Fabriksverk, Ordnance Division, Eskilstuna, Sweden
Type Gas-operated, selective fire
Caliber 5.56mm
Barrel 13.4in (340mm)
Weight (empty) 7.7lbs (3.5kg)
Magazine capacity 35 rounds
Cyclic rate of fire 650 rounds/minute

The Swedish Army have, for some years, been using the 'AK4' rifle which is, in fact, the German Heckler & Koch G3 manufactured by FFV under licence. This is in 7.62mm NATO caliber and in recent years the Swedes have decided to follow the examples shown by several other forces and move down in caliber to 5.56mm. Nothing, though, is ever simple in Sweden, and the environmental, ecological, pacifist and other lobbies were extremely vociferous over the allegedly excessive wounding power of the contemporary 5.56mm bullet. As a result the Swedish Army could not simply buy an existing 5.56mm weapon but had to ask FFV to do something which would placate the objectors.

The Model 890C which resulted is nothing more than a slightly modified Israeli 'Galil' rifle, FFV having obtained the necessary licence and permission to make the changes. Most of them are designed in order to improve functioning in extreme cold conditions, familiar to the Swedes but not really considered in the original Israeli design. The front handguard has been enlarged and more deeply ribbed so that it can be securely held by a gloved hand in cold and wet conditions; the trigger guard has been enlarged for the same reason; and a gas regulator has been incorporated, with a blocking position for firing rifle grenades. The major technical change is in the rifling and ammunition; in order to reduce the wounding power FFV developed a new 4.0 gramme (61.6 grains) bullet, heavier than the standard M193, and then rifled the Galil barrel with a new twist of one turn in 41 calibers. The previous standard was one turn in 55 calibers, so that the new bullet is spun more rapidly and has greater stability, thus tending to tumble less on impact, so (it is hoped) wounding the enemy but not too severely.

Finnbiathlon .22

Manufacturer Tampereen Asepaja Oy, SF-33100, Tampere 10, Finland
Type Bolt action, magazine, rimfire
Caliber .22 Long Rifle RF
Barrel 22.8in (580mm)
Weight 9.25lbs (4.2kg)
Magazine capacity 5 rounds

The Biathlon event is an Olympic Games contest which involves skiing across country and stopping four times to carry out target shooting in prone and standing positions; the whole affair is intended to simulate a hunting expedition in the frozen North. When it was first invented, by the Scandinavians many years ago, it probably did; the contestants used military rifles and fired at realistically varying ranges. Since it has been absorbed into the artificial world of Olympic sports, however, the rifle has become a .22 rimfire and the range is fixed at 50 yards. Needless to say, as soon as it became an organized sport, the sportsmen began looking for an edge and a highly specialized design of rifle has resulted.

The Finnbiathlon is a good example of this rare class, and it exhibits some unusual features. Its angular appearance makes it obvious that it is a target rifle, but the unusual collection of straps marks it out as something out of the ordinary. These are the carrying slings which allow it to be slung from both shoulders and worn in the middle of the back, pointing up, so as to be out of the way when skiing; the sling ends in cords which can be passed through any pair of eight holes in the butt, so adjusting the height of carry.

The bolt action is also unusual, being a straight pull type; these are exceptionally rare in modern weapons. The T-shaped handle is simply pulled straight back and pushed forward again, a sleeve with cam track taking care of rotating the bolt. This leads to a very fast action and one which gives minimal aim disturbance when per-

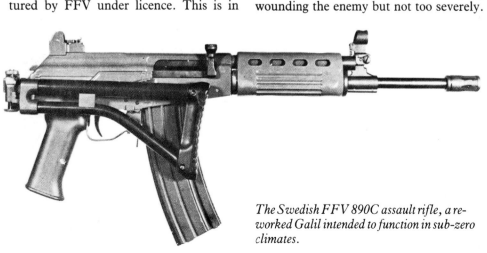

The Swedish FFV 890C assault rifle, a reworked Galil intended to function in sub-zero climates.

formed at the shoulder, both desirable features in the Biathlon where time is at a premium. Another unusual item is a 'snow guard' around the muzzle, which prevents the sights or barrel becoming blocked with snow during traveling or even when diving for the ground for the prone shoots. When the muzzle is closed off, so are the sights, so there is no danger of accidentally loosing off a round when the cover is in place.

The trigger is adjustable for tension and position, and is a two-pressure military type. The rear sight is an aperture type, fully adjustable for elevation and windage, while the front sight is a hooded aperture. Weights can be fitted inside the fore end in order to achieve the desired balance, the maximum additions taking the overall weight of the rifle up to 11lbs. As a final touch, the fore end has four slots in its right side into which four loaded magazines can be fitted, their bases out, so that they can be rapidly reached and changed during the progress of the event, avoiding the necessity of hunting through pockets.

The center ring of the Biathlon target is 40mm in diameter (1.57in) and the rifle is quite capable of putting a string of shots into this at 50 meters. Its accuracy is first class, giving half- to three-quarter-inch groups at that range when fired from a rest. But of course, shooting a string of five from the standing position after traveling across miles of snow isn't exactly shooting from a rest.

Galil Assault Rifle

Manufacturer Israeli Military Industries, Tel Aviv, Israel
Type Gas operated, selective fire
Caliber 5.56mm (.223)
Barrel 20.6in (524mm)
Weight 8.8lbs (4.0kg)
Magazine capacity 35 rounds
Cyclic rate of fire 650 rounds/minute

The Israeli Army decided to adopt the 5.56mm cartridge after the Six-Day War of 1967, and in the following two years every 5.56mm rifle in existence was bought and tested. In view of their location, much emphasis was placed on reliability under hot dusty conditions. Of the various models tested, the Galil, designed by Israel Galil and Yaacov Lior, most closely met the requirements and development went ahead; it was approved for adoption in 1972 but it was some time before it actually got into service and it is not, even now, a universal issue throughout the Israeli armed forces. It has been exported to some other countries, and a modified version is being adopted by Sweden as the FFV 890.

The Galil has been designed to fill the place of three weapons – the rifle, the submachine gun and the squad automatic or light machine gun. It can also fire a variety of grenades, and a short-barreled version has been developed for use by Special Forces.

Mechanically, the Galil leans heavily on the Kalashnikov; it uses a similar method of gas operation, with a cylinder above the barrel, and a similar gas piston-cum-bolt carrier assembly. The bolt has two locking lugs and a cam pin which follows a track in the carrier which drives it to rotate for locking and unlocking. The cocking lever is attached to the bolt carrier so that it can be used for positive bolt closure in the event of fouling, and the change lever for single shot or automatic fire is on the right and when moved to the 'safe' position closes up the cocking handle slot against dust and also restricts the movement of the handle and bolt. The trigger and firing mechanism use a hammer and are very reminiscent of the Garand design.

The Galil may be found with a wood or plastic stock and handguard (Model ARM), or with a folding metal stock and plastic handguard (Model AR); the ARM is fitted with bipod and carrying handle for use as the squad automatic. There is also the Model SAR which resembles the AR but has a shorter (13in–332mm) barrel.

The foresight is a post, adjustable for elevation for zeroing and concealed within a ring shroud, and a flip-over rear sight set for 300m and 500m ranges. Both sights have auxiliary night sights folded down behind them; when raised, these exhibit three white or pale green spots of light, generated by 'Betalight' radiological sources. To sight the weapon the three dots

Above: The Finnbiathlon, a highly-specialized weapon intended for just one Olympic event.
Below: The Israeli Army's Galil rifle comes in several forms; this is a 7.62mm Short Assault Rifle (SAR) version.

RIFLES

are lined up horizontally and the center one alined with the target. The barrel has a flash hider which doubles as a grenade launching spigot, and the bipod joint incorporates a wire-cutter.

In service the Galil appears to have lived up to its expectations; it is simple, robust and accurate and it can withstand desert conditions probably better than any other comparable rifle.

Heckler & Koch G-11

Manufacturer Heckler & Koch GmbH, Oberdorf Am Neckar, West Germany
Type Gas operated, selective fire, caseless
Caliber 4.7mm
Barrel 21.25in (540mm)
Weight 9.4lbs (4.26kg)
Magazine capacity 50 rounds
Cyclic rate of fire 600 rounds/minute

This is probably the most revolutionary weapon to appear anywhere in the last 30 years or more, involving a totally new type of mechanism and a caseless cartridge. It will be adopted as a service weapon by the West German Army before the decade is out and it is likely to start a complete new phase of small arms development for the remainder of this century.

It began in the late 1960s when the Bundeswehr, looking ahead, asked for designs of a new rifle. They laid down few conditions except that it had to be able to fire a three-round burst with dispersion not more than 2.0 mils between shots. This means that at 500 meters the extreme spread between the three shots had to be not more than one meter – and we are talking about a three-round burst, not three individually aimed shots.

Heckler & Koch soon realized that this meant a rate of fire in excess of 2000 rounds per minute in order to get the rounds off before the barrel moved from the point of aim, and this, in turn, meant devising some totally new mechanical solution.

Their first move was to develop a caseless cartridge in conjunction with Dynamit Nobel. This has two advantages; it is lighter than a conventional round, so the soldier has less weight to carry both on his person and in the loaded weapon; and the rifle mechanism no longer has to cater for extraction and ejection of the spent case. This development took time; the first round was a block of nitro-cellulose propellant and plastic binder with a bullet in the front end and a combustible cap in the rear. It worked but overheated the rifle, leading to cook-off problems in which a round loaded into a hot chamber suffered from spontaneous combustion by the heat of the chamber. This problem has now been overcome by the development of a new type of propellant which requires a temperature some 100°C more than nitrocellulose before it cooks off.

The mechanism of the rifle is a German state secret, but the makers have revealed sufficient for us to have a basic knowledge of how it works. The heart of the weapon is the breech block, a circular unit with the chamber bored through it. It revolves around an axis across the rifle so that the chamber lies in prolongation of the barrel when ready to fire. By operating an external knob the bolt is turned through 90° until the chamber is vertical whereupon a caseless cartridge is fed down into it from the magazine which lies above the barrel. Another rotation and the cartridge is lined up with the barrel. Pressing the trigger allows a firing pin to strike the cap and the propellant and cap are entirely consumed and the bullet leaves the barrel. Gas is tapped off to operate the mechanism and the bolt is rotated to reload and rotated again to the firing position.

The mechanism, together with the barrel, is completely concealed in an all-enveloping plastic casing. This is formed into a butt, into a pistol grip and into a carrying handle which also contains a low-power optical sight with battery-illuminated reticles for night firing. On firing the entire mechanism recoils inside this casing, about an inch, being damped by buffer springs. As a result the recoil felt by the firer is more in the nature of a push than a violent blow.

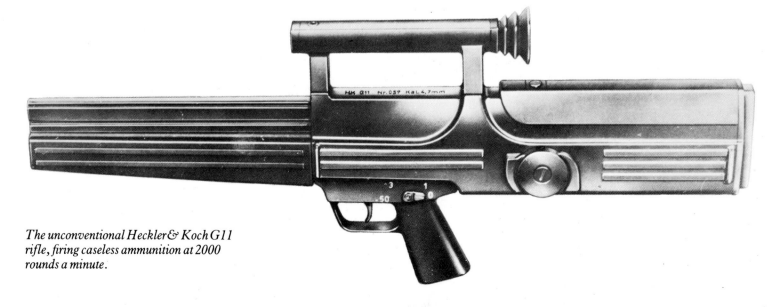

The unconventional Heckler & Koch G11 rifle, firing caseless ammunition at 2000 rounds a minute.

Above: The Heckler & Koch HK81 police rifle.
Left: The HK81 rifle in use; notice the quick-release barrel.

If the selector switch is turned to the three-round burst position, the sequence of events for the first shot is the same as before. But as the first shot is fired and the mechanism begins to recoil, control is assumed by an automatic device which now operates the bolt to reload and fire a second shot, while the weapon is still moving backwards on the recoil stroke from the first. This second shot adds to the rearward momentum, and a third shot is chambered and fired. Only then does the weapon complete its recoil stroke and return to battery. The recoil stroke is about 2.5 inches, but the blow to the firer's shoulder is still not excessive due to the internal buffering. But the noise of the three rounds going off merges into one rasping report and the three bullets have left the barrel before the firer feels any recoil and before the barrel has started to move off the aim. In this way the demand of the Bundeswehr has been met.

At automatic fire the high-speed mechanism is out of action and the rifle merely repeats the single-shot action at about 600 times a minute. Here the individual recoils can be felt, but even so the buffering keeps most of them in the target area.

The G-11 is currently undergoing final development preparatory to its acceptance trials. The company's intention is to reduce the weight still further, to 3.6kg (7.9lbs) and the number of parts to 100, so that mass-production will be easier.

A practical test with the G-11, fired at Heckler & Koch's range at Oberndorf, was enough to convince the writer that this is a practical weapon. A series of three-round bursts all hit the target about an inch apart, while accuracy at single shot was remarkable for a service weapon which had not been zeroed to my eye. The repercussions of this design are going to make something of a stir throughout NATO.

Heckler & Koch HK81 Rifle

Manufacturer Heckler & Koch GmbH, Oberndorf Am Neckar, West Germany
Type Delayed blowback, selective fire
Caliber 7.62mm NATO
Barrel 17.7in (450mm)
Weight 19.05lbs (8.65kg) (with bipod and telescope sight)
Magazine capacity 5, 20 or 30 rounds
Cyclic rate of fire 800 rounds/minute

Mention was made in the introduction of the gradual change in the attitude towards firearms of various European police forces, now that they are more regularly confronted with armed opposition. The HK81 rifle is an interesting example of how gunmakers are tailoring their products to suit the special requirements of police forces, and it is also a lesson in how to acquire firepower without upsetting the populace at large.

On the face of it the HK81 is little more than the basic G3 military rifle with a few small changes. It uses the same two-part, roller-locked bolt which every H&K weapon shares, but the barrel is somewhat heavier than the military standard and is carefully fitted so that the rifle is capable of extremely high accuracy. There is also a light but strong bipod attached to the fore-end so that the rifle can be rested during long periods of surveillance. While iron sights (front hooded post and rear aperture) are fitted, the rifle is always supplied with a variable-power telescope sight. The trigger mechanism can be either a standard military two-stage trigger or an adjustable set trigger for increased accuracy. So the basic weapon is a robust and highly accurate sniping or general-purpose rifle.

Above the trigger, however, there is a change lever which allows automatic fire; and on the right side of the rifle there is a release for the quick-change barrel. So the HK81 can also function as a light machine gun, using the 30-round magazine. Thus while the police force has ostensibly bought

rifles, it has in fact equipped itself with machine guns.

Further, by changing the barrel and bolt the gun can be rapidly converted to fire either the 7.62mm×39 cartridge or the 5.56mm×45 cartridge should the need arise. And by removing the magazine housing and replacing it with a belt adapter, it can be turned into a belt-fed machine gun in any of the three calibers. As if this were not enough, a laser projector can be fitted, placing a spot of light on the target to permit accurate aiming at night; image-intensifying sights can be fitted to the telescope mount; tear gas grenades can be projected from the flash hider (which doubles as a grenade-launching spigot), and there is even a tripod mount for heavy duty.

The HK81 is a remarkable example of versatility; it is also a depressing example of the lengths to which European police forces are being driven by political extremists.

Heckler & Koch HK 91

Manufacturer Heckler & Koch GmbH, Oberndorf Am Neckar, West Germany
Type Delayed blowback, semi-automatic
Caliber 7.62mm NATO (.308 Winchester)
Barrel 19in (482mm)
Weight 10.25lbs (4.65kg)
Magazine capacity 20 rounds

The German Army's service rifle, the Heckler & Koch G3 is widely distributed throughout the world and enjoys a high reputation for serviceability. It is too well-known to warrant a separate entry here, but it is perhaps worth reminding readers that it is descended from the Mauser design of Sturmgewehr developed in 1945, whisked off to Spain to become the original CETME, and later returned to Germany and polished into G3 form. Like many military rifles of today the G3 has a selective fire option which prevents it being legally acquired by sport shooters, and therefore Heckler & Koch have developed a semi-

The Heckler & Koch Model 91 is a civilianized version of their highly successful Gewehr-3 military design.

automatic-only version, now on sale as the Model 91.

The HK91 is typical of today's military firearms, having a stamped steel receiver, plastic fore end, butt and pistol grip, and a very simple takedown procedure. The bolt moves on ribs formed in the receiver walls, and the barrel is pinned into the receiver. Above the barrel is a tubular sleeve carrying the cocking handle and bolt extension. The bolt is Heckler & Koch's renowned two-piece unit with roller locking, described elsewhere in these pages, which delays the opening of the breech long enough for the bullet to clear the muzzle, after which the action is straightforward blowback. One problem with blowback action is that the initial extraction of the cartridge tends to be somewhat abrupt, and this can cause trouble with necked high pressure cases. The HK91 uses a grooved chamber to allow gas to flow back down the grooves to the outside of the case and so 'float' it on a layer of gas, making extraction more easy and generally foolproof. The cases are ejected streaked with carbon and generally looking rather sorry, but experience has shown that they are perfectly safe to reload several times.

The sights are standard Bundeswehr service pattern, a post inside a ring for the foresight and a rotating rear sight with apertures for 200, 300 and 400 meters. There is also an open notch 'battle sight', and the entire rear sight unit can be adjusted to compensate for individual zeroing and for differences in ammunition.

The standard model uses a fixed plastic butt; there is also a version with telescoping metal buttstock. There is also the HK93, similar to the 91 but chambered for the 5.56mm cartridge.

The accuracy of the HK91 is rather better than average for this class of rifle; it will generally make four- to five-inch groups at 200 yards with European service ammunition, rather worse with other types. With handloaded ammunition it should be possible to get slightly under four inches if a telescope sight is used.

Heckler & Koch HK270

Manufacturer Heckler & Koch GmbH, Oberndorf Am Neckar, West Germany
Type Blowback semi-automatic
Caliber .22 Long Rifle RF
Barrel 19.7in (500mm)
Weight 5.5lbs (2.5kg)
Magazine capacity 2, 5 or 20 rounds

This sporting rifle from Heckler & Koch has an interesting amalgamation of civil and military features and there is a suggestion that it may have originated in a design for a military training rifle. However it started, the resulting rifle is one of their best, being light, rapid and accurate.

The 270 is a conventional sporting rimfire model, using a plain blowback bolt action. The stock is of walnut and might be called 'semi-Monte Carlo' since while the comb is fairly high there is no prominent cheek rest. Its finish is excellent and it complements the well-blued finish of the metalwork.

The magazine enters beneath the action; as with other German designs, regulations restrict the home market to a two-round box, but larger magazines are provided for export, the five-round as standard and the 20-round as an optional alternative or extra.

The foresight is a ring shroud containing a diaphragm unit carrying a central post; by removing a pin this diaphragm can be changed for different thicknesses and heights of post. The rear sight is the standard German Army G3 sight, which is the clue to its possible military training origin. This is an aperture sight which can be varied for set ranges by rotating an obliquely-set drum. The whole sight can be adjusted for elevation and windage very easily by use of a special tool supplied with the rifle. In addition, the receiver top is grooved for a telescope mount.

The 270 is by no means a target rifle, but on the other hand it should not be dismissed simply as a 'fun gun' either. Once zeroed it is capable of impressive accuracy and it makes an excellent hunting weapon for the vermin and small game found in Europe.

Heckler & Koch HK300

Manufacturer Heckler & Koch GmbH, Oberndorf Am Neckar, West Germany
Type Blowback, semi-automatic
Caliber .22 Winchester Magnum RF
Barrel 19.7in (500mm)
Weight 5.7lbs (2.59kg)
Magazine capacity 2, 5 or 15 rounds

The HK300 might be called a 'de luxe' version of the 270; it is built to take a more powerful cartridge, but retains the same basic blowback mechanism and is generally to a higher standard of fit and finish. The manufacturers claim that it is 'Specially intended for the close season and for hunting small predatory game and controlling stray domestic animals.'

Heckler & Koch's Model 270 rimfire rifle, a semi-automatic of high quality

The stock is of walnut, well checkered and oil-finished, and with a cheek rest on the butt. The barrel is somewhat heavier than that of the 270, as befits the heavier cartridge, but the bolt mechanism is basically the same. The sights comprise a front blade set on a ramp and adjustable for elevation, and an open blade rearsight adjustable for windage. The receiver top is slotted to take the HK05 universal telescope mount, which can be attached or removed in seconds, firmly locked in place by a lever, and retains the zero whenever replaced. As with other German designs, there is a two-round magazine for the domestic market and five or 15-round models for export.

The combination of heavier barrel and .22 Magnum cartridge have produced a rifle of superlative accuracy, capable of stretching most marksmen to their utmost ability.

Heckler & Koch HK770

Manufacturer Heckler & Koch GmbH, Oberndorf Am Neckar, West Germany
Type Delayed blowback semi-automatic
Caliber .308 Winchester
(7.62mm NATO)
Barrel 19.7in (500mm)
Weight 7.04lbs (3.20kg)
Magazine capacity 2, 3 or 10 rounds

Thanks to somewhat more intelligent gun legislation than the rest of Europe and to their natural advantages in respect of forests and hunting areas, the Germans still

have a thriving home market for firearms which helps to form a sound base for their export activities. Most German gunmakers, irrespective of their primary product, have an eye to this home market and ensure that they have a suitable product, if only to remind people of their existence. Thus it comes about that Heckler & Koch, generally associated in most non-German minds with military firearms, have an impressive range of sporting weapons, and the Model 770 is the civilian equivalent of the well known G3 military rifle.

In saying that we do not imply that it is a conversion for civil purposes; this role is played by the HK91 already discussed, but this sort of conversion is less popular in Europe than in the U.S.A. The HK770 is a well built sporting rifle and looks it; its military heritage is only seen in the mechanical arrangements, which include the same two-part roller-locked breech block.

The 770 is a handsome weapon, with a graceful walnut stock, finely checkered and well finished. The receiver has a somewhat unusual steel cover over the bolt mechanism, and there is a folding cocking handle on the right side. A box magazine is inserted beneath the action; in Germany this is restricted to a model holding two rounds, to comply with various regulations, but for export magazines holding 5 or 10 rounds can be provided. The magazine retaining catch is in the front of the trigger guard and the safety is on the left side, just above the trigger area.

The foresight is a flat-topped blade

Top: The Heckler & Koch 300 uses the .22 Magnum cartridge.
Above: The Heckler & Koch Model 770 is an elegant and powerful sporting rifle which uses the same semi-automatic mechanism as their G-3 service rifle.

adjustable for elevation, while the rear sight is an open notch, adjustable for elevation and windage. The top surface of the 'upper receiver' (receiver top cover) is prepared for H&K's HK05 Claw Mount which will accept virtually any type of telescope mount.

On the range the 770 performs extremely well; those unaccustomed to H&K rifles will find the recoil perhaps less than they anticipate, due largely to the buffering action of the two-part bolt in soaking up some of the recoil force. Its accuracy is reputed to be high, but my experience has been confined to a 30-meter range which is not sufficient for me to make fair comment. One major advantage over most semi-automatics derived from military design is that the vast production of the G3 and its allied models over the years enables this rifle to be turned out to a high standard of manufacture but at a most competitive price.

There are two parallel models to this; the HK630 is chambered for .223 Remington (5.56mm) cartridges, and the HK940 for the .30-06 cartridge. Apart from small differences in barrel length to accommodate the differing ballistics of the cartridges they are substantially the same as the 770.

Heckler & Koch PSG-1 Sniping Rifle

Manufacturer Heckler & Koch GmbH, Oberndorf Am Neckar, West Germany
Type Semi-automatic, delayed blowback, magazine
Caliber 7.62mm NATO (.308 Winchester)
Barrel 25.6in (650mm)
Weight 15.8lbs (7.2kg)
Magazine capacity 5 rounds

This rifle has been developed by Heckler & Koch to satisfy the current demand from military and police authorities for a high-precision weapon for use by snipers and skilled marksmen. It uses the standard basic breech mechanism in which the bolt is a two-part unit and its opening is delayed by a roller-locking system. In this way the rifle's operation is already familiar to most service personnel and its repair and maintenance present no fresh problems.

To suit it to its specialist role, some modifications have been made. The bolt system has been designed so that its closing action, when loading and cocking, is almost silent; the trigger is adjustable for its break point and for width; the abruptly-contoured stock is adjustable for length and for height of the cheek-piece; there is a T-rail underneath the fore end which permits the mounting of a hand-stop, a sling or even a light bipod or tripod; and the weapon is equipped with a telescope sight as standard. This has been carefully designed to suit the weapon and is unusual in that adjustments for elevation and azimuth are made by movement of the internal optical system, giving a high degree of precision; one click of either adjustment will move the bullet strike 1cm at 100m range.

The PSG-1 is heavy but well-balanced

and it shoots extremely accurately; 10 shots in a two-inch circle at 300 yards is well within its capabilities, though as with any other precision weapon it is best to test it with several makes of ammunition and bullet weights to find the one which suits it best. The PSG-1 has only recently been announced, and so far as I am aware there have been no major sales, though several German police authorities are evaluating it.

Heym SR-20 Rifle

Manufacturer Fried. W. Heym, D-8732 Munnerstadt, West Germany
Type Bolt action, center-fire, magazine
Caliber .270 Winchester
Barrel 20.5in (520mm)
Weight 6.5lbs (2.94kg)
Magazine capacity 5 rounds

Friedrich Heym is a long-established German gunmaker whose principal fame comes from his hand-built sporting guns – rifles, shotguns, drillings – which are virtually tailor-made for his clients. But for those with less wealth, he also makes a stock rifle which can be bought off the shelf – though even this has sufficient variations of barrel length and caliber to be able to suit almost all applicants.

The SR-20 is basically a Mauser action, but furnished in three lengths to suit short, medium and magnum cartridge lengths. It is assembled to three possible barrel

lengths; 20.5in (520mm), 24in (610mm) and 26in (660mm); generally the three barrel lengths parallel the actions, the two shorter lengths being found with either of the two shorter actions and the 26in with the magnum action, but this is not immutable and Heym will marry whatever barrel and action you wish.

The shortest barrels are usually stocked to the muzzle in Mannlicher carbine style, while the longer ones are partially stocked in the usual sporting rifle manner. Whatever the stock type it will be of high-grade walnut, oil-finished and hand checkered, fitted to the barrel and action in a faultless manner. The sights are usually a front post with removable hood, and a rear notch fully adjustable for elevation and windage. The receivers are always drilled and tapped for telescope mounts. The trigger is fully adjustable, and the magazine has a hinged floor-plate released by a catch in the trigger guard. There is a three-position safety catch which gives the shooter a choice of 'bolt & trigger locked,' 'trigger only locked' and 'all free' positions.

As for accuracy, all one can say is that it lives up to its promise and reputation; Heym rifles will group to two minutes of arc as they come from the box. They are not inexpensive weapons by any standard of comparison, but the customer gets an accurate weapon, beautifully hand-finished and flawless in operation, and what more can he ask of a sporting weapon?

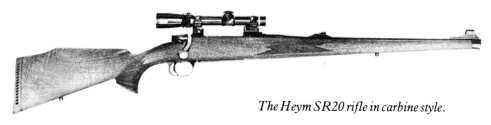

The Heym SR20 rifle in carbine style.

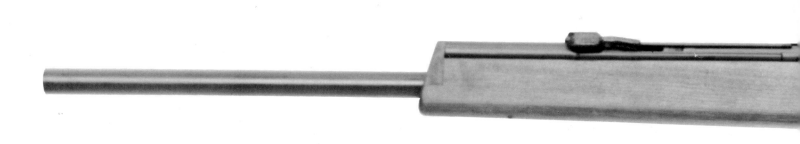

The PSG-1 sniping rifle uses the normal Heckler & Koch roller-locked bolt, delivers superb accuracy, and is capable of a wide range of individual adjustment.

Interdynamics MKR Assault Rifle

Manufacturer Interdynamics Forsknings AB, Stockholm, Sweden
Type Assault rifle, selective fire
Caliber 4.5mm rimfire
Barrel ca 26in (670mm)
Weight, loaded 6.39lbs (2.9kg)
Magazine capacity 50 rounds
Cyclic rate of fire Not stated

This interesting and innovative design comes from Sweden; due to the fact that there are still patent applications outstanding, the company are careful not to divulge too many details of the design, but we do have sufficient information to allow us some description and some assumptions.

The picture indicates that the Interdynamic uses a plastic stock and receiver casing and the magazine is located behind the pistol grip, in the front edge of the butt. In spite of this it can hardly be classed as a 'bullpup' since the length is more or less that of a conventional assault rifle and the action is forward of the butt.

The magazine is a disposable pre-packed plastic unit containing 50 rounds. It is fitted into the forward edge of the butt, feeding upwards into the action. This configuration appears to have been adopted in order to protect the magazine, enabling it to be made in a light material. Once emptied it is removed and thrown away, and a fresh one fitted.

A short 'carbine' version of the MKR has also been developed; this is stocked to the muzzle but otherwise appears to use the same basic mechanism as the rifle. Both weapons have conventional sights raised

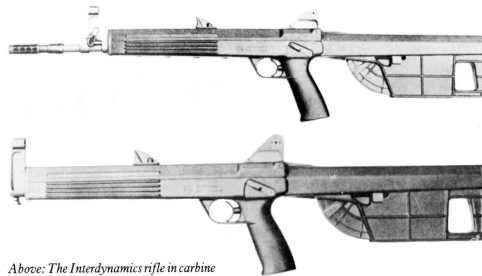

Above: The Interdynamics rifle in carbine form.

Top: The Swedish Interdynamics rimfire military rifle; the semi-circular protrusion in the front of the butt is the magazine.

well above the receiver and barrel, and there is a prominent cocking handle above the receiver.

The most remarkable feature of this new rifle is its ammunition. Rimfire ammunition has long been thought to be impractical for military use due to the high chamber pressures and the malleability of the rimfire case, the two combining to give danger of perforated cases. But Interdynamics have taken the commercial .22 Winchester Magnum Rimfire case as their starting point and re-formed it to suit their design of 4.5mm bullet. In the re-forming the case takes on a double taper which permits cartridges to be packed in the rifle magazine without danger

of the rims overlapping and causing jams; this is no doubt the reason for the sharply-curved shape of the magazine. The bullet is solid copper, with a long tapering nose, a short cylindrical section and a flat base. It weighs 1.58gm (25 grains) and has a muzzle velocity of 1000 meters per second (3280ft/sec), and it is claimed that for all practical purposes it matches the trajectory of the conventional .223 M193 bullet. There are proposals for development of a boat-tailed bullet of 1.93gm weight, since this would be a better vehicle for developing tracer and armor-piercing variants, but it would probably demand a different twist of rifling.

So far as we are aware the MKR rifle has appeared only in prototype form and has not been publicly demonstrated, though it is said that various military forces have expressed an interest.

Iver Johnson's carbine differs from the original only in its perforated handguard.

Iver Johnson .30 Carbine

Manufacturer Iver Johnson Arms, Middlesex, NJ 08846, U.S.A.
Type Gas-operated semi-automatic
Caliber .30 Carbine
Barrel 18in (457mm)
Weight 5.5lbs (2.49kg)
Magazine capacity 15 rounds

We have observed elsewhere the attraction which the U.S. Army's .30 Carbine holds for many people. In addition it has been adopted by a dozen armies at one time or another and is highly popular with police forces around the world. With a potential market of this size, it is hardly surprising that several people have, at various times, tried to duplicate the carbine with varying degrees of success. The latest in this endeavour is the Iver Johnson model, from a company perhaps more renowned for pistols than for long arms.

The Iver Johnson is, except for a better quality of finish and the use of a perforated metal handguard above the barrel, an identical copy of the original M1; identical even to the degree of omitting the bayonet lug, which was not fitted to the first issue M1s. Its operation, by gas cylinder and short-stroke tappet to operating rod and rotating bolt, is sufficiently well-known not

to require any further description here. The sights are also in the original style, a blade front and aperture rear, adjustable for windage and elevation.

Regrettably, it shows little or no improvement in accuracy over the original, though this is hardly to be expected given the hard ballistic facts of life. Five-inch groups at 100 yards are about par for the course. But, also like the original, it's a lot of fun and a supremely handy weapon.

Kalashnikov AK-74

Manufacturer Soviet State Arsenals
Type Gas-operated, selective fire
Caliber 5.45mm
Barrel 15.75in (400mm)
Weight 7.93lbs (3.60kg)
Magazine capacity 40 rounds
Cyclic rate of fire 650 rounds/min

It was to be expected that with the western nations turning to small calibers for their military rifles the Soviets would eventually follow suit. They had developed a necked-down version of their standard 7.62mm M43 cartridge with a 5.56mm bullet in the 1960s, though this appears never to have had any military applications other than as a research vehicle. What was also to be expected was that when they did move, it

would be to a caliber and chambering entirely unlike anything in the west and totally incompatible with any capitalist weapon system.

The resulting rifle was first seen by outsiders in 1979, since when numbers of them have become available to western agencies (mainly from Afghanistan). In general the AK-74 is a modified AK-47 insofar as it uses the same receiver and stock, pistol grip, trigger unit and general configuration. The bolt is smaller, but the bolt carrier and gas piston are the same. The magazine is of thick and tough plastic, thick so that it can fit into the AK-47 magazine housing without demanding any modification. It holds 10 more of the smaller cartridges than did the AK-47 magazine. The wooden fore end grip has a horizontal groove, useful as a recognition feature if nothing else.

The most obvious change is in the addition of a muzzle brake, designed to divert some of the ejected gases sideways and upwards to counter recoil and upward climb during automatic fire. In this it appears to be very successful, since numbers of tests have shown that the rifle can be controlled quite well when firing automatic, the recoil force having been reduced to a level approximately that of a .22 rimfire sporting rifle. Unfortunately, muzzle brakes are a two-edged sword; they make life easier for the shooter but they make life difficult for the men next to him, diverting the muzzle blast sideways, and Soviet medical publications have printed one or two articles on the dangers of ear damage on firing ranges with the new rifle.

The new cartridge is conventional enough, the case being slightly shorter and

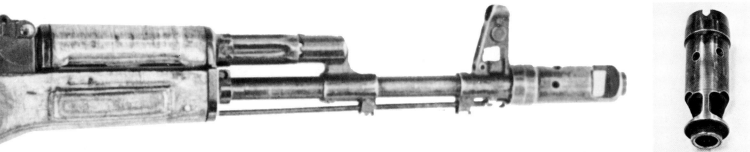

Top: Evidence of the universal distribution of the AK74 is this picture of an infantry recruit being ceremonially issued with his personal rifle upon graduating from basic training.
Above: The newest Soviet rifle, the AK74 in 5.45mm caliber.
Above right: The muzzle brake/compensator from the AK74 rifle; notice the assymetric vents which counter the upward climb during automatic fire, and also the peripheral slots which direct gas forward so as to reduce the side-blast.
Right: One of the first AK74 photographs to reach the West was this casual shot taken on an East German rifle range.

fatter than the .223. The bullet weighs 53 grains, is full jacketed and boat-tailed and has a muzzle velocity of 900 meters/second (2950 ft/sec). This is rather low for this class of weapon, but appears to be adequate for combat purposes. Internally, the bullet is remarkable for having a vacant space in the nose; the major part of the core is mild steel, with a short lead section at the front. This combination appears to facilitate expansion, bent noses and tumbling on impact so as to deliver a severe wound. It is also somewhat complicated to mass-produce with any accuracy. The rifling twist is very steep – one turn in 26 calibers – and the rifling is bevelled on its leading edge so as not to incise the bullet jacket during its travel up the bore. Tracer and armor-piercing bullets have also been reported, though there is no information available on the penetration ability of the armor-piercing type.

Two types of rifle have been seen; the standard AK-74 has a wooden butt, while the AK-74S has a folding steel butt and appears to be issued to paratroopers and special forces only. The AK-74 appears to have now completely replaced the AK-47 in Soviet service, since photographs have been seen of artillery and Frontier Guard troops using these new rifles.

Kimber Model 82

Manufacturer Kimber of Oregon, Clackamas, OR 97015, U.S.A.
Type Bolt action, rimfire, magazine
Caliber .22 Long Rifle RF
Barrel 22.5in (572mm)
Weight 6.56lbs (2.97kg)
Magazine capacity 5 or 10 rounds

The bolt action .22 rifle was common in the U.S.A. in years gone by, but in the past decade American makers have become extremely scarce, and in order to remedy this the Kimber company was formed for the sole purpose of making and selling this rifle.

The Model 82 is not a cheap and cheerful boy's rifle but a finely executed precision weapon. The oil-finished walnut stock is of conservative line, without cheek-rest, but is well finished and elegantly checkered – as is even the butt-plate. The receiver is tubular, milled from the solid, and attached firmly to the one-piece trigger and magazine

housing. The bolt is sturdy and the handle positioned above the trigger, while the trigger is easily adjustable for pressure and over-travel. Five- or ten-round magazines are available; the five-round fits flush with the bottom of the fore end and is released by a small catch at its rear. Even the trigger guard has been milled from solid metal and not stamped from sheet steel as some sort of afterthought.

The rifle can be supplied with sights to choice, but the normal case is for it to have no iron sights but be grooved for Kimber telescope mounts. The barrel is heavy, extremely well finished inside and out, and with the chamber dimensions on the low side of the permitted tolerances. Accuracy is excellent; half-inch groups at 50 yards, firing from a rest, are easily attained, provided one takes the trouble to try various brands of ammunition to discover that which is best suited.

Marlin Model 375 Rifle

Manufacturer Marlin Firearms Co., North Haven, CT 06473, U.S.A.
Type Lever action, center fire, magazine
Caliber .375 Winchester
Barrel 20in (508mm)
Weight 6.75lbs (3.06 kg)
Magazine capacity 5 rounds

John Mahon Marlin began making lever-action rifles and carbines in 1881 and the fact that the company he founded is still making them is sufficient proof of their excellence. There have been some small changes, but since 1889 the significant

feature of the Marlin has been the solid top to the receiver and the side ejection port.

The Marlin Model 375 gets its nomenclature from being chambered for the .375 Winchester cartridge, which was introduced specifically for use in lever-action rifles in order to give them a medium-to-high powered round for use in forests and close country. Note that it is a rifle rather than a carbine; the barrel is much longer than the magazine tube and the whole weapon is three to four inches longer than the average carbine.

The Marlin action retains the solid top receiver and has a cylindrical bolt which, on operating the lever, comes out from the rear of the receiver to cock the external hammer. At the same time the cartridge lifter pivots to raise a fresh round from the magazine, and on the return stroke the bolt chambers the round, is locked, and the rifle is ready to fire.

One advantage of the solid top and side ejection Marlin is that it makes life easier for fitting a telescope, and the receiver is factory drilled and tapped for a mount. Marlin have also aided telescope shooters by making an extension hammer spur which protrudes to one side (either side, to choice) so that there is no danger of trapping the thumb between hammer and telescope when cocking or lowering the hammer. Iron sights are fitted, a gold-bead foresight and a step-adjustable rear sight with a rotatable insert which provides a choice of four notches.

The short magazine makes the rifle somewhat lighter at the muzzle than one normally expects with lever-actions,

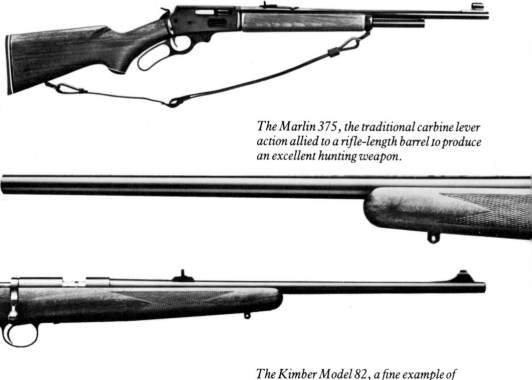

The Marlin 375, the traditional carbine lever action allied to a rifle-length barrel to produce an excellent hunting weapon.

The Kimber Model 82, a fine example of precision manufacture.

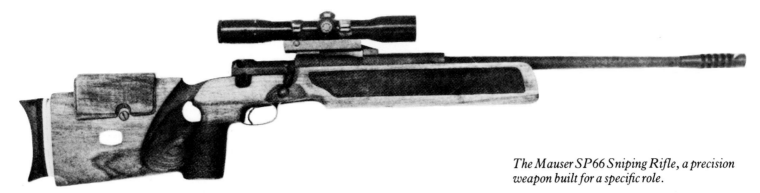

The Mauser SP66 Sniping Rifle, a precision weapon built for a specific role.

though this certainly helps when attempting to follow a moving target. Accuracy leans heavily upon the ammunition in use, but with the correct choice made, then groups between two and three inches are possible at 100 yards range for the moderately practised shooter.

Mauser SP66 Sniper's Rifle

Manufacturer Mauser-Werke Oberndorf GmbH, Oberndorf Am Neckar, West Germany
Type Bolt action, magazine
Caliber 7.62mm NATO
Barrel 26.7in (670mm)
Magazine capacity 3 rounds

When the armies of the world adopted semi-automatic rifles, most of them slapped a telescope on those which proved-out best in their acceptance tests and issued them to snipers. The theory was that semi-autos made good sniping weapons since the firer did not have to move his arm to operate the bolt and therefore was less likely to disclose his position. This seems to have arisen because of the Soviet Army's policy of giving semi-autos to snipers during World War Two, but in my view the reason for this was more that their semi-autos were somewhat temperamental unless properly looked after, and a sniper is more likely to devote care to his rifle than the average front line

soldier. In any event, after some years the snipers of the Western armies began complaining that stealthy reloading was of little use unless you could hit the target in the first place, and that military semi-autos, no matter how good, were simply not accurate enough for sniping purposes. As a result, there has been a gradual move back to bolt action rifles for snipers, and this Mauser is the issue for the West German and at least a dozen other armies.

In appearance you would be excused for thinking that it is a high quality match rifle; the stock is strictly functional and non-military, with a near-vertical pistol grip, thumb-hole, deep comb and adjustable cheek-rest and deep stippled fore end. All this, of course, simply permits the sniper to get the best 'hold' he possibly can, which is half the battle. The action is a short Mauser bolt locking into the receiver with forward lugs and feeding from an integral three-round magazine concealed within the depth of the fore end. The bolt handle is at the forward end of the bolt, just behind the locking lugs, so that it is close to the trigger and reduces the action length to about half the normal. The firing pin spring is stronger than normal to give a fast movement to the striker and the 'lock time' (the time between pressing the trigger and the exit of the bullet from the muzzle) is about half of that with a conventional Mauser action.

No sights are fitted; the user is expected

to specify what he wants and the receiver is then adapted to it; Mauser recommend using a Zeiss Diavari optical telescope or a Varo or Smith & Wesson image-intensifying sight. The muzzle is fitted with a complex muzzle brake and flash hider which is designed to prevent the firer being dazzled by his own flash at night, a feature of particular importance when image-intensifying sights are in use.

I have been unable to fire this rifle, but reports indicate that its inherent accuracy is well in excess of the capabilities of stock military ammunition. Most countries are now taking steps to produce special batches of cartridges which have been more carefully assembled than the run-of-the-mill issue stuff, for use solely by snipers, and with this available the Mauser will undoubtedly come into its own.

Midland Model 2100

Manufacturer Midland Gun Co., Birmingham, England
Type Bolt action, center-fire, magazine
Caliber Various
Barrel 24in (610mm)
Weight (empty) 6.6lbs (3kg)
Magazine capacity 5 rounds

The Midland Gun Company is a subsidiary of Parker-Hale Ltd which manufactures sporting guns, largely for export. The Model 2100 is also called the '98/03' to indicate that it has an exterior configuration based upon the Mauser Gewehr 98 rifle and the bolt of the Springfield M1903 rifle. In fact the bolt stop adheres to neither of these but is an entirely Midland design.

The gun is best described as plain but

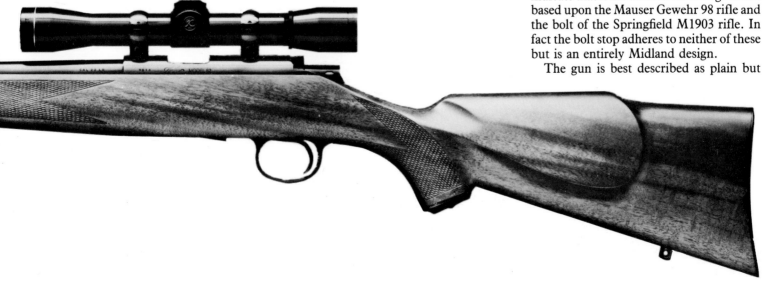

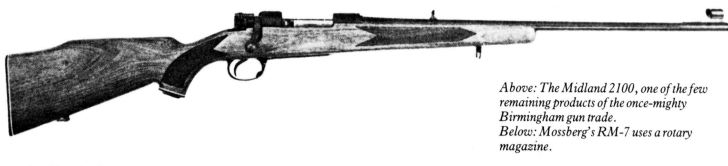

Above: The Midland 2100, one of the few remaining products of the once-mighty Birmingham gun trade.
Below: Mossberg's RM-7 uses a rotary magazine.

serviceable; the finish throughout is excellent but there are no frills and this is definitely a working gun. The walnut stock is well shaped and well fitted to the action and the checkering is neatly done. The barrel is of steel, while the receiver is of investment cast steel and is not so highly polished as the barrel.

The foresight is a hooded bead, mounted on a ramp, while the rear sight is a folding open blade which can be adjusted to provide either a 'V' or 'U' notch; it can be adjusted for elevation by loosening the retaining screws and for windage by drifting it across its dovetail seating. The receiver is drilled and tapped for a Parker-Hale telescope mounting.

The trigger is adjustable for weight of pull and for slack, and it is noteworthy that if the adjustment is badly done and the trigger slack completely eliminated, the rifle will not cock.

Accuracy is very good, averaging two-inch groups at 100 yards from rest. The rifle is available in .243, 6.5mm, .270, .308 Winchester and .30-06 calibers.

Mossberg RM-7

Manufacturer O.F. Mossberg & Sons, North Haven, CT 06473, U.S.A.
Type Bolt action, center-fire, magazine
Caliber .30-06; 7mm Remington Magnum
Barrel .30-06: 22in (560mm); 7mm Rem Mag: 24in (610mm)
Weight 7.87lbs (3.57kg)
Magazine capacity 4 rounds

Mossberg are well-known for the long series of shotguns and rimfire rifles produced by the company since before the turn of the century; their center-fire rifles are less well-known outside the U.S.A. This is their latest center-fire model, and one which repays study.

The appearance is conventional, with a conservatively styled walnut stock having a graceful pistol grip and good crisp checkering. Two heavy steel crosspins go through the stock behind the recoil shoulder and magazine in order to reinforce it.

The bolt is of Mossberg's own design using four front lugs for very positive locking and with the body fluted, with polished bearing surfaces, to ensure smooth action. The bolt knob is checkered for a firm grip, and there is a prominent safety

catch on the bolt sleeve where it can be easily operated by the right thumb.

The magazine is unusual in being a rotary type, though not totally mechanical as, say, the Mannlicher-Schoenauer. The magazine has a curved inner wall against which the cartridges ride, propelled by a sprung follower arm which tracks them round their curved path to deliver them to the feedway. There is a magazine release lever which permits the contents to be emptied without having to work the bolt; the bolt is opened and the lever pressed, withdrawing the stop arm and allowing the follower to push the cartridges out and into the feedway where they can be removed.

The foresight is a gold bead on a ramp; the rear sight an open folding leaf in the mid-position, capable of adjustment for elevation and windage. The receiver is factory drilled and tapped for telescope mounts.

Accuracy is good, averaging two-inch groups when rest-fired at 100 yards, and the rifle is well-balanced and handy in practical use.

Nikko Model 7000

Manufacturer Nikko Firearms Co., Tochigi, Japan
Type Bolt action, center-fire, magazine
Caliber Various
Barrel 24in (610mm) or 26in (660mm)
Weight 8.5lbs (3.86kg) with 24in barrel
Magazine capacity 3 (Magnum) or 5 (regular)

Although ostensibly manufactured in Japan, this is something of an international weapon; the action is made in Japan, the barrel in Belgium, and the wood for the stocks comes from the U.S.A. The whole design is very much tailored for the American market.

The action is a five-lug bolt having an opening arc of 60°, the lugs being at the rear end of the bolt. The bolt body is nicely engine-turned, the face is counterbored, and the firing pin cocks on opening. There

is a sliding safety catch alongside the rear of the bolt which locks the trigger but leaves the bolt free to be operated.

The stock is quite heavy and amply-proportioned; there is a high Monte Carlo comb and cheekpiece and the finish is quite good, if somewhat glossy. The interior fit and finish is not so good.

The magazine has a spring-loaded floor plate and a release catch at the front of the trigger guard. Sights are provided only on two calibers, .375 and .458; all others are without sights and are drilled and tapped for telescope mounts. Calibers available run from .22-250 to .458 Winchester Magnum and include all the commercial standards currently available.

I have been unable to fire this rifle, and reports from other sources are mixed; the general opinion seems to be that as it comes, the barrel is not always well bedded, giving rise to inconsistent shooting, but that with a little adjustment this can be overcome, resulting in a very good hunting rifle at a reasonable price.

Parker-Hale 1200H

Manufacturer Parker-Hale Ltd., Golden Hillock Road, Birmingham, England
Type Bolt action, magazine
Caliber .270
Barrel 24in (610mm)
Magazine capacity 4 rounds

Parker-Hale have been making firearms for many years, though their name is inevitably associated with their highly specialized sights which have had a high reputation for

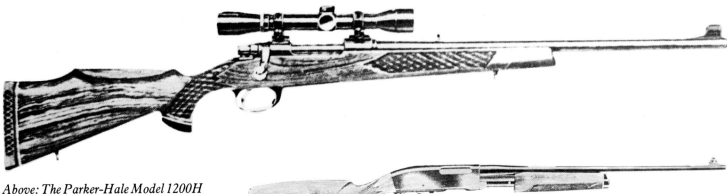

Above: The Parker-Hale Model 1200H Super sporting rifle.

Slide action rifles are few and far between; this is the Remington Model Six, an excellent example of the class.

decades. They have largely tended to concentrate on the export market, but in recent years have begun promoting their 'British' series of rifles for home consumption, a series in which quality is allied to a reasonable price to give exceptional value.

The Model 1200H Super is a handsome and well-proportioned rifle with Monte Carlo stock, recoil pad, elegant checkering and neatly fitted caps on the pistol grip and fore end. The action is a standard Mauser bolt with twin front lugs locking into the receiver, and the face is shaped to ease the passage of the cartridge from magazine into feedway. Indeed, with this shaping and with the extractor bearing on a large sector of the cartridge rim, magazine feed is essential; hand-loading single rounds into the feedway for loading is not to be recommended, since the extractor bearing surface finds it difficult to snap over the rim if the cartridge is not fed smoothly from below. The four-round magazine is concealed, Mauser-style, within the depth of the stock and has a hinged floor plate.

The barrel is heavy, tapered, and fully bedded into the stock. The trigger pull is adjustable and there is no difficulty in tuning it to any shooter's precise liking.

Parker-Hale claim that this rifle will produce consistent one-and-a-half-inch groups at 100 yards and a brief sampling on the range, together with comments and reports from other users, suggests that they are being very conservative and that a good shot should be able to better this figure once he has got used to the rifle. The Model 1200H Super is also available in .243, .270, .308, .30-06 and 7mm calibers, so that most tastes are catered for and, we would repeat, this rifle represents one of the best bargains in sporting rifles today.

Remington Model Six Slide Action

Manufacturer Remington Arms Co., Ilion, New York, 13357, U.S.A.
Type Pump action, center-fire, magazine
Caliber Various
Barrel 22in (560mm)
Weight 7.5lbs (3.40kg)
Magazine capacity 4 rounds

Slide action guns ('pump guns' or 'trombone guns') are usually associated, at least in Europe, with low-powered .22 rimfire rifles or with shotguns, but providing the design is properly done there is no reason why the system should not be used with high powered rifles. Remington, though, seem to be the only people to have made a success of it, and they have featured a center-fire slide action rifle in their catalogs for several years. The Model Six is the latest version, introduced in 1981 and replacing the earlier Model 760.

One advantage of the slide action, if only a cosmetic one, is the 'streamlined' shape of the receiver, which flows from the line of the stock. This box-like receiver is immensely strong and has an ejection slot in the right side. The box magazine enters below the receiver. Below the barrel is a rod assembly which acts as a bearing surface for the slide grip to move upon. When the slide is operated, a connecting link cams the breech block out of engagement with a locking recess in the receiver, then withdraws it, ejecting the spent case. The forward stroke then propels the block forward to load the cartridge and cams the

block into the locking recess. By careful design of the leverages the action can be made very smooth and it barely disturbs the aim; the only defect is that there is no mechanical gain to deal with the occasional sticky case.

The Model 760 has a checkered walnut Monte Carlo stock with pistol grip, and the slide grip is of similar material. The foresight is a gold bead on a matt ramp, while the rear sight is open, step-adjustable for elevation and also adjustable for windage. The receiver is factory drilled and tapped for telescope mounts.

The rifle is available in 6mm, .243, .270, .30-06 and .308 calibers, and its accuracy is good, with groups of just over two inches at 100 yards. In view of the extraction hazard, it pays to try a variety of ammunition to find which particular brand suits this rifle.

Remington Model 700 7mm Express

Manufacturer Remington Arms Co., Bridgeport, CT 06602, U.S.A.
Type Bolt action, center-fire, magazine
Caliber 7mm Remington Express
Barrel 22in (559mm)
Weight 7.25lbs (3.29kg)
Magazine capacity 5 rounds

The 7mm Remington Express cartridge is the new name for what used to be the .280 Remington; dimensionally identical, the new version has improved ballistics and Remington are promoting it as a long range hunting cartridge. And the best way of doing that is to produce a good rifle to shoot it from, hence the Model 700 in 7mm Express.

The Model 700 has been in production for some time in a wide variety of calibers from .17 to .458, so it is a thoroughly proven design. Elegantly proportioned and well-finished, with a Monte Carlo stock and inlaid fore end, the Model 700 balances well and comes easily to the shoulder. The action is basically a Mauser bolt, amply strong for this loading, while the barrel is

The Nikko 7000, the result of international collaboration.

The Remington 700 Express, a powerful and accurate conventional bolt-action design.

smoothly tapered and appears to be light in weight, which probably accounts for the good balance.

The front sight is a post set on a ramp, hooded to obviate glare, and can be drift-set to compensate when zeroing. The rear sight is open, adjustable for elevation and windage. The receiver has been factory drilled and tapped for mounting any type of telescope sight mount base or for the addition of more specialized receiver sights.

The 7mm Express cartridge generates some 2800 feet per second (853 meters/sec) muzzle velocity in this rifle, and 200 meters is the theoretical cross-over point at which bullet and sight line should coincide. As a result the rifle shoots particularly well at that range and is capable of producing better than four-inch groups straight from the box and with factory ammunition.

Rossi Model 92SRC Carbine

Manufacturer Amadeo Rossi Lda., São Leopoldo, Brazil
Type Lever action, tubular magazine
Caliber .357 Magnum
Barrel 20in (508mm)
Weight (empty) 5.94lbs (2.69kg)
Magazine capacity 8 rounds

In the days of the Old West the carbine chambered for a handgun cartridge (or vice versa, as you prefer) was the common saddle gun, but the concept seems to have withered over the years, with the riflemen looking to more exotic calibers and better ballistic efficiency. But there is still a good case for the combination, especially in those parts of the world where there is a need for a general-purpose rifle with no frills, on farms, ranches, the backwoods and the few remaining frontiers. For this reason Rossi have marketed this carbine, which enjoys good sales throughout South and Central America and is now being exported further afield.

The 92SRC makes no bones about being an almost identical copy of the Winchester Model of 1892 in appearance, though there are some minor differences internally. The receiver is an investment casting, attached

to a steel barrel, and the woodwork is well-fitted and polished while the metalwork is well blued. The breech mechanism is the traditional Winchester lever action, feeding from the tubular magazine beneath the barrel. This holds 8 rounds of .357; but the weapon can be used with .38 Special cartridges, and nine of these can be accommodated in the magazine. The foresight is a blade, while the rear sight is open, with step adjustment for elevation and capable of being drifted sideways for windage and drift zeroing.

The carbine appears to be somewhat touchy about ammunition; naturally, with a tubular magazine only flat-nosed bullets should be used, but different brands appeared to have tolerances which did not mate well with the tolerances of, for example, the cartridge guides in the breech. Length is also fairly critical, and while factory loads mostly work well, hand-loads need to be tailored to suit the characteristics of the breech. The accuracy is adequate, with two-inch groups at 50 yards possible with the right ammunition.

Ruger No. 3 Carbine

Manufacturer Sturm Ruger & Co., Southport, CT 06490, U.S.A.
Type Single shot, center-fire
Caliber .223 (5.56mm)
Barrel 22in (558mm)
Weight 7.18lbs (3.26kg)

The Ruger No. 3 Carbine was introduced in 1969, chambered for the .45-70 cartridge; it was later made available in other calibers, and the latest to appear is the .223 Remington, also widely known as 5.56mm in military parlance.

The No. 3 Carbine is a functional single-shot weapon, using a dropping breech block controlled by an under-lever. The walnut stock is plainly finished and is in two pieces, fore end and butt, the latter being a straight grip contour in keeping with the traditional carbine appearance. The barrel is rifled one turn in 45 calibers, a tighter twist than is used on military weapons in this caliber and one which will ensure ample bullet stability during flight, leading

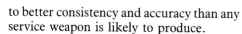

to better consistency and accuracy than any service weapon is likely to produce.

The foresight is a gold bead, the rear sight a folding leaf, adjustable for elevation. The receiver is also drilled and tapped for the attachment of telescope mounts. The trigger is adjustable for tension and travel.

As a result of the long barrel and steep rifling, the Ruger No. 3 is extremely accurate; it is capable of producing groups under one inch at 100 yards range with selected ammunition.

Ruger Mini-14 Series

Manufacturer Sturm Ruger & Co., Southport, CT 06490, U.S.A.
Type Gas operated, semi-auto or selective fire
Caliber .223 (5.56mm)
Barrel 18.5in (470mm)
Weight 6.39lbs (2.9kg)
Magazine capacity 5, 10, 20 or 30 rounds
Cyclic rate of fire 750 rounds/min (AC556 & 556K only)

Sturm Ruger & Co introduced their Mini-14 carbine in 1973, a lightweight weapon using the well-proven Garand system of gas operation and rotating bolt, allied to the .223 cartridge. As might be imagined, such a useful combination of reliability and light weight, allied to a modern service cartridge, attracted several military and para-military forces, to the extent that Sturm Ruger have developed some specific variants of the Mini-14 for use by such agencies. In the expectation that readers might be less familiar with these models, we append some notes on them.

The *Ruger Mini-14/20GB Infantry Rifle* is a conversion of the standard Mini-14 to meet general military standards. The front sight is protected, moved back on the barrel, and incorporates a bayonet lug; there is a flash hider on the muzzle, and the handguard is of heat-resistant glass-fiber reinforced plastic material. The flash hider is shaped so as to function as a grenade launching spigot. In other respects, and in general dimensions and weight, the Infan-

The Rossi 92, a traditional saddlegun using revolver cartridges.

Ruger's No. 3 single shot carbine in 5.56mm caliber.

Above: Close up right view of the breech of the Ruger Mini-14 .223 caliber rifle.
Below: The same rifle field-stripped.

RIFLES

Right view of the Ruger Mini-14 .223 with scope.

try Rifle version is the same as the commercial Mini-14 and is available in blued steel or stainless steel.

The *AC-556 Selective Fire Weapon* resembles the Mini-14/20 Infantry Rifle but incorporates modifications to the trigger mechanism to permit the firing of single shots, three-round bursts or full automatic fire.

The *AC-556K Selective Fire Weapon* is the AC-556 modified to have a steel folding stock, a pistol grip, and a shorter (16.7in or 425mm) barrel. Due to the added weight of the stock the complete weapon now weighs 6.9lbs (3.15kg). It is a particularly compact model, well suited to airborne or armored troops. These models are only for sale to law enforcement agencies or governments.

Below: Left view of the Mini-14's action.

Below: Left profile of the Mini-14.
Bottom: Left close up view of the action and scope mounting.

RIFLES

St. Etienne 'FA-MAS' Assault Rifle

Manufacturer Manufacture d'Armes de St. Etienne, St. Etienne, France
Type Delayed blowback, selective fire
Caliber 5.56mm (.223)
Barrel 19.2in (488mm)
Weight 8.73lbs (3.96kg)
Magazine capacity 25 rounds
Cyclic rate of fire 950 rounds/minute

The peculiar shape of this rifle has led to it being nicknamed 'The Trumpet' by today's poilus, and in the hands of a well-built soldier it looks like a toy. But it is a very efficient and ingenious design, and production at St Etienne is intended to have it in the hands of every French soldier by 1990. At present it has only been seen in service use with paratroops, but infantry units are now being equipped and trained, and it will eventually become the standard 'personal weapon' acting as rifle, carbine or sub-machine gun.

The system of operation relies upon delayed blowback of the breech block and carrier. The carrier has two 'delay arms' which, when the bolt is closed, contact a hardened steel rod lying across the receiver. When the rifle fires the cartridge case attempts to move back against the face of the bolt; this movement is transferred to the carrier, but when this attempts to move the delay arms, held against the cross-bar, resist. They now have to rotate on their pivot, so that their upper section moves

back and, in doing so, begin to move the bolt carrier backwards. But the differing lengths of the two sections of the delay arms ensures a mechanical disadvantage which delays the movement. When the arms have moved about 45° they clear the cross-bar and the bolt and carrier now move to the rear, ejecting the spent case. In order to avoid hard extraction, the chamber has longitudinal grooves machined in it so that the fired case is 'floated' on a layer of gas during the extraction phase.

The rifle is a bullpup design, the bolt and chamber being alongside the firer's face and the trigger ahead of the magazine; this permits a long barrel in a short rifle, since the otherwise wasted length of a naked butt is avoided. The butt carries a buffer unit in its upper surface so as to cushion the recoil, and there is a rubber recoil pad. The bolt can have its extractor moved across, and the butt cheek-piece can also be moved, so that the rifle can be quickly adapted to left or right-handed firers. The cocking handle lies centrally, underneath the carrying handle; this handle is of plastic and grooved; within it lie the sights, a blade foresight and an adjustable aperture rear sight calibrated to 300 meters.

The firer can select single shots, three-round bursts or full automatic fire; the three-round burst mechanism is separate from the rest of the trigger group so that should it fail the remaining options are still available. This means that there has to be two separate controls, one for fire selection and one for burst selection, but careful

training avoids any problems with this. The rifle can also be readily adapted for firing grenades, and there is a light bipod which folds beneath the handle and steadies the rifle when firing automatic.

The FA-MAS (which means 'Fusil Automatique, Manufacture d'Armes St. Etienne) is comfortable to fire, in spite of its size and unusual appearance. It is very accurate at battle ranges and is easily controlled during burst fire. Its length allows it to be used in the submachine gun role quite effectively, and its adoption by the French Army is expected to increase the basic squad's fire power and also reduce the variety of weapons carried.

Sako P-72

Manufacturer Oy Sako AB, SF-11100 Riihimaki 10, Finland
Type Bolt action, magazine
Caliber .22 Long Rifle RF
Barrel 23.375in (594mm)
Weight 6.53lbs (2.96kg)
Magazine capacity 5 rounds

Sako have been making firearms for many years, concentrating particularly on center-fire sporting rifles in their export markets, but they have always made .22 rimfire rifles for home consumption. They have now begun exporting this rimfire rifle and as well as making it in the standard .22 Long Rifle chambering offer models in .22 Winchester Magnum RF and a center-fire version in .22 Hornet.

Below: The 'Trumpet'; The French Army's FAMAS 5.56mm assault rifle.
Left: A French soldier using the FAMAS rifle fitted with an infra-red aiming spotlight and wearing infra-red goggles to permit accurate shooting in darkness.

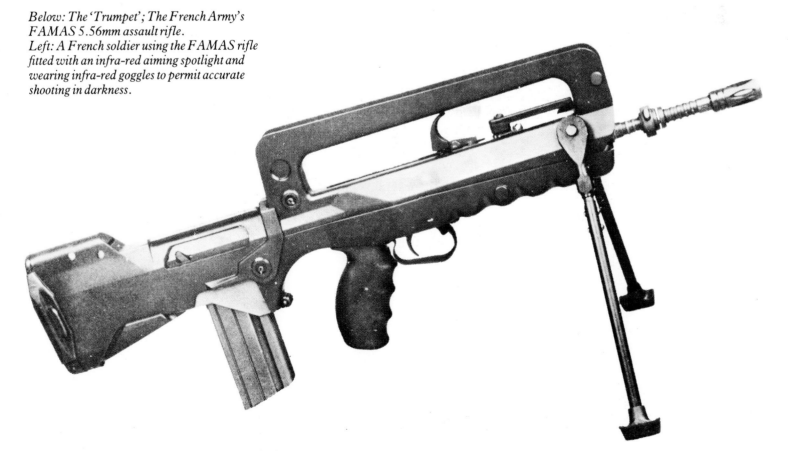

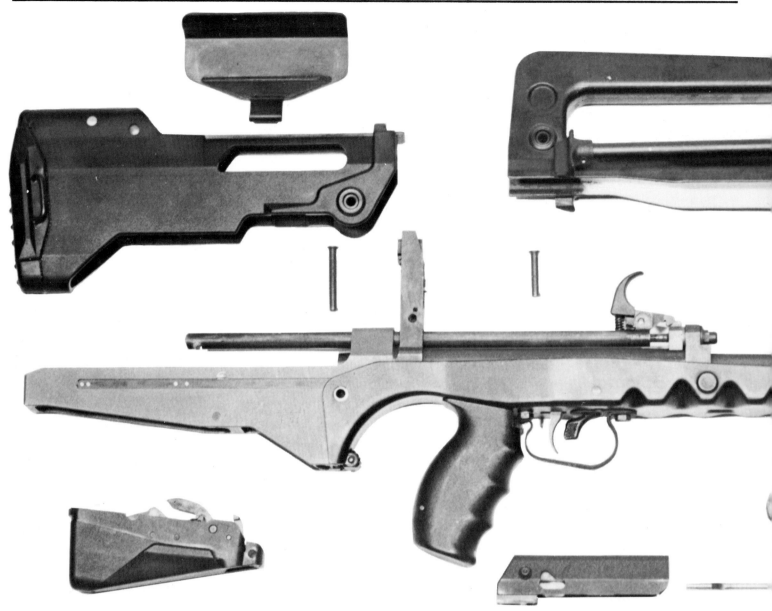

The general appearance echoes the lines of their larger-caliber sporting rifles, and the Sako is definitely not intended as a child's first gun or a plinker. The action gives the impression of immense strength, the bolt having two extractors and two locking lugs, while both receiver and bolt are large by conventional .22 rimfire standards. The bolt is an interesting three-piece design in which the firing pin floats free, held back by its own spring, and the cocking piece, driven by the mainspring, is released by the sear to strike the pin. The cocking piece is retracted as the bolt lever is lifted to open the bolt, so that the firing pin spring moves the pin back before the chamber is opened.

The stock is checkered and oil-finished, and there is a substantial pistol grip; the comb of the Monte Carlo butt is somewhat low, though this may be an individual impression. The sights incorporate the Williams Guide Line and comprise a ramped front sight with hooded bead and an open rear sight adjustable for windage and elevation; the receiver also has dovetail bases for mounting a telescope.

Accuracy is good, one-inch groups at 50 yards being easily accomplished from a rest. I have seen reports of misfeeding with this rifle but was unable to fire sufficient rounds to make any conclusions of my own.

Savage 110-S Silhouette Rifle

Manufacturer Savage Arms Div. of Emhart Industries Inc., Westfield, MA 01085, U.S.A.
Type Bolt action, magazine
Caliber .308 Winchester (7.62mm NATO)
Barrel 22.125in (562mm)
Weight 8.5lbs (3.85kg)
Magazine capacity 5 rounds

We have commented elsewhere on the recent rise in 'silhouette shooting' in which metal representations of animals and birds are engaged at long range in a competitive simulacrum of hunting, and this is one of several weapons which have been devised to suit its particular demands.

The Savage 110-S stems from their standard 110 series, modified as necessary. The stock is functional, with a good-sized pistol grip and a high comb but without a cheekpiece so that it can be used by right- or left-handed shots. There is ample stippling in the areas likely to be gripped, and the magazine does not pass through the stock so that there is the maximum amount of rigidity.

The barrel is heavy and free-floating,

The Sako P-72, a rimfire rifle from Finland.

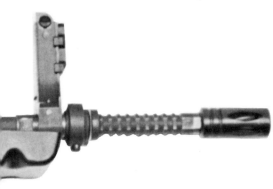

The component parts of the FAMAS rifle.

counterbored at the muzzle, and excellently finished inside and out. It is screwed into the receiver and retained there by a barrel nut which also locates the recoil lug. The bolt locks on two forward lugs and has the face recessed to enclose the head of the cartridge.

No sights are provided, as is customary with silhouette rifles, but the receiver is drilled and tapped for the attachment of telescope mounts.

The rifle balances well and operates smoothly. Its accuracy is such that it is well capable of two-inch groups at 100 yards,

provided that care is taken over selecting ammunition. It appears to be admirably suited to its designed purpose.

Savage-Anschutz Mark 12 Rifle

Manufacturer Savage Arms Div. of Emhart Industries Inc., Westfield, MA 01085, U.S.A.
Type Bolt action, single shot, rimfire
Caliber .22 Long Rifle RF
Barrel 26in (660mm)
Weight 7.8lbs (3.54kg)

The Anschutz company have been making target rifles in Germany for longer than most of us can remember, while the Savage company have been making hunting rifles in the U.S.A. for much the same length of time. For some time now Savage have marketed Anschutz target rifles in the U.S.A., and now they have collaborated with Anschutz in making a target rifle aimed at the less-serious competitive market, the local contests rather than the international affairs demanding heavy and expensive weapons.

The stock is plainly styled but well finished, with a hand-filling swell to the pistol grip; there is a track under the fore end carrying an adjustable plastic hand-stop and a fixed sling swivel. The barrel is cylindrical, amply proportioned but not as heavy as might be expected in international classes, and counterbored at the muzzle to protect the rifling.

The bolt and trigger mechanism represent Anschutz' contribution (everything else is made by Savage). The bolt locks by the handle turning into a recess in the receiver wall and the striker is cocked on the opening movement of the handle. There is a safety catch on the left side which locks the trigger.

The foresight is a hooded unit carrying a diaphragm which can be changed; the rifle is supplied with seven different posts and

The Savage-Anschutz Model 12, a precision target rifle from the collaboration of two highly-skilled makers.

apertures for this. The aperture rear sight is click-adjustable for elevation and windage and can also be moved back and forth to give eye relief. The sighting disc which carries the aperture is also interchangeable, though no alternatives are supplied.

As to accuracy, a skilled shot should be able to put ten rounds into a one-inch circle at 50 yards, so the rifle is capable of performing as well as its operator is likely to do. Bearing in mind its purpose in life, we feel that the accuracy is more than adequate, and in view of the quality of material and finish exhibited, this rifle is excellent value and would make a first-class introduction to competitive shooting.

SIG SG-541 Rifle

Manufacturer Schweizerische Industrie Gesellschaft (SIG), Neuhausen-Am-Rheinfalls, Switzerland
Type Gas-operated, automatic, magazine
Caliber 5.56mm (.223)
Barrel 14.05in (357mm); or 21in (533mm)
Weight (empty) 8.26lbs (3.75kg); or 7.36lbs (3.34kg)
Magazine capacity 20, 25 or 30 rounds
Cyclic rate of fire 750 rounds/minute

The Swiss Army has used a powerful 7.5mm cartridge since the turn of the century, but in recent years it decided to investigate a lighter caliber and asked both its own Federal Arsenal at Berne and the SIG Company to develop some new rifles in smaller calibers. As a result both establishments produced prototypes in 5.56mm and in a new 6.45mm caliber; government testing is by no means complete but already it is known that the 6.45mm has been eliminated and that no further work will be done.

The SIG 541 is their answer to the request and as well as being formally evalu-

The Savage 110-S, a heavy rifle designed for metallic silhouette shooting.

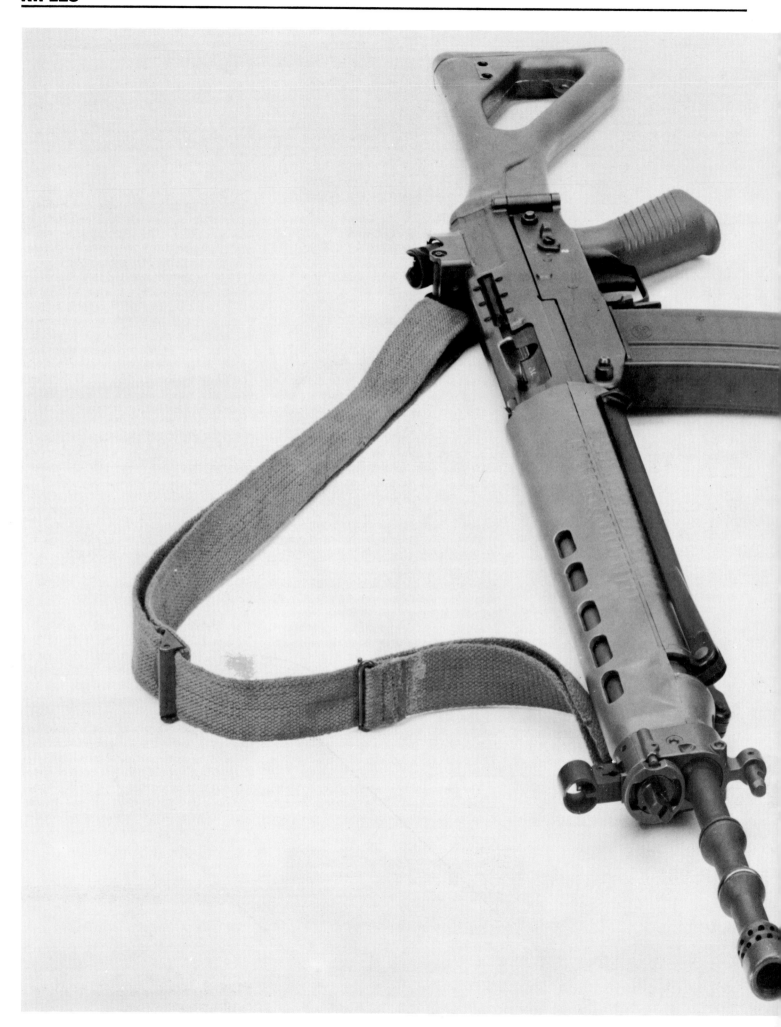

The SIG 541 assault rifle (left) and headquarters weapon (right).

The Swiss SIG SG541 assault rifle, currently undergoing trials by the Swiss Army.

ated it is now available for commercial sale to approved customers. It is a conventional gas-piston-operated rifle using a rotating bolt inside a bolt carrier. High-quality plastic material has been used for the folding stock and the fore-end guard, and also for the transparent magazine. Two lengths are available; the longer model is the 'Assault Rifle' while the shorter model is known as the 'Headquarters Weapon' and, with the butt folded, can be used in the submachine-gun role.

The sights are an aperture rear and blade front, with luminous dots for night sighting; there are mounting points for a telescope or for a variety of electro-optical sight units. There is a three-round burst facility, plus single shots or full automatic fire, and a light bipod can be fitted to steady the weapon when used in the squad automatic role.

Singapore Assault Rifle 80

Manufacturer Chartered Industries of Singapore
Type Gas operated, selective fire
Caliber 5.56mm (.223)
Barrel 18.07in (459mm)
Weight 8.15lbs (3.70kg)
Magazine capacity 20 or 30 rounds
Cyclic rate of fire 700 rounds/minute

Chartered Industries is a government-sponsored company set up in Singapore in 1967 to produce 5.56mm ammunition and to manufacture the M16 rifle under license. After this the Singapore Armed Forces asked the company to investigate the possibility of a new rifle, one which would be simple, rugged and effective and capable of entirely local manufacture; one drawback to the M16 was the contractual requirement to purchase several major components from the U.S.A.

The SAR 80 was designed by Sterling Armaments of England in 1976; prototypes were made and tested in 1978, design improvements were made and production got under way late in 1980. Approximately 45 percent of the components are fabricated by casting or pressing, and another 40 percent are readily available commercial items. Issue to the Singapore Armed Forces has begun, and there have been expressions of interest from other Far Eastern countries.

The mechanism is the conventional one of gas cylinder above the barrel, gas piston

The Singapore Assault Rifle SAr 80, designed by Sterling Armaments of Britain.

driving a bolt carrier, and rotating bolt. The gas cylinder is fitted with a regulator so that more or less gas can be admitted to compensate for fouling or changes in ammunition, or it can be shut off completely to convert the weapon to a single-shot hand loader when launching grenades with blank cartridges. Firing is performed by a hammer which strikes the firing pin; there is also an auto-sear safety device which prevents the hammer being released until the breech is closed and locked. A selector switch permits firing single shots or full automatic.

The standard rifle has a plastic butt and fore end, and may be fitted with a light bipod. The 20- and 30-round magazines of the U.S. M16 rifle are interchangeable with those made for the SAR 80. A folding-stock version has also been developed, and its compact dimensions make it a useful weapon for airborne troops. The sights are the usual front post and rear flip-over aperture, and the receiver is prepared for mounts to take telescopes or night vision devices.

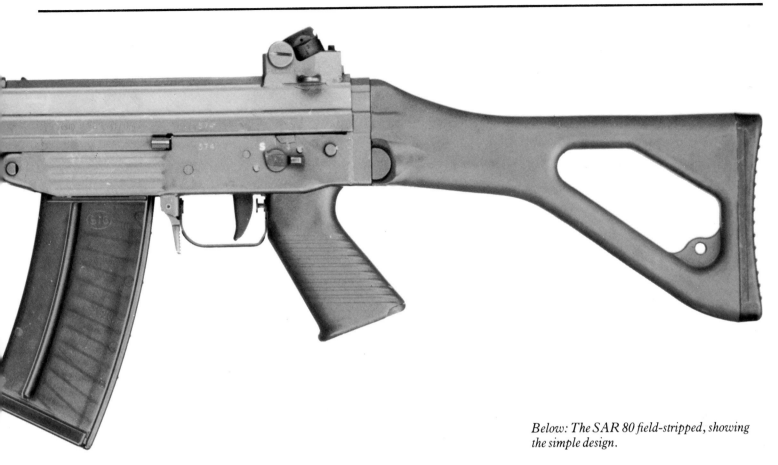

Below: The SAR 80 field-stripped, showing the simple design.

Smith & Wesson Model 1500

Manufacturer Howa Machinery Co., Japan
Marketed by Smith & Wesson, 2100 Roosevelt Avenue, Springfield, MA 01101, U.S.A.
Type Bolt action, magazine
Caliber .30-06; .243; .270; 7mm Magnum
Barrel 7mm Magnum; 24in (610mm); other calibers: 22in (558mm)
Weight 7.44lbs (3.37kg)
Magazine capacity 5 standard, 4 Magnum

Smith & Wesson entered the rifle market in the late 1960s, marketing Swedish Husqvarna sporting rifles, but after Husqvarna got out of the arms business in the early '70s, were rifle-less until 1979 when they bought this one from a Japanese maker.

Two grades are available, the 'Standard' and the 'De Luxe', the differences being largely cosmetic. The Standard has a fairly plain wooden stock with coarse checkering and sling swivel studs and is fitted with iron sights. The De Luxe grade uses a better quality of wood, has a Monte Carlo stock with finer checkering, has engine-turned finish on the bolt, is fitted with sling swivels and provided with a sling, and has no iron sights but has the receiver drilled and tapped for mounts.

The bolt action might be described as modified Mauser, using front locking lugs, and the face is counter-bored. The action is partially cocked as the bolt handle is lifted to open, and completely cocked during the closing stroke. There is a thumb-operated safety at the right of the trigger which shows a red dot when in the 'fire' position. The box magazine has a hinged floor plate which can be released by a catch in the front edge of the trigger guard. The trigger mechanism is provided with adjusting screws to alter both pull and engagement; as supplied the trigger tends to have very little travel before or after the pull-off point, though the release is crisp.

Accuracy is reasonably good, giving three-inch groups at 50 yards 'as is' and could probably be improved by attention to the sights and the selection of matched ammunition. One noticeable point was that the cartridges tend to set forward in the magazine rather violently when a shot is fired, leading to some hammering of the tips of soft point bullets.

Sterling AR-180

Manufacturer Sterling Armament Co., Dagenham, England
Type Gas-operated semi-automatic
Caliber 5.56mm
Barrel 18.25in (464mm)
Weight 7.2lbs (3.26kg)
Magazine capacity 5, 20, 30 or 40 rounds

The original AR-18 military selective fire rifle was designed by Eugene Stoner and developed in the mid-1960s as an alternative to the existing AR-15. The reason for this was to have a design which could be

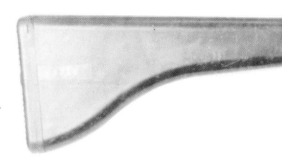

The Sterling AR-180 semi-automatic rifle is based on the Armalite AR-18 design, intended for easy production in developing countries.

made on fairly simple plant, so that the design could be sold to developing countries for them to make their own. The idea was a good one but it didn't work that way, since the developing countries were quite happy to buy their AR-15s from the U.S.A. During the Vietnam war there was a short-lived attempt to make the AR-18 in Japan for supply to South Vietnam, but the Japanese Government, nervous about arms sales, stepped in and forbade the deal. Finally the rights of manufacture were acquired by Sterling of Britain and numbers have been made for various security forces and some smaller armies. Now they have moved across to the commercial world by developing the AR-180.

The AR-180 was actually intended as a police weapon for those forces which abhor

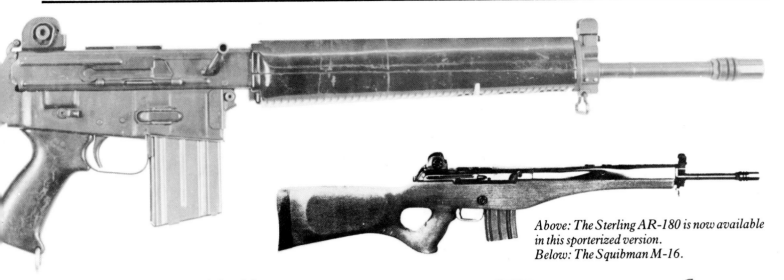

Above: The Sterling AR-180 is now available in this sporterized version.
Below: The Squibman M-16.

the use of automatic weapons; it is solely a semi-automatic rifle with the AR-18's selective fire capability removed. Now it is being offered in the U.S.A. as a possible sporting rifle for those who prefer military-style weapons. Like most of its type it makes extensive use of steel stampings and plastic materials, but it is extremely robust. The gas actuation is by a gas cylinder and short-stroke tappet which impinges on the bolt carrier and drives it back; this cams the rotating bolt round to unlock the eight lugs holding it to the receiver.

The plastic stock is hinged behind the receiver and can be folded round to the left side of the rifle, a useful feature for those who wish to keep the weapon in a car or boat. The foresight is a post, adjustable for elevation, while the rear sight is a two-leaf

flip-over with apertures for short and long range use.

The accuracy of the AR-180 can be surprisingly good if the firer takes trouble over selecting his ammunition, and it can be quite astonishing with a carefully worked out handload. It has the 'old' rifling twist of one turn in 55 calibers, which will suit the M193 ball but may not work so well with some more modern 5.56mm ammunition, particularly of European origin.

Squibman M-16 Rifle

Manufacturer Squires, Bingham Mfg. Co., Marikina, Philippines
Type Semi-automatic, blowback
Caliber .22 Long Rifle RF
Barrel 16in (406mm)
Weight 6lbs (2.72kg)
Magazine capacity 15 rounds

'Squibman' is the brand name of the Squires Bingham Company and they have produced a variety of rifles, shotguns and pistols under this name. Their M-16 is one of several attempts to make a cheap rimfire weapon which resembles a combat rifle.

The configuration of the rifle is, as the title implies, based upon that of the American M16, though the detail execution is considerably different. There is the 'straight-line' stock layout, the carrying handle with rear sight, the elevated foresight and the muzzle flash hider. But the mechanism is a simple blowback unit and the barrel and receiver are in a tubular assembly which simply drops into the stock. Below is the pistol grip and magazine housing assembly.

The stock is of mahogany, finished in ebony black, while the metal components are either blackened steel or anodized alloy. The rear sight is a fixed elevation aperture, adjustable for windage.

The M-16 shoots quite well, with acceptable accuracy, and makes a good general purpose 'fun gun' or vermin shooter. The design has not copied the M16 so slavishly as to finish up with bad proportioning, as have some others, and there is sufficient length of butt to allow the rifle to be held comfortably and firmly.

The Smith & Wesson Model 1500 rifle, made in Japan to a high specification.

The De Luxe version of the Model 1500 features best quality wood, finer checkering, a Monte Carlo stock and mounts for a scope.

Sterling Model 81 Rifle

Manufacturer Sterling Armament Co.,
Dagenham, England
Type Bolt action, magazine
Caliber 7.62mm NATO
(.308 Winchester)
Barrel 26.5in (673mm)
Weight (empty) 10.37lbs (4.70kg)
Magazine capacity 4 rounds

Another one of the many rifles now being
offered to military and police units as a
sniping or marksman's rifle, the Sterling
Model 81 sticks to well-tried mechanisms
and contours rather than trying to woo the
customer with new technology and fancy
shapes.

The bolt mechanism is of Mauser type,
using a bolt machined from a single forging
and with front locking lugs. The very heavy
barrel is fully-floating in the stock, and the
whole weapon is made with smooth contours and a minimum of frills. The stock
has a rubber butt plate with a vertical

The Sterling Model-81 Sniper rifle.

adjustment slide and two spacers to give a
full range of adjustment, and there is a well-
proportioned cheek piece. There is a track
under the fore end which mounts an adjustable hand stop with sling swivel and an
optional bipod. The trigger is adjustable for
tension and for length of pull.

No iron sights are fitted, but the receiver
is machined for mounting a wide variety of
telescopes or electro-optical sighting systems.

Steyr Armee-Universal-Gewehr

Manufacturer Steyr-Daimler-Puch,
Steyr, Austria
Type Gas-operated, selective fire
Caliber 5.56mm (.223)
Barrel Various
Weight 7.9lbs (3.6kg) (508mm barrel)
Magazine capacity 30 rounds
Cyclic rate of fire 650 rounds/minute

The Steyr AUG gets its name from its
ability to be configured in four different
ways, depending upon the length of the
barrel and the presence or absence of a
bipod. The basic mechanism, receiver and
stock remain the same in all cases.

In appearance the AUG is, to say the
least, futuristic, the plastic stock material
and shape giving it the appearance of a
child's toy or something from a space opera.
But its performance puts it well into the
front rank of contemporary assault rifles
and it has already been adopted by the
armies of Austria, Argentina, Saudi Arabia
and Tunisia, with others currently making
evaluations and comparisons preparatory to
possible orders.

The plastic stock unit forms a major part
of the weapon; the principal feature is the
main pistol grip with an enormous trigger
guard which accepts the whole hand.
Behind this is the magazine and its housing
and release, and then the shoulder stock. It
follows from this sequence that the AUG is
a 'bullpup', having the action under the

*The space-age Steyr AUG in standard form;
note the transparent magazine, optical sight
and forward hand grip.*

Above: The Steyr AUG with alternative barrels; from top to bottom, the squad machine gun, rifle, carbine and submachine gun barrels.
Below: The Steyr AUG field-stripped.

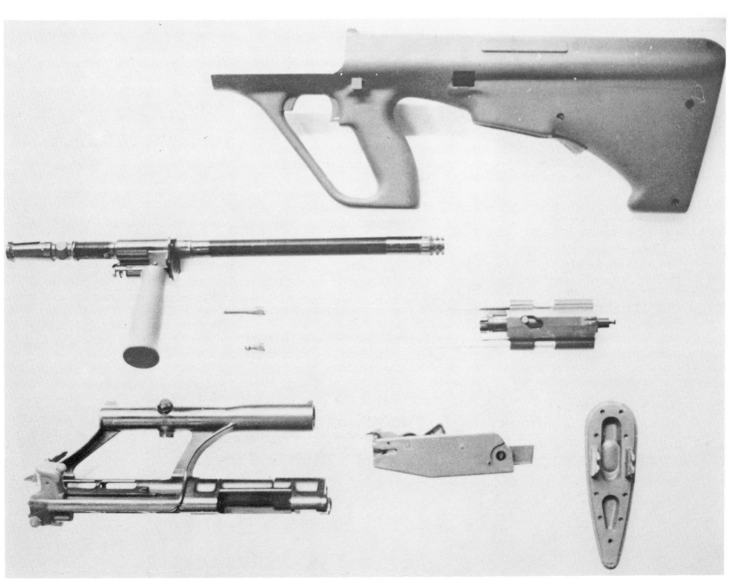

firer's cheek and the trigger well forward of the bolt and magazine.

The receiver unit is an aluminium die-casting which includes the seating for the barrel, bearings for the two bolt guides, the carrying handle and the optical sight. The bolt is the usual rotating multi-lug type held in a carrier, and this carrier moves back and forth on two machined steel bolt guide rods which are held in the receiver; thus there is no direct contact between receiver and bolt and therefore no need for expensive machining of the boltway. The return springs are concealed within the guide rods; in addition the left-hand rod acts with the cocking lever to operate the bolt when loading, and the right-hand rod acts as the gas piston.

The barrel unit consists of the barrel, gas port and cylinder, gas regulator and a folding forward hand grip. This grip can be used to change barrels, since the barrel locks into the receiver by interrupted lugs. Once the barrel is aligned, the gas cylinder unit, which carries a short-stroke piston, lines up with the right-hand bolt guide rod. One might expect some degree of imbalance with the gas impulse working off-axis, but in practice there is no torque effect and no deviation of shooting is detectable.

The magazine is a clear plastic unit, so that its contents can be seen at all times. The trigger group, containing the safety and selective fire mechanism, is a removable unit, much of it plastic. Selective fire is achieved by trigger pressure; a light pressure gives single shots, a harder pressure automatic fire. Again, this is something which, at first, one would expect to lead to inaccuracy, but once the technique is mastered it gives no trouble and automatic fire can be delivered as accurately with the AUG as with any other comparable rifle.

The various models are as follows: 'Commando' with 14in (315mm) barrel; 'Machine Carbine' with 16in (407mm) barrel; 'Assault Rifle' (the standard version) with 20in (508mm) barrel; and the 'Heavy Barrel Rifle' or 'Squad Automatic Weapon' with 24in (610mm) barrel and bipod. All models can be modified by removing the receiver casting and replacing it with another type which carries a low telescope mount instead of the optical sight and integral telescope; this is intended to cater for sniping telescopes or night vision sights.

Firing the AUG holds no surprises; it can be set up for left or right-hand firing very quickly by changing the ejector to one or other side of the bolt and rotating the ejection port cover in the butt to expose the port on the selected side. For those not accustomed to bullpup rifles, the weight distribution feels strange and distinctly light at the muzzle, but this is soon mastered and the rifle is extremely handy for use in quick combat situations. Accuracy is as good as, if not slightly better than, most other rifles of this caliber. The rifling is one turn in 41 calibers, tighter than the usual 1/54, which suggests that it will shoot equally well with a wide variety of service ammunition types.

Steyr-Mannlicher SSG-69 Sniper's Rifle

Manufacturer Steyr-Daimler-Puch, Steyr, Austria
Type Bolt action, magazine
Caliber 7.62mm NATO
Barrel 25.6in (650mm)
Weight 8.6lbs (3.9kg)
Magazine capacity 5 rounds

I have previously commented upon the recent rise in the use of bolt-action rifles for military sniping, replacing the earlier semi-automatics. One of the first to make this move was the Austrian Army, and the Steyr SSG-69 was the weapon developed to their specification.

When this rifle first appeared, most commentators suggested that it was simply the Greek Army Mannlicher-Schoenauer Model 1900 revived, but this was a gross simplification. In the first place the bolt is unusual in having its six locking lugs, in three pairs, at the rear and not in the front; in theory this is liable to give rise to compression stresses in the bolt and consequent inaccuracy, but in practice it seems not to matter. By way of compensation the barrel is set extremely deeply into the receiver and the receiver itself is strengthened, so that the whole assembly is rock-rigid.

The magazine is the Schoenauer rotating spool type, not seen on a military rifle since the aforementioned 1900 model, and it can be quickly removed from the bottom of the

Right: The Steyr SSG in exploded form.

stock by squeezing in two grips on its base. The rear face of the magazine is closed by a transparent panel, so that the firer can slip the magazine out and, without moving it, can check on its contents and replace it. There is a specially-adapted 10-round box magazine which will fit in place of the spool should this be desired.

Iron sights are fitted for emergency use, a blade foresight and 'V' notch backsight. In normal use this weapon will be aimed by a telescope and the receiver is ribbed to take the Kahles 'Helia 6S2' which is standard issue. The same mounting can also be used for infra-red or image-intensifying night sights.

The stock and butt are made of olive-drab self-colored glass-reinforced fiber plastic material which is rot-resistant, impervious to rain, and fairly resistant to casual impact damage. It is also less likely to be seen than a wooden stock and has a matted surface which gives a good grip at all points, though the pistol grip and fore end have additional stippling.

In use this weapon is very accurate, giving 3½-inch groups at 300 yards, though as with most rifles of this type the accuracy relies greatly upon the quality of the military-grade ammunition. It is now available commercially, with a walnut stock and with Walther match-grade adjustable sights, and in this form should make an excellent full-bore match rifle.

Stirling M-20 Rifle

Manufacturer Squires, Bingham Mfg Co., Marikina, Philippines
Type Semi-automatic, blowback
Caliber .22 Long Rifle RF
Barrel 19.5in (495mm)
Weight 6lbs (2.72kg)
Magazine capacity 15 rounds

The Stirling is another product of the Philippine Islands company of Squires Bingham. It is, in essence, the same blow-back action used in their 'Squibman M-16' combat-style rifle but installed into a more conventional form of stock.

The stock is of Philippine mahogany; the standard model is sanded and oil finished

The Steyr SSG military sniping rifle is now available in civilian form.

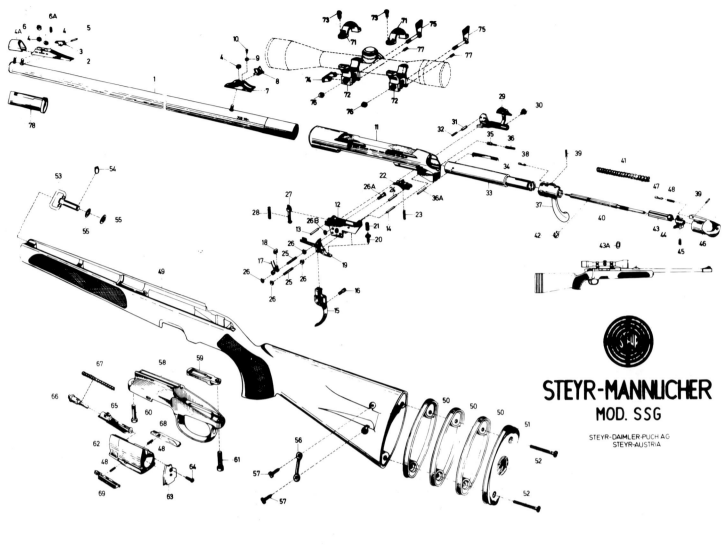

STEYR-MANNLICHER
MOD. SSG

STEYR-DAIMLER-PUCH AG
STEYR-AUSTRIA

Above: The Stirling M20 uses the Squibman M16 mechanism in a more traditional shape.

while the De Luxe Model has the grain well figured and is with a polished finish. Both have machined checkering on pistol grip and fore end, and butt pads and pistol grip caps with white spacers; the De Luxe model also has the fore end capped.

The mechanism is a straightforward blowback bolt working in a tubular receiver attached behind the barrel; the trigger mechanism and magazine housing are fitted through the stock, and the box magazine goes in from beneath. There is a combined muzzle brake and compensator, though just how much of its effect is practical and how much cosmetic is a moot point in this caliber. The whole of the mechanism can be removed from the stock by simply taking out one screw, after which disassembly into the various component parts for cleaning is very simple.

The Stirling is a sound little rifle, excellent for vermin and general plinking and

sufficiently accurate for all practical purposes. It is well finished, and of first-class material, and the manufacture and assembly appears to be to a high standard for a reasonably-priced weapon.

Tikkakoski Model 55 Heavy Barrel

Manufacturer Tikka AB, Tikkakoski, Finland
Type Bolt action, magazine
Caliber .22-250; .243; .308 Winchester
Barrel 24in (610mm)
Magazine capacity 3, 5 or 10 rounds

The Tikkakoski company began making firearms as far back as 1918 but it is only in the last few years that their products have begun to be widely exported. Their Model 55 has been well received and has been made available in various calibers, and it

has now been produced in a heavy barrel version.

The bolt action is Tikkakoski's standard two-lug bolt which locks deeply into the receiver and is provided with vents for the escape of gas in the event of a pierced primer. The bolt head is a large 1.25in-diameter plastic ball, which makes operating easy no matter what the shooter may be wearing on his hands. Safety cams prevent the striker from going forward unless the bolt is completely closed and locked.

The receiver is strong and is dovetailed for a telescope mounting, and the safety catch is mounted at the left side where it can be easily operated with the thumb. The heavy barrel (1.125 inches thick at the chamber end) is completely free-floating and finished to a high standard. The stock is of high-grade wood, and the butt is exceptionally deep, with a cheek rest and an excellent pistol grip, while the fore end swells at its lower edge to make a hand-filling grip. There are rails under the fore end for taking a sling swivel. The magazines are detachable, and available in differing capacities.

The rifle may be had with either target iron sights – post front and fully adjustable rear – or without iron sights for use with a

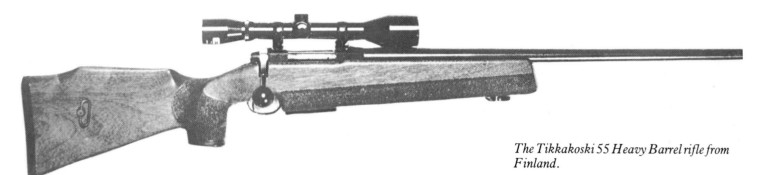

The Tikkakoski 55 Heavy Barrel rifle from Finland.

telescope. On the range the bolt action proved to be well-fitted and sweet in operation, allowing rapid firing, while the accuracy was such that one-inch groups at 100 yards must be considered the average. The weight of this rifle makes it a good target weapon, while it is also perfectly suitable for sporting applications.

A change in bolt dimensions produces the Model 65, which can be had chambered for longer cartridge cases such as the 6.5mm, .270 Winchester and .30-06; apart from that there is little or no difference between the various models.

Unique T-66 Rifle

Manufacturer Manufacture d'Armes des Pyrenees, Hendaye, France
Type Bolt action, rimfire, single shot
Caliber .22 Long Rifle RF
Barrel 25.6in (650mm)
Weight 11.38lbs (5.16kg)

The Manufacture d'Armes Pyrenees has long been known for its 'Unique' series of auto pistols, but in the late 1970s decided to begin production of a match target rifle as a complement to its target pistols.

The T66 rifle is of more or less conventional form, somewhat angular in appearance but carefully designed to meet the exacting demands of International Shooting Union competitions. The stock is of oil-finished walnut, stippled in the grip areas and of quite generous proportions for a good handful. The butt-plate is adjustable for angle and drop, and by removing a spacer the butt length can be shortened. The heavy barrel floats freely and is counter-bored at the muzzle to avoid damage to the rifling.

The bolt locks securely by a lug which

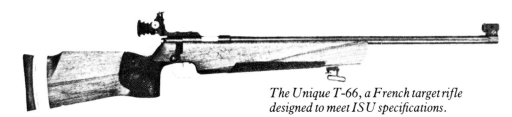

The Unique T-66, a French target rifle designed to meet ISU specifications.

engages in the left side of the receiver and by the root of the bolt-handle engaging on the right side. There is a loading groove beneath the bolt, from which the cartridge is fed into the chamber after being placed by hand. The trigger is fully adjustable for tension, slack and let-off point, and the trigger itself can be repositioned to suit personal choice.

The foresight is the usual competition aperture carried in a hood, with removeable diaphragm to give a choice of aperture sizes or to replace the aperture with a solid post. The rear sight is an aperture fully adjustable for elevation and windage and with a rubber eyecup. The sight is mounted so that it can be moved back and forth to give the desired eye relief.

Accuracy is average for this class of rifle, giving better than one-inch groups at 50 yards, fired from rest; as with most target rifles, this could probably be improved had we time to experiment with different brands of ammunition to find the one best suited to the weapon.

Valmet M76 Rifle

Manufacturer Valmet Oy, Jyvaskyla, Finland
Type Gas-operated, selective fire
Caliber 7.62×39mm Soviet
Barrel 16.5in (420mm)
Weight 7.7lbs (3.5kg)
Magazine capacity 15 or 30 rounds
Cyclic rate of fire 650 rounds/minute

The Finns adopted the Soviet armory at the end of the war and the Kalashnikov AK47 rifle in the early 1950s. However, like the Czechs, they have ideas of their own on what a good rifle consists of, and in a few years time they were at work modifying the Kalashnikov design. They have now gone through three stages of change and their latest version is known as the M-76. Though it looks like a standard Kalashnikov (though with far better exterior finish) there are some major differences. It has been adopted by the forces of Qatar, in the Middle East, and a semi-automatic-only version is sold as a sporting rifle in the U.S.A.

The receiver is of stamped steel rivetted together, and there is no wood whatever in the construction; the pistol grip and fore end are of steel, covered in plastic. Earlier versions (M60 and M62) have cooling holes in the fore end, but these have been omitted on the M76. There is a three-pronged flash hider on the muzzle, one prong of which carries a bayonet lug. The foresight is a hooded, adjustable, post, while the back

The latest offering from Valmet is the Model 255-470 bullpup, here seen with plastic furniture.

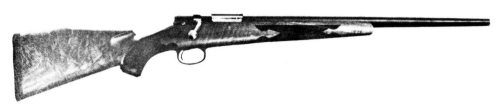

sight is an aperture type protected by two wings. Instead of using the Soviet position in front of the chamber, the Finnish rear sight, being an aperture, is at the rear end of the receiver. It is also fitted with Tritium light beads for night aiming, as is the foresight.

The trigger guard has no forward part, so that heavily-gloved fingers can get in to the trigger; there is a hinged bar at the front end to prevent accidental release of the magazine. Four types of butt-stock are produced: the M76T has a tubular unit, very thick, plastic-covered and rigid; the M76F has a folding skeleton butt; the M76M has a plastic stock of conventional appearance, and the M76W has, unusually, a wooden butt.

In 1981 Valmet announced the existence of a new experimental rifle, the M76 Short; this uses the same Kalashnikov mechanism of the M76 but fitted into a bull-pup stock. It is chambered for the 5.56mm cartridge. The stock of the prototype is entirely of wood, but it is said that if the rifle were to go into production, then a plastic stock would be developed. We understand that the Finnish army are conducting evaluation trials with this design.

Whitworth Express Rifle

Manufacturer Whitworth Rifle Co., Manchester, England
Type Bolt action, center-fire, magazine
Caliber .375 Holland & Holland
Barrel 24in (610mm)
Weight 8.5lbs (3.85kg)
Magazine capacity 3 rounds

The day of the big game rifle may be drawing to its close, but it is not yet over and there are still people who need the most powerful rifle they can find. The 'Express' rifle is a phrase which conjures up the Great White Hunter and similar images, and it might be as well to explain the term; it began in the 1850s when Purdy, the famous English gunmaker, produced a rifle which he called his 'Express Train' model because

of its high (for those days) velocity. The term caught the popular fancy and was shortened to 'Express' and came to denote a rifle which developed a higher-than-normal velocity for its caliber. The term 'Magnum' has largely replaced it, but the English gunmakers still stick to the old word.

The Whitworth Express is a conventional bolt action rifle based on a Mauser bolt which is, in fact, made in Yugoslavia by Crvena Zastava, the old state arsenal at Kragujevac. The actions are sent to England where the Whitworth company fit the barrel, stock and sight the weapon and it is distributed in the U.S.A. by Interarms.

The Mauser bolt is sufficiently well-known to require no further description. The rifle is fitted with an English walnut stock, oil-finished and elegant, with fine checkering and a small but efficient cheekpiece. The trigger is adjustable for tension and let-off. The sights are the traditional Express type, a bead foresight and a three-leaf backsight; the 100-yard leaf with notch is permanently fixed; the 200- and 300-yard leaves are hinged and can be flipped up when required. These are calibrated to the rifle during manufacture and there is no elevation adjustment, which means that the shooter has to determine precisely what ammunition the weapon is meant to fire. The rear sight can be adjusted for windage by drifting it sideways in its seat. Once set they are perfectly capable of delivering two-inch groups at 100 yards.

The rifle is available in four calibers; 7mm Remington Magnum, .300 Winchester Magnum, .375 Holland, and .458 Winchester; the two latter will unfailingly kill anything to be met with on this planet, while the two former will cope with anything on the North American continent.

The Wichita 'Varminter', a no-frills rifle capable of considerable accuracy.

Wichita 'Varminter' Rifle

Manufacturer Wichita Arms, Wichita, KS 67211, U.S.A.
Type Bolt action, single shot, center-fire
Caliber .308 Winchester (7.62mm NATO)
Barrel 22in (560mm)
Weight 9.125lbs (4.14kg)

The first response to this rifle is to wonder what vermin needs 7.62mm NATO bullets to see it off; but this interesting rifle is also available in smaller calibers such as .222, .22-250 and 6mm, so perhaps vermin comes in varying sizes.

Levity aside, the Wichita company have produced an excellent rifle using their own action machined from the solid to give a most rigid receiver, and their own design of bolt with three forward locking lugs and counterbored to shroud the cartridge base. The barrel is Atkinson rifled, of generous dimensions and weight, and is bedded into the receiver by glass fiber. The stock is well styled in walnut, with a Monte Carlo comb, good pistol grip, and excellent checkering where it matters.

The trigger is adjustable for tension, so that a smooth pull and crisp let-off can be adjusted to suit individual whims. The rifle is supplied without sights but with drilled and tapped holes for fitting telescope mounts.

The makers claim that it is capable of shooting well under one-inch groups at 100 yards; I have been unable to fire it, but reports indicate that the claim is not unwarranted.

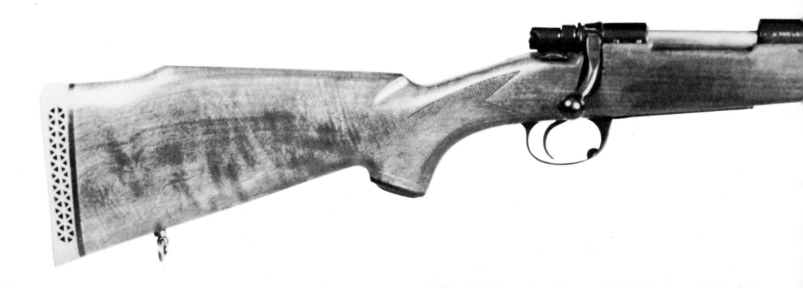

Sold under various names, the Zastava is a well-built sporting rifle based on the proven Mauser action.

Zastava 70 Rifle

Manufacturer Zavodi Crvena Zastava, Kragujevac, Yugoslavia
Type Bolt action, center-fire, magazine
Caliber Various
Barrel 23.6in (600mm)
Weight 7.5lbs (3.4kg)
Magazine capacity 5 rounds

This rifle is a product of the Yugoslavian national armaments factory 'Red Flag', which in years gone by was known as 'Voini Techni Zavod' or 'Army Technical Factory' and before that was the Serbian State Arsenal. It is sold in the U.S.A. under the Interarms name as their 'Mark X' rifle.

Throughout its existence, the Kragujevac factory has constantly been making or modifying Mauser military rifles, so it is not surprising that this weapon is a modified Mauser '98 pattern action. Some of the more military aspects have been omitted and the action made more smooth; the bolt handle is swept down and back, there is no cutaway in the sidewall for the thumb when clip-loading, the safety is a sliding pattern instead of the Mauser 'flag', and the magazine floor plate is hinged, with a release inside the trigger guard. The trigger is fully adjustable.

The stock is well proportioned, with a somewhat swept-back pistol grip and a low cheek rest. The finish appeared to be a synthetic varnish, not conducive to a firm grip. The foresight is a brass bead on a ramp, while the backsight is an open notch, adjustable for elevation and windage. The receiver is drilled and tapped for telescope sights.

The Zastava shoots well, delivering two-inch groups at 100 yards.

Center: Soviet troops advance on exercise. The Kalashnikov AK-47 has been produced in greater volume than any other current small arm.
Above: The English Whitworth sporting rifle is available in several choices of caliber.

Assault Rifles

Although the assault rifle is, by definition, entirely a military affair, the fact remains that it has several attractions to the sport shooter and, of course, as a self-defense weapon. For sport, the principal benefit is the combination of high velocity and light weight; there is a school of thought which considers that the ideal hunting rifle is the heaviest one which can be carried all day without fatigue, but there is another point of view which suggests that the lightest rifle which will achieve the aim of killing specified types of game is a more practical weapon. As a self-defense weapon the lightness scores once more, but so too do the military attributes of reliability and ruggedness and the ability to deliver fast, aimed, semi-automatic or automatic fire.

One anomaly which is little understood is the considerable cost difference between automatic rifles built in the conventional 'gunsmith' way – machined receivers, wooden furniture and so forth – and the modern assault rifles built by production engineering methods – pressed-steel receiver, investment-cast components, plastic or tubular steel stocks. One of the much-touted advantages of this latter type of manufacture is its cheapness; no time-consuming machining and expensive machinists to do it, simply stamp, cast and weld. On the face of it, this sounds a reasonable statement, but when the actual prices are examined something seems to have gone wrong. A recent catalog, for example, lists the Springfield Armory M1 Garand rifle, as conventional as you can get, at $525, while the FN-FNC, one of the latest representatives of the assault rifle world, is listed at $1695 and the SIG AMT, the civilianized version of the Swiss Army's SIG 510-4 rifle, is listed at $2200.

One reason for this high price for what is supposed to be cheaper is that assault rifles on the commercial market usually have to be somewhat modified from their military specification, if only to restrict them to semi-automatic firing only. If this is done properly, so that the weapon cannot be transformed back into a full-auto by some simple home gunsmithing, then it involves non-standard components which usually have to be made by hand and certainly will have to be hand-fitted, and once extra hands get into the business, then the price begins to spiral. Another reason is that although 'pressing, casting and welding' sounds simple, in the case of firearms these process have to be to an exceptionally high standard of accuracy, far higher than, for example, pressing, casting and welding in the automobile or other general engineering industries. To press to this sort of accuracy requires extremely expensive and accurate machinery, the cost of which has to be spread across the product, and although an order for, say 100,000 rifles may sound impressive, it is a derisory figure in the context of modern press technology which is more accustomed to production runs in the order of millions. A three-million-dollar computer-controlled machine, which is by no means excessive today, will thus add $30 to the price of each rifle, and there is more than one machine involved in the production process.

Another factor which adds to the price is the inclusion of military standards of reliability and robustness in the design. A hunter whose rifle malfunctions occasionally is probably in no more danger than of missing his supper, but a soldier in similar straits stands to get killed. The average commercial rifle is unlikely to be able to survive a military-style acceptance test, with prolonged firing, dunking in sand and mud, hot and cold temperature testing and similar rigors, and designing a military rifle to meet this sort of specification, and then building the design, are, again, sources of expense which have to be amortized in the cost of the final weapon.

The last factor to be considered is that the commercial buyer is a one-off customer. He buys the rifle, leaves the store, and except for occasional purchases of ammunition, that's the last the gunshop or manufacturer knows. The military customer, on the other hand, starts out by being a buyer in quantity – from 100,000 rifles up – adds on a few million dollars worth of spares and accessories such as specialist sights, spare barrels, cleaning kits or bayonets, decides perhaps on a side-order of trench mortars or submachine guns, and will be back in 15 or 20 years for the next generation rifle. For him, a hefty discount on the unit price of the rifles is a foregone conclusion.

Left: The start of it all; a British General examining a captured German Sturmgewehr in the winter of 1944.
Below: The German MP44 or Sturmgewehr introduced the 'straight-line' recoil path, pressed-steel components and mass-production techniques to the military rifle.

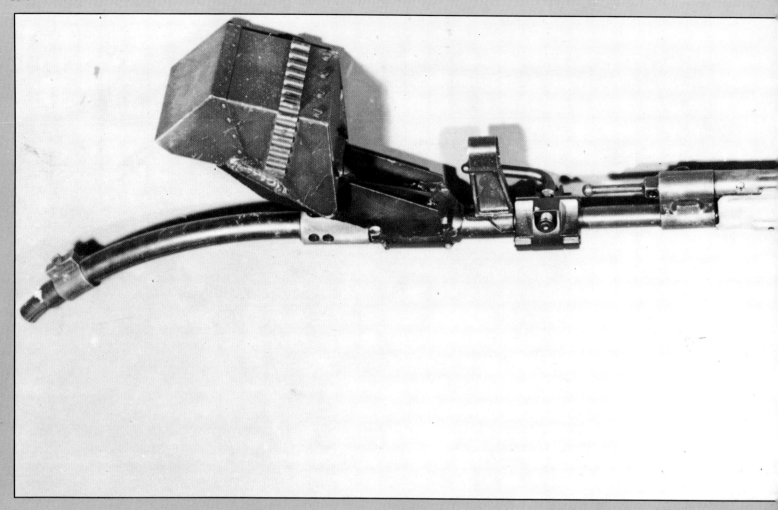

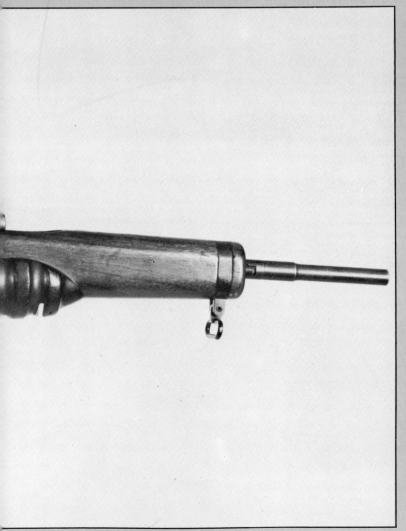

Above: The short bullet of the Sturmgewehr allowed the use of this muzzle attachment which permitted the firer to shoot around corners.
Left: The British .280 EM2 rifle, the first military bullpup to be approved for service and the first postwar application of the assault rifle.

Even so, there are still plenty of weekend shooters and seasonal hunters who lust after the latest assault rifle, sure that its military heritage will give them the reliability and accuracy that they crave. Whether or not it will do so is another matter, and to understand why there could be debate on this subject it is as well to reflect on the background of the assault rifle.

Back at the start of World War I all the combatants were armed with much the same sort of rifle; a bolt-action, magazine weapon firing a bullet around .30 caliber from a sizeable cartridge giving about 2600ft/sec velocity and with a maximum range of about 2500 yards. Most regular soldiers of that era were sufficiently well trained to be able to hit a six-foot target at 1000 yards range, and at shorter ranges they were lethal. The South African War and the Russo-Japanese War, both of which had taken place in open country and had featured long-range rifle fire, had conditioned soldiers and designers to the idea that such weapons were mandatory.

But when World War I came along, the long-range rifle shot became a rarity. Instead, soldiers sat in trenches, often no more than 50 yards apart, and shot at each other. Hastily-trained conscripts missed more often than they hit, and when the armies of the world abandoned red and blue uniforms and merged into the background in field-gray, khaki or olive drab, it was a hawk-eyed soldier who could even *see* a target at more than 3-400 yards, let alone hit one.

In the 1930s, when Hitler's Wehrmacht was building up, a group of German officers sat down to contemplate the future armament of the infantryman, and after studying reports on World War I, and taking into account their own experiences in it, reached the conclusion that the infantryman was, in fact, over-gunned. If, as had been made plain, he was unable to detect targets over 400 yards, and if hasty wartime training was such that he had no better than a fifty-fifty chance of hitting a distinct target at 300 yards, then there was no logical reason to give him a rifle and ammunition designed to kill at 2000 yards.

Once you accepted this premise, certain conclusions stemmed from it. If the operational range was defined as, say, 500 yards, then the current cartridge was too powerful

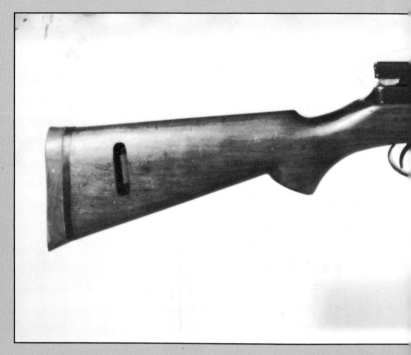

Below: When the 7.62mm NATO cartridge was agreed upon, the British tried to convert their EM2 design, but it was not a success. Right: An assault rifle in the conventional mould was this British BSA P-28, designed for the .280 cartridge. The cartridge was superseded before the rifle could be finally perfected.

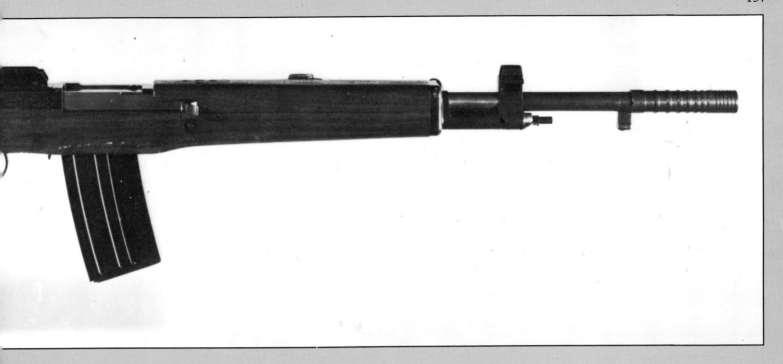

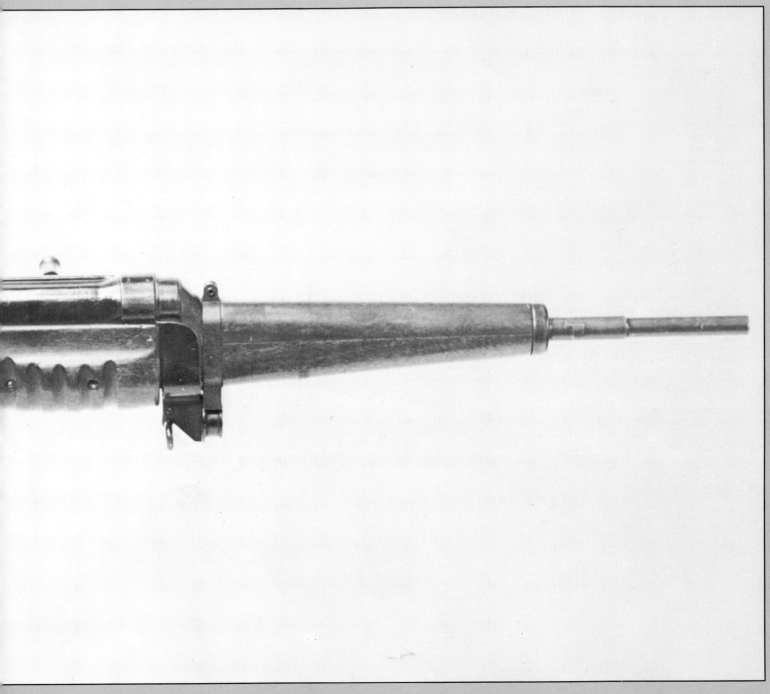

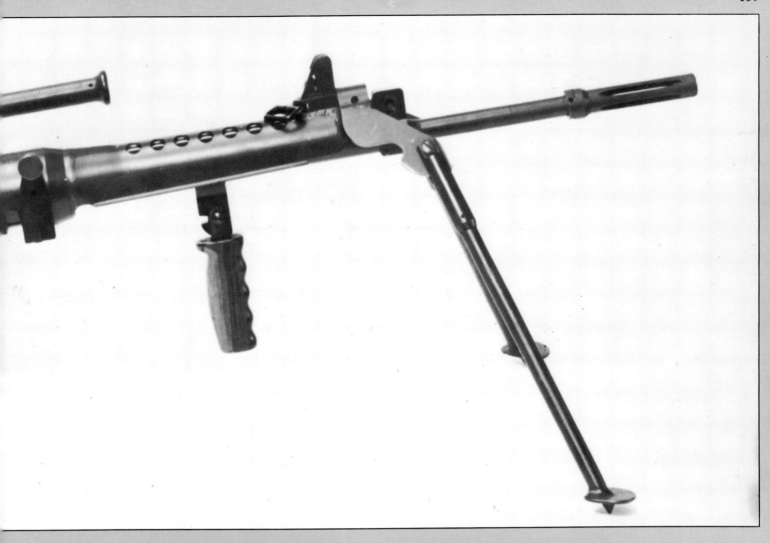

Above: One of the earliest Armalite designs was the AR-10, which was license-built in Holland but found few customers.
Left: The designers of the Mauser Sturmgewehr 45 fled from Germany after the war and settled in Spain to make this early CETME rifle.

and a less powerful round could be designed. A less powerful round, ie one with a shorter bullet and less powder, would require a shorter case so that the whole thing would be more compact. The action of a rifle is governed by the length of cartridge it is required to feed, so a shorter cartridge meant a shorter action. If long range was not required, then the rifle's barrel could be shorter. If the ammunition was shorter, it would weigh less, so the soldier with his 'day of fire' or basic load (usually 200 rounds) would have less weight to carry. Moreover his shorter rifle would weigh less. As a result he would be less fatigued or, alternatively (and more in line with most military thinking) he could have some extra piece of equipment hung on him to make up the weight.

The result of all this thinking was a contract to a major ammunition manufacturer to design a totally new short 7mm cartridge. Once that was successful, the design of a rifle could come along afterwards. And by about 1938 DWM had produced the required cartridge and proved that it worked well. The next problem for the brains trust was to sell the idea to the Wehrmacht and, more particularly, to the Ordnance Supply Office. Here they ran into a problem, which was simply that the Army had scores of billions of 7.92mm Mauser cartridges on hand and several plants set up to turn them out in quantity, and the prospect of throwing all

One of the virtues of a light assault rifle is that it can carry a heavy sight without becoming too cumbersome; this is the American Litton night sight on a Heckler & Koch HK33 rifle.

that away and starting again was too much for anyone to swallow. So they went back to DWM and had the cartridge designed in 7.92mm caliber, which meant that existing machinery could be used for its manufacture and for the manufacture of barrels to suit.

Now two companies, Walther and Haenel, were given contracts to develop suitable rifles. These had to be light and handy, but were also to incorporate automatic fire, since it was reasoned that a lighter cartridge would develop a lower recoil force and would thus allow the weapon to be fired on automatic without the need for bipods or similar aids. The two prototypes were tested on the Russian Front and the Haenel model, which was designed by Hugo Schmeisser, was accepted for development. It eventually became the 'Machine Pistol 43', a title given in order to sneak it through the production schedules at a time when Hitler was encouraging submachine guns and discouraging rifle design. Once fully accepted, Hitler was converted into being a supporter of the project and it was he who gave it the name 'Sturmgewehr' or 'Assault Rifle', and the name has stuck ever since.

As might be imagined, the assault rifle and the short cartridge were intensively studied after the war was over, and while everybody agreed what a good idea it was, few people actually got down to doing very much about it. The first people to move were the Russians, who set about developing their own version of a short cartridge before the war had ended. This became the 7.62×39mm which is now standard throught the Warsaw Pact and with many other nations who have adopted Soviet weaponry. Though longer than the German 7.92mm 'Kurz' round, it is still shorter than any other medium-caliber cartridge, and it led to the famous Kalashnikov rifle, which probably outfits more troops around the world than any other design does or has ever done.

Above: Another experimental rifle from the middle 1970s was this Mauser, developed for a caseless cartridge.
Right: It is generally easy to develop variant models, such as these 'standard' and 'carbine' versions of the Belgian FN-FNC rifle.
Below: The hunt for small calibers stopped here; the Heckler & Koch 4.6mm HK 36 experimental assault rifle, developed in 1975.

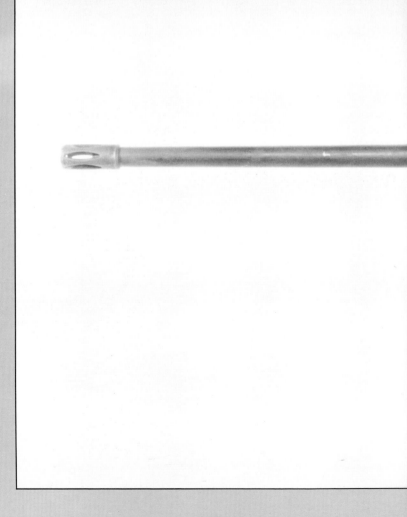

In March 1983 the Swiss Army announced that they had selected this SIG 514 4.45mm rifle as their new service weapon, subject to approval and finance being granted by their Parliament.

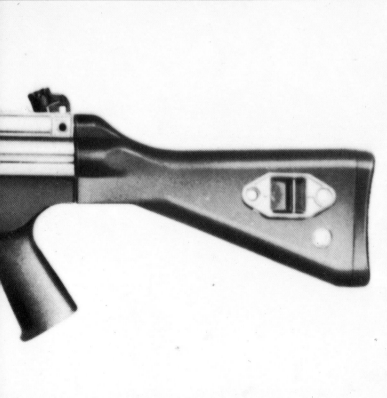

The rest of the world experimented with scores of designs of short cartridge but none of them ever got into service use. Britain had developed a very good .280 short cartridge, but in the name of NATO standardization they had to abandon the idea when the US Army complained that it lacked velocity and had a poor long-range performance. The more the British tried to explain the assault rifle concept, the less the US Army listened, and eventually NATO settled on the 7.62×51mm which was little more than the .30-06 slightly trimmed so as to pay lip service to the idea of a short round.

There were, though, American designers who could understand what the assault rifle idea meant, and they began working on their own, and out of that came the famous Armalite rifle. But this started a move in another direction, that of reducing the caliber; in effect the Armalite uses a full-length cartridge, but since the caliber is smaller, so is the overall size. And eventually, in the middle 1960s, the US Army caught up with the assault rifle concept and wholeheartedly adopted the .223 rifle as its standard infantry weapon in Europe, thus blowing NATO standardization straight into the weeds.

Now, with that background sketched in, what can we say about assault rifles and their application to sport shooting? Bearing in mind that they were designed for combat out to ranges of about 300-400 yards, then it is not to be expected that they will perform with much accuracy at ranges in excess of that, but accuracy is a comparative thing. What suits a soldier will not suit a deer-hunter; one is satisfied to get a wounding hit anywhere on the body, the other wants a killing shot which will drop the animal where it stands. The soldier, if he is skilled in the use of his rifle, will probably be able to get wounding hits out to 600 yards; the hunter, intent upon clean kills, would be wise to restrict his shots to under 200 yards.

This is not to say that the .223, or any other assault rifle, cartridge is inaccurate; far from it. In a good conventional rifle any of these cartridges will deliver perfectly acceptable accuracy on a target range or against live targets. But we are talking of military assault rifles, and the accuracy specification for these is not so tight as it is for conventional hunting rifles. Remember we said that they are produced by modern techniques, and they are produced in vast quantities under mass-production conditions. After that they are given an acceptance firing, and so long as they group within whatever the military consider acceptable, they're in. Some are, without any doubt, very good; equally, some are scraping the edge of acceptance, and what you get is purely the luck of the draw. Those rifles which are 'sporterized' and converted for commercial sale are, most certainly, selected from the best and will be as accurate as they can be, but there is always that limitation, that they were designed to a specification which, so far as accuracy is concerned, is not up to the standards of the better conventional hunting rifles.

To emphasize the point, it should be noted armies do not use their assault rifles for sniping. Every major army has adopted some other rifle for this purpose; it may be a close

Above left: This Kalashnikov look-alike is the Yugoslavian M70AB2 in 7.62mm (.308 Winchester) caliber, available on the export market.
Left: The Heckler & Koch G41, a new design which adds a three-round burst facility to the standard G3 model.

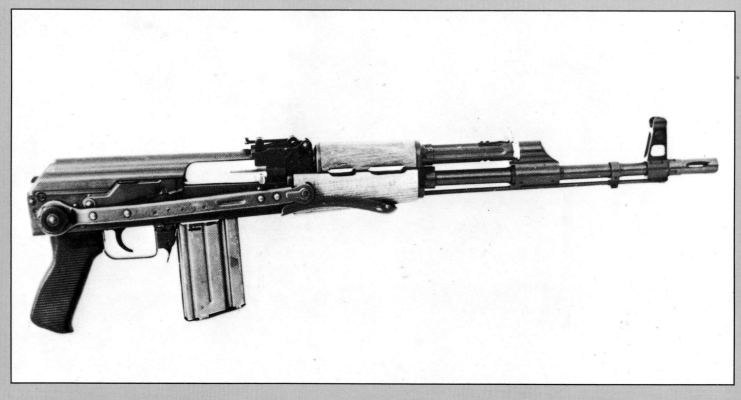

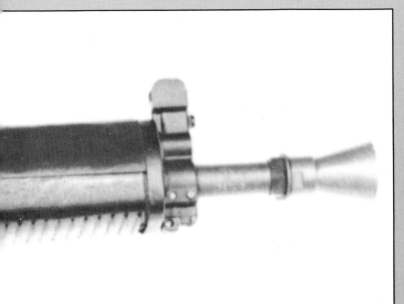

relative of the assault rifle, but it is sufficiently different to be designed and built to a higher specification, and the results show.

What else is our hunter going to get from his assault rifle? For one thing, reliability of a sort he has probably never before experienced in a firearm. Soldiers expect their rifles to accept virtually any kind of abuse and continue to work, and even when the soldier tries to cosset the weapon (as most soldiers do) the rigors of operational life soon make themselves felt. It can be dropped in water, dunked in mud, dragged through sand, thrown into a truck, used to drive tent-pegs, and, given a quick wipe with the hand, it will still continue to function. Even the plastic material used on military rifles is of a grade which is rarely met in civil life.

He will also get the clean kills he requires on game, particularly if he adopts the .223 caliber, because the military would only accept this small bullet after it was sure that it would do the job required of it, which is, not to be too mealy-mouthed about it, to kill men, or at least severely wound them. Wounding is, in fact, preferable, on a cold statistical basis, because a wounded man uses up medical facilities and keeps people tied up in evacuating him and nursing him. And, human nature being what it is, the wounded man frequently gets the assistance of a buddy to help him back to the aid post, so one shot has removed two enemies from the battlefield.

The .223 achieves this wounding capability by being carefully matched to its rifling so that the bullet is just sufficiently spun to keep it stable during flight. As soon as it strikes anything thicker than air, then it tumbles and delivers up its latent energy in a massive blow. No mushrooming, since such bullets are outlawed for military use, but the combination of marginal stability and a soft- or hollow-point hunting bullet is absolutely lethal on game of any sort.

As it happens, though, and as we have mentioned elsewhere, NATO have recently standardized on a new bullet which demands a different twist of rifling. The .223 standard, since its inception has been one turn in 305mm (12 inches), giving the desired degree of stability. But the new SS109 bullet requires one turn in 178mm (7 inches) for optimum stability, so it will pay the potential assault rifle purchaser to check out what rifling twist he is likely to get and figure out how that will sit with his chosen ammunition.

For home defense and survivalists the assault rifle cannot be bettered, particularly those models which have short-

Above; The Sterling-Armalite AR-18S is a carbine version of the AR-18, with folding butt and short barrel, made by the Sterling Armaments Company in England.
Left; Another Yugoslavian export offering is this 5.56mm assault rifle, also based on the world-famous (and infamous) Kalashnikov design.
Below: The Soviet AK74 in 5.45mm caliber, currently being used in Afghanistan.

Above: The exception that proves the rule; this is the newly-announced Sniper version of the Israeli Galil rifle. But although it is based on the assault rifle design, its manufacture is more carefully done, the barrel is heavier, and the whole weapon is a high-precision job. Notice how the telescope sight is clamped to the side of the receiver by a massive bracket, easily removeable without disturbing the zero.

Left: The Colt-Armalite AR-18 was designed so as to be capable of being made by less industrialized countries and can be turned out by any press shop or small engineering factory.

barrelled 'carbine' versions available. The short barrel makes the weapon as handy as a submachine gun, but the bullet gives it the reach of a full-sized rifle for short-range engagements. Accuracy may be slightly down compared to the long-barrel versions, but would probably only show up under bench-test conditions, and certainly not in combat-style firing. The reliability factor is of value here since these rifles will continue to function with minimal maintenance; a loaded assault rifle can be laid aside and virtually forgotten for months on end and will still operate perfectly when called on in an emergency.

Above left: Little heard of is this carbine version of the U.S. M-16A1; with its collapsible butt it would make a good brush or survival rifle.
Below left: The M-16A1 carbine in pieces, illustrating the simplicity of modern rifle design and construction.
Above: Something unusual; the Colt M-231 'Firing Port Weapon' is solely for use from inside armored fighting vehicles. The screwed fore-end fits into special firing ports in the armor, and the firer takes aim through a periscope. The sliding butt allows it to be used as an ordinary rifle, out of the vehicle, in emergencies.

There is, though, one field in which I am of the opinion that a military assault rifle is the wong choice, and that is in police employment. In some European countries the police are regarded (rightly or wrongly) as a para-military force, and so no eyebrows are raised when they appear with military-style weapons. But in Britain and in the United States the police are regarded as an essentially civil force, with no military overtones, and I feel that for such a force to appear on the streets with military-style weaponry is to invite undue criticism and, from some sections of society at least, open hostility. Moreover the military rifle has only limited applications in civil policing; and situations which call for a rifle can be equally well served with a commercial weapon of sporting outline, a weapon with an appearance which sits better with the civilian image of the local police force. Perhaps the happiest solution is to adopt what amounts to a military assault rifle action wrapped up in a sporting-style wooden stock; such rifles are available in Europe and are attracting attention from police forces.

And what of the future for the assault rifle? There seems little doubt that within the next decade it will have taken over the role currently held by the 'standard' military rifle in practically every armed force of any consequence and will, itself, have become the standard infantry weapon. As for its technical development, that is harder to foresee; in strict fact

there have been very few innovations in design in assault rifles over the past twenty years, and they all seem to have settled down on a well-tried formula. The norm is now a .223 caliber gas-operated weapon using a rotating bolt and feeding from a 30-round box magazine and with a folding butt. Some nations have adopted the 'bullpup' configuration, but inside, the mechanism conforms to the norm. The only revolutionary idea has been the caseless cartridge weapon developed in Germany and now under development in the USA, but the indications are that this may prove to be too revolutionary for many people to accept. Moreover the timing of the development has, unfortunately, worked out badly; the major NATO countries had already made up their minds – and put down their money – some time before the Germans announced the success of their design. At least two European countries who have committed themselves to other types of rifle might have made a different decision had the caseless weapon been perfected a year or two earlier.

Then again, one must never fail to take chauvinism into account; some countries would rather lose a war than equip their troops with a foreign design, no matter how much better it may be. Fortunately for the soldiers this attitude is seen less and less as time goes by, but it still exists and it is still a factor to be thought of when designers are postulating possible markets for their wares.

All in all, therefore, the end of the century will probably see things much as they stand today; the British Enfield, US Armalite, Beretta, Galil, FN-FNC, SIG and Heckler & Koch models will have more or less divided up the major armies, while smaller forces will have outfitted with the lesser-known designs such as CETME and Singapore. That goes for the Western-aligned countries of course; those on the opposite side of the fence have less choice; Kalashnikov first, the rest nowhere.

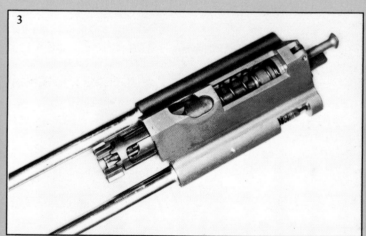

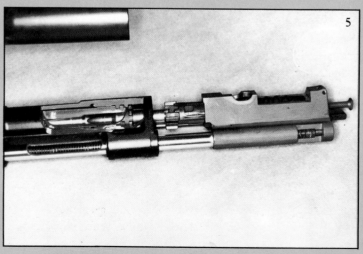

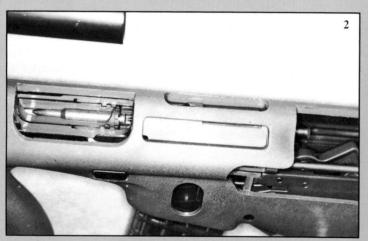

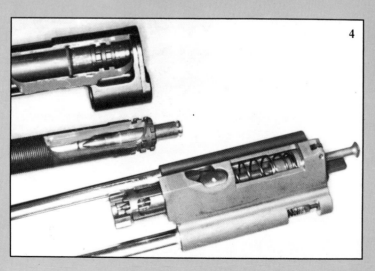

8

1) The Steyr AUG Assault Rifle in light machine gun form, with bipod, 40-round magazine and Kahles telescope sight.

2) The Steyr factory made this special cutaway AUG to enable its mechanism to be seen in operation. This shows the cartridge seated in the chamber, the bolt locked behind it, and (right) the hammer, cocked and ready to strike the firing pin.

3) The bolt unit of the cutaway model, showing the firing pin and its retracting spring, the bolt lug in its camway, and the rotating bolt head.

4) It all fits together; top, the receiver of the cutaway AUG; below it the barrel, with a 5.56mm cartridge partly entered into the chamber. The interlocking lugs on barrel and receiver can be clearly seen. Below is the cutaway bolt.

5) When fitted together it looks like this; the barrel is locked into the receiver, and the bolt rides on two rods which pass through bearings in the receiver. Here the bolt is loading a cartridge into the chamber. Notice the recoil spring concealed within one of the guide rods.

6) After the shot; the bolt has extracted a fired case from the chamber and is about to eject it. The tube at the top of the picture is the integral optical sight unit.

7) The AUG firing mechanism, with the hammer cocked and held by the sear. With the exception of the wire springs, every part of this mechanism is of high-quality plastic mouldings.

8) 'I think there's a sniper up there . . .' The aiming mark and sight picture seen through the AUG 1.6X telescope sight.

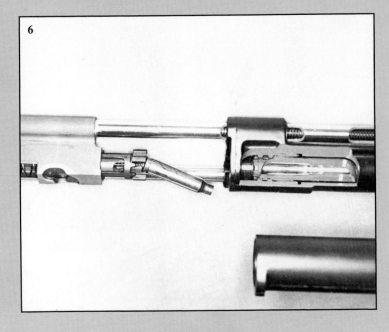

6

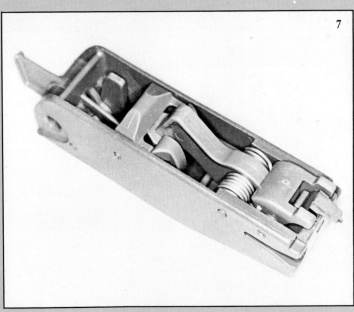

7

MACHINE AND SUBMACHINE GUNS

A Federal German Army machine gunner with his MG3.

MACHINE AND SUBMACHINE GUNS

American 180 Carbine

Manufacturer Voere GmbH, Austria
Type Blowback, auto or semi-automatic
Caliber .22 Long Rifle RF
Barrel 16in (406mm); 9in (230mm)
Weight (empty) 7.38lbs (3.35kg)
Magazine capacity 177 rounds
Cyclic rate of fire 1500 rounds/minute

The American 180 submachine gun was first developed in 1971 in the U.S.A., but manufacture was subsequently taken over by the Voere Company of Austria. It has been tested by several military authorities, and is believed to have been taken into service by some special forces; it has also been purchased by several police and prison authorities.

The idea of a .22 rimfire submachine gun may, at first, seem something of a joke, but the considerable magazine capacity and the effective bullet make it quite a serious proposition, as U.S. Army tests have shown. It is capable of piercing service nylon-armored body vests at 50 yards range, and a burst of 25-30 rounds at the same range can penetrate a standard steel helmet. As a deterrent for prison riots its worth has been proved, and the relatively low noise level makes it an attractive proposition for use by commando and similar forces.

In addition to being made in submachine gun form, it is also sold commercially as the SAM-180, in semi-automatic form, in which case it can be used either as a police weapon or as a somewhat unusual sporting rifle. In this form it is extremely accurate, though with a heavy trigger pull which reminds the shooter of its quasi-military background.

The general outline of the weapon resembles that of a Thompson submachine gun, with its square receiver, side cocking knob and tapering barrel. There is a pistol grip for the trigger hand and a grooved fore end for the supporting hand, both of plastic material grained to resemble wood; there is also a short-barreled model made in the submachine gun pattern in which the foregrip is a pistol grip which makes the Thompson resemblance even greater.

The magazine, however, is a flat pan which sits on top of the receiver rather like that of a Lewis or Degtyarev machine gun. The drum mechanism is roughly that of the Thompson, using a spring-driven 'spider' to propel the rounds to the feedway. As the last round is fired, the spring drive releases itself with a loud snap, so that the firer is in no doubt that the magazine is empty.

The sights are basically military in style, the foresight blade being protected between two substantial ears, and the rear sight being an aperture moving on a ramp to give elevation, very much like the sight on the M1 Carbine. The full-automatic versions can also be fitted with a 'Laser-Lok' sight, a system which mounts a small helium-neon laser beneath the barrel and projects a tight beam of light in alignment with the weapon's bore axis. Once correctly zeroed, this sight unit gives infallible results in poor light, being capable of projecting its light to any range at which a man-sized target is visible. The operator merely triggers the laser, moves the weapon until the spot of light falls on his target, and then fires; the bullets go exactly where the laser points.

On the range, this weapon gives the impression of having been carefully aligned before leaving the factory; using the service sight, straight from the box, it proved possible to put a string of single shots into a half-inch circle at 50 yards, firing from a rest, with no adjustment at all. At full automatic the recoil force is low in comparison to the more usual 9mm caliber submachine gun, but it needs a great deal of practice to avoid over-long bursts, due to the extremely high rate of fire.

Auto-Ordnance Model 27 A-1 Carbine

Manufacturer Auto-Ordnance Corp., West Hurley, NY 12491, U.S.A.
Type Delayed blowback, semi-automatic
Caliber .45 ACP
Barrel 16in (406mm)
Weight 11.5lbs (5.22kg)
Magazine capacity 30 rounds

The Thompson submachine gun has the dual distinction of holding both an honored place in American firearms history as well as owning a particularly dishonorable reputation of its own; it was the first weapon to actually use the term 'submachine gun', it was the first such weapon to be developed outside Europe, and its shape became so familiar in movies and comic strips that in 1939 most people were surprised to find that there were other submachine guns in existence. The Auto-Ordnance Company, founded by Thompson, has passed through several changes of ownership, but during all this it managed to hold on to the patents and to some of the original tools, and from time to time limited numbers of Thompsons have been produced for military or police customers.

There was, though, a constant demand for Thompson guns from collectors and gun buffs, and Auto-Ordnance finally came to the conclusion that their best course would be to revive the Thompson M1927 model, a semi-automatic designed for use by police forces, make some modifications (notably in lengthening the barrel) to comply with current U.S. regulations, and place it on commercial sale. The result was the Model 27 A-1.

In appearance it is identical to the original Thompson guns except for the longer barrel; this is not surprising since many of the parts are made from the original tools, and even the original title and Thompson

The AM-180 .22 rimfire submachine gun.

Auto-Ordnance's Thomspon M1927A1 semi-automatic carbine continues the 'Tommy-Gun' tradition of reliability and accuracy while still retaining an authentic appearance.

'bullet' trade-mark are faithfully reproduced. Internally the mechanism differs from a standard Thompson so that only single shots can be fired and it is impossible to convert the weapon to full automatic fire; the frame, sear, sear lever and selector lever are all different and some other components are added.

Two versions are offered; the 'standard' has a smooth barrel and horizontal fore end; the 'De Luxe' has a finned barrel and pistol-grip fore end. In addition there is the 'Model 1927 A-5' which has a short barrel and no butt, and is legally a 'pistol', and the A-3 which is similar to the De Luxe A-1 but chambered for the .22 Long Rifle rimfire cartridge. Mechanically this is totally different to the other weapons; the receiver is of light alloy and the mechanism is a simple blowback.

These Thompson designs are faithful reproductions of a highly original weapon; the long barrel gives them good accuracy and the weight gives them good control. Though expensive, they are carefully made from machined components, just as were the originals, and I suspect that demand for them will continue for many years to come.

Beretta Model 12S

Manufacturer Armi Beretta SpA, Gardone Val Trompia, Italy
Type Blowback, selective fire
Caliber 9mm Parabellum
Barrel 7.87in (200mm)
Weight (empty) 7.05lbs (3.2kg)
Magazine capacity 20, 32 or 40 rounds
Cyclic rate of fire 550 rounds/minute

The Beretta Model 12 submachine gun has been in use by several armies since the late 1950s and has been produced under license in Indonesia and Brazil. Beretta have now brought it up to date in a new and slightly modified version which has been issued to the Italian forces and has also been exported to Tunisia and other countries.

The basic Model 12 is a sheet steel submachine gun of outstanding robustness and simplicity. The breech block is of the 'overhung' type and surrounds the barrel at the moment of firing, while the pistol grips, magazine housing and trigger housing are all in one piece. There is a grip safety in the pistol grip which ensures that the bolt cannot move unless the weapon is being properly held in the firing position. It has a reputation for smooth action and controllable fire, largely due to its balance and the fact that most of the barrel is inside the receiver so that the turning movement

about the forward pistol grip is very small.

The Model 12S differs in having the fire selector and safety catch in a single lever unit, instead of two; the front sight has been made adjustable for windage and elevation; the attachment of the receiver rear cap has been strengthened and its locking catch moved to the top of the receiver for easier visual checking; the butt plate of the folding metal stock has been modified by the addition of a catch which ensures positive locking folded or unfolded position.

Though these are relatively small changes, they have made a positive difference to the weapon and turned a good design into a better one.

CETME CB-64

Manufacturer Centro de Estudios Tecnicas de Materiels Especiales (CETME), Padilla 46, Madrid, Spain.
Type Blowback, selective fire
Caliber 9mm Parabellum or 9mm Largo
Barrel 8.35in (212mm)
Weight (empty) 5.85lbs (2.65kg)
Magazine capacity 32 rounds
Cyclic rate of fire 600 rounds/minute

This weapon has been developed by CETME, the Spanish official firearms development center; some reports suggest that it may be put into production for the

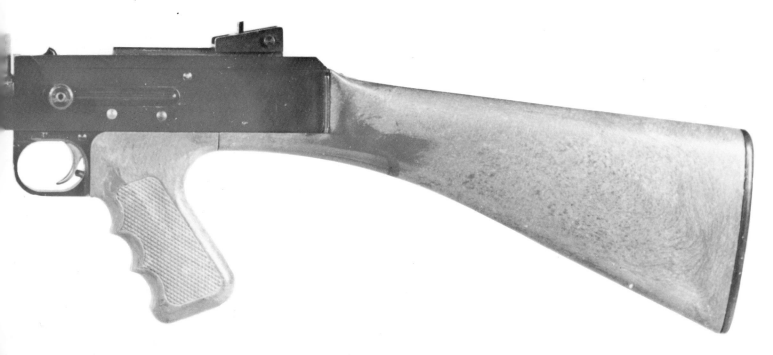

Above: The Model 12S with butt folded.
Far right: The Model 12S field-stripped;
observe how the bolt 'telescopes' around the
barrel so as to give a compact receiver.

Above: The Beretta Model 12S, a slight modification to a highly respected design.

The CETME CB-64, a little-known weapon from Spain.

Spanish military forces, others that it may be intended as an export item. So far as is known no large-scale production has yet taken place.

The casual observer might be excused for thinking he was looking at a British Sterling submachine gun; there is considerable outward resemblance, though there are some minor differences in the configuration of the folding butt and the cocking handle. Internally, however, there are major differences; the CB-64 uses a movable firing pin and a rocking hammer unit within the bolt; as the bolt reaches the closed position, so the tip of this hammer strikes a lug in the receiver, and this rotates it about an axis pin so that the other end delivers a blow to the firing pin to fire the cartridge. There is also an unusual automatic safety device, another pivoted lever which blocks the forward movement of the bolt before it can reach the magazine to commence loading a cartridge; this safety lever is only moved out of the path of the bolt by pressing the trigger.

Firing the CETME light machine gun.

CETME 5.56mm Machine Gun

Manufacturer Centro de Estudios Tecnicos de Materiales Especiales (CETME), Madrid, Spain
Type Delayed blowback belt-fed machine gun
Caliber 5.56mm (.223)
Barrel 15.7in (400mm)
Weight 13.88lbs (6.3kg)
Magazine capacity Belt fed
Cyclic rate of fire 1,000 rounds/minute

The CETME design office and research center was set up by the Spanish Government in the early 1950s and much of the original staff were refugees from Germany, where they had been employed in a similar capacity before and during the war. As a result one can trace the original parentage of some of their designs right back to the Mauserwerke of 1943-4, and by the look of this weapon to some other wartime establishments as well. It looks to have been influenced by the famous MG42.

Full details of the new CETME design have not yet been made public, but knowing their predilections I feel fairly certain that this weapon will employ the same two-part roller-locked breech mechanism used in the CETME rifles and perpetuated in the German designs of Heckler & Koch. The MG42 used a fully locked breech along similar lines, but I feel safe in predicting that this weapon will be a delayed blowback, using a fluted chamber to obviate problems with sticking cases. It is obviously belt fed and, like the MG42, has a high rate of fire. The only photographs

The Chinese Type 64 silenced submachine gun, without magazine.

available are, unfortunately, of the left side, so that we do not know whether the MG42 barrel change system (in which the barrel was released from the receiver and removed via a long slot in the right side of the barrel jacket) is in use, though I would expect it to be. An interesting minor point appears to be the incorporation of the rear sight into a carrying handle.

The CETME is still undergoing final development and improvement, and it is for this reason that the center is reluctant to publish details, since these could very easily change before the final model is perfected. I understand that a number are in the hands of the Spanish Army for practical trials.

Chinese Type 64 Silenced

Manufacturer Chinese State Arsenal
Type Blowback, selective fire, silenced
Caliber 7.62mm Soviet Pistol
Barrel 9.6in (244mm)
Weight (empty) 7.5lbs (3.4kg)
Magazine capacity 30 rounds
Cyclic rate of fire Not known

This weapon is far from new, its Type number being an indication of its date into service, but it was not generally known in the west until the latter 1970s. It is completely Chinese-designed and constructed and appears to be an amalgam of ideas taken from various European designs. So far as is known, the Type 64 is only used by the Chinese Communist Army.

The basic mechanism is that of the Soviet PPS-43, a plain blowback weapon using a stamped and welded steel receiver to house a very basic bolt and return spring. The trigger mechanism, which incorporates a selective fire mechanism, is a copy of that used on the Bren machine gun, several hundred of which, in 7.92mm Mauser caliber, were made in Canada and supplied to China during the 1939-45 war. The chamber is fluted, a step probably devised to ease extraction with the necked cartridge case, and the curved magazine fits into the bottom of the receiver.

The forward section of the barrel is perforated with four rows of holes which follow the rifling grooves, after which there are a series of disc-shaped baffles with a central hole through which the bullet passes. This

The CETME 5.56mm light machine gun, a delayed blowback weapon with considerable potential.

whole assembly is surrounded by a jacket which forms the external 'barrel' section of the weapon. The result is unique because it is a rare example of a weapon designed from scratch as a silenced gun, and not one which has had the silencer added as an afterthought or modification. It is moderately effective, though not so efficient in silencing as the British Sterling or American Ingram designs, but it has the added bonus of being an efficient flash hider, so that the result is a useful weapon for ambushes and guerilla operations. The principal drawback is the loss of velocity due to the escape of gas through the barrel vents; this is intended to reduce the bullet to subsonic speed, but obviously has a deleterious effect on its range and penetrative power.

Commando Arms Carbine

Manufacturer Commando Arms Inc., Knoxville, TN 37919, U.S.A.
Type Blowback, semi-automatic
Caliber .45 ACP or 9mm Parabellum
Barrel 16.5in (419mm)
Weight 8lbs (3.63kg)
Magazine capacity 5, 15, 30 or 90 rounds

The Commando Carbine is one of several attempts to produce a quasi-submachine gun which satisfies the demands of the Bureau of Alcohol, Tobacco and Firearms, and it appears to be one of the better ones. Its outline is an unabashed appeal to nostalgia in that it is based on the familiar Thompson shape; indeed, the resemblance is sufficiently close for the Commando to be able to use Thompson 30-round magazines.

Inside, though, the design is much different. The Commando uses a simple blowback mechanism, but fires from a closed bolt. The pistol grip and trigger housing are metal, while the butt and hori-

Commando Arms' Carbine closely resembles the Thompson.

zontal fore end are of walnut; alternatively, a vertical pistol grip fore end is available, which includes a slotted cooling vent unit which gives the gun the appearance of the original Thompson ribbed barrel.

The Commando was first made available in .45 ACP chambering, and several thousand were sold as the 'Mark III'. It was then made in 9mm Parabellum caliber, and the title changed to indicate the caliber, as the 'Mark 9' or 'Mark 45'. Except for caliber the two models are the same. The magazines are in a variety of sizes to cater for individual choice and also to conform with legal requirements in some areas. It should be noted that all of them are box magazines, and that the 90-round magazine is actually three 30-round boxes welded together, one mouth-up and two mouth-down, so that as one is emptied the unit can be released and reversed to place a full box in the magazine housing.

The length of barrel makes the Commando very accurate for its caliber, and the size and weight also help in damping down recoil. It has become popular as a hunting weapon, while its appearance makes it extremely effective as a home defense weapon.

Fabrique Nationale 'Minimi' Machine Gun

Manufacturer Fabrique Nationale d'Armes de Guerre, Herstal, Belgium
Type Gas-operated light machine gun
Caliber 5.56mm (.223)
Barrel 18.3in (465mm)
Weight 14.32lbs (6.5kg)
Magazine capacity 30 rounds, or belts
Cyclic rate of fire 850 rounds/minute

When Fabrique Nationale developed their 5.56mm CAL rifle in the late 1960s, they felt it logical to continue work and develop a 5.56mm machine gun to accompany it. In fact the CAL was somewhat ahead of its time, and has since been replaced by the

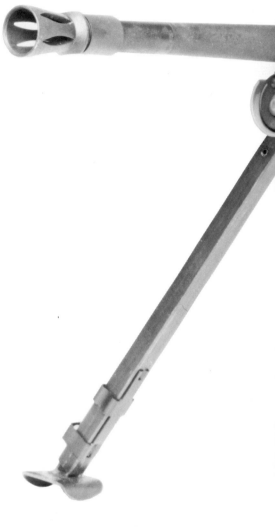

The 'Minimi' with box magazine fitted; note the belt-feed aperture above.

FNC, an improved design, but the 'Minimi' machine gun appeared in 1974 and was well-timed to catch the first stirring of enthusiasm for the 5.56mm caliber. It has been adopted by the armies of Belgium, Indonesia, Thailand and other countries and also approved for the U.S. Army as the M249 Squad Automatic Weapon (SAWS).

The Minimi is of conventional type, using gas tapped from the barrel to drive a piston which propels a bolt carrier. This contains a rotating bolt which is unlocked by cam action. The unusual feature of the Minimi is its feed system; it is capable of feeding from a box magazine or from a belt. The bolt is provided with two sets of feed horns which will strip cartridges either from an overhead belt or from a side-mounted magazine, while a simple mech-

Below: Fabrique Nationale's 'Minimi' 5.56mm machine gun, adopted by the U.S. Army as the M249 Squad Automatic Weapon.

anism prevents any attempt to feed both at once. Thus the gun can be normally operated as a belt-feed weapon but in an emergency can be fed from the standard M16A1 30-round box. The belt is carried in a transparent box which acts as a carrier when not on the gun and then locks securely to the gun when installed for feeding. Two sizes are available, one for 100 rounds and one for 200 rounds.

The standard model has a fixed metal butt; there is a variant model for airborne or special forces which has a shorter barrel (335mm) and a folding metal butt. Both types have quick-release barrels so that they can be changed when over-heating. The standard sights consist of a protected blade mounted on the gas regulator and an elevation-adjustable aperture rear sight. The receiver will also accept NATO standard mounts for image-intensifying sights.

Trials by the U.S. Army, preparatory to accepting it for the SAWS program, showed the Minimi to be remarkably free from stoppages and breakages during prolonged firing. By adopting the Minimi the U.S. Army looks like having a good light machine gun for the first time in its history.

Heckler & Koch HK21A1 GP Machine Gun

Manufacturer Heckler & Koch GmbH, Oberndorf-Am-Neckar, West Germany
Type Delayed blowback general-purpose automatic
Caliber 7.62mm NATO
Barrel 17.7in (450mm)
Weight 17.63lbs (8kg)
Magazine capacity Belt feed
Cyclic rate of fire 900 rounds/minute

The HK21A1 is the latest development of the HK21 gun, which has been in military service for some years, and the aim has been to produce a one-man machine gun which

will improve the firepower of the infantry squad without adding to their logistic load. As well as being the squad light gun it can be tripod-mounted and used as a company support weapon.

The layout of the gun is similar to the company's rifle design, and it uses the same roller-locked delayed blowback breech mechanism. A major change has been to do away with the magazine-loading option and make this a belt-fed-only gun. The belt feed unit has been redesigned to make belt loading much quicker than previously. The barrel can be quickly changed by cocking the weapon, releasing the barrel latch, and then easing the barrel forward and sideways through a slot in the ventilated barrel guard. There is a bipod which can be mounted in the usual place, at the front end of the jacket, or can be moved to a position just in front of the feed unit, at the center of balance, if preferred.

A variety of specialized mountings are available; there is a spring-buffered tripod with panoramic sight for support fire roles; a column mount which fits on light vehicles and uses spring balancing gear to take the weight of the gun; and two different 360° tracks for ground, vehicle or anti-aircraft defense.

The HK21A1 is understood to have been purchased by several African and Asian armies, but no firm details have been released.

Heckler & Koch MP5

Manufacturer Heckler & Koch GmbH, Oberndorf-Am-Neckar, West Germany
Type Delayed blowback, selective fire
Caliber 9mm Parabellum
Barrel 8.8in (225mm)
Weight (empty) 5.4lbs (2.45kg)
Magazine capacity 15 or 30 rounds
Cyclic rate of fire 650 rounds/minute

The Heckler & Koch company made their G3 rifle the foundation of their business and by adapting its mechanism they have parlayed it into a number of formats. This submachine gun is somewhat unusual in that it uses a delayed blowback mode of operation and incorporates the roller-locked breech mechanism used in the G3 rifle to do it. As a result several of the parts of the MP5 are common to the G3 rifle, a point which has attractions for military procurement officers. The MP5 is in use by West German police and Border Guards, by the Swiss and Netherlands and several other police and military forces, and has also been seen in the hands of the British Special Air Service operating against terrorists.

The two-part breech block of the MP5 locks the forward section by two rollers, forced out into recesses in the receiver by the forward motion of the rear section during the closing movement. The force on

Below: The Heckler & Koch HK21A1 general-purpose machine gun.
Bottom: Heckler & Koch's MP5 submachine gun in standard form.

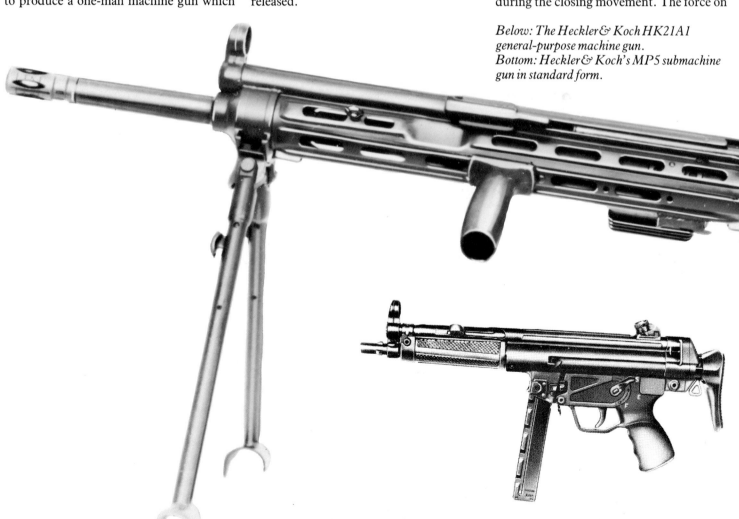

Above: The H&K MP5K extra-short version of their submachine gun, for concealment on the person, carriage in a car's glove box or in a briefcase.

Above: The H&K MP5SD with butt fitted and silencer casing removed.

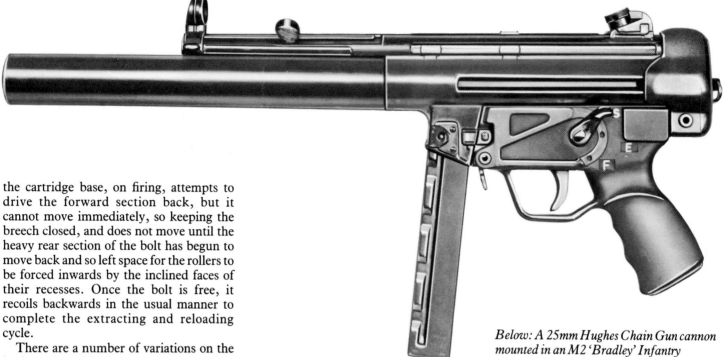

the cartridge base, on firing, attempts to drive the forward section back, but it cannot move immediately, so keeping the breech closed, and does not move until the heavy rear section of the bolt has begun to move back and so left space for the rollers to be forced inwards by the inclined faces of their recesses. Once the bolt is free, it recoils backwards in the usual manner to complete the extracting and reloading cycle.

There are a number of variations on the basic model, which is known as the MP5A2 and has a plastic buttstock and fore end. The MP5A3 has a telescoping metal buttstock. The MP5SD has a permanently-fixed silencer around the barrel and sub-divides into three versions – MP5SD1 with no butt, MP5SD2 with fixed plastic butt, and MP5SD3 with telescoping butt. The MP5K is a specially shortened version for concealed use by anti-terrorist squads and similar people; it can also be fitted inside a special briefcase for use by bodyguards; it can be fired from this concealment and performs faultlessly, the empty cases being carefully channelled and collected so as not to bounce around and jam the weapon. There are also attachments to permit these various models to be fired from ball-mounts in armored vehicles or from specially-developed turrets.

Hughes Chain Gun®
Machine Gun

Manufacturer Hughes Helicopters, Culver City, CA 90230, U.S.A.
Type Mechanical, belt fed, machine gun
Caliber 7.62mm NATO
Barrel 22in (558mm)
Weight 29.1lbs (13.2kg)
Magazine capacity Belt fed
Cyclic rate of fire Variable up to 600 rounds/minute

Mechanical machine guns are as old as the industry, names like Gatling, Gardner and Nordenfelt having been prominent in this field in the 1870s, but with the development of the self-powered Maxim they were rendered obsolescent. They reappeared when it became obvious that only mechanical solutions could provide the high rate of fire demanded by modern aerial combat, and

Below: A 25mm Hughes Chain Gun cannon mounted in an M2 'Bradley' Infantry Fighting Vehicle.

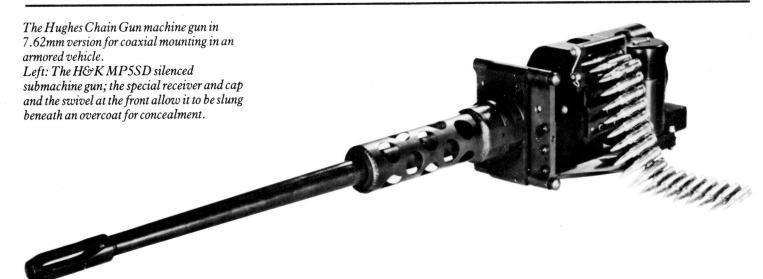

The Hughes Chain Gun machine gun in 7.62mm version for coaxial mounting in an armored vehicle.
Left: The H&K MP5SD silenced submachine gun; the special receiver and cap and the swivel at the front allow it to be slung beneath an overcoat for concealment.

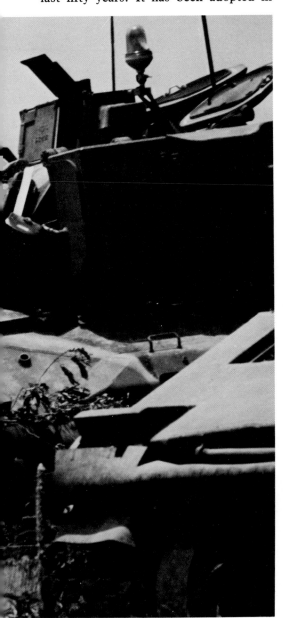

the Gatling was revived as the electrically-driven 'Vulcan' aircraft cannon. But for land force use they seemed to be out of the question until Hughes perfected this design, one of the most significant developments in small arms technology in the last fifty years. It has been adopted in 7.62mm caliber as a tank and armored vehicle gun by the U.S. and British armies and is likely to be taken into use by several others in the future. In 25mm and 30mm caliber it is in use by the U.S. forces as a helicopter weapon and is also being evaluated by the British Army as armament for their 'Fox' armored car.

The heart of the Chain Gun is a loop of commercial roller chain which lies on the bottom of the receiver and is driven round by a gear, driven by an electric motor. Attached to this chain is a lug which engages in the bolt carrier, so that as the chain moves forward, along one side of the receiver, so the carrier is moved forward, a cartridge is fed into the breech, and the bolt is rotated and locked. As the chain lug moves, following the loop path, across the front of the receiver there is no motion of the bolt carrier; the breech stays locked and the cartridge is fired. Then as the chain lug turns the corner and begins to run back, down the other side of the receiver, the bolt is unlocked and opened, the carrier pulled back, the case ejected. As the chain lug makes its fourth side of the receiver, again there is no motion on the carrier and there is a brief pause which permits cooling of the open barrel.

The delay, or 'dwell', with the closed bolt acts as a safety in case of a hangfire (delayed ignition of the cartridge), and if the cartridge has not fired by the time the lug has made its crossing, the gun stops and the operator has to re-start it, thus giving ample time for the longest hangfire to discharge itself safely. If the round is a misfire, then once the gun is re-started the dud round is extracted and ejected safely. Ejection is done down a forward-facing tube, since this gun is designed for use in armored vehicles and the empties (and any unfired rounds) are thrown clear of the turret. Since the gun is sealed, fumes cannot escape into the vehicle but are ejected either through a jacket sleeve around the barrel or through the ejector tube, keeping the air in the tank relatively clean.

It will be apparent that the rate of fire is infinitely variable by simply controlling the speed of the drive motor, though in practice the controls are such that either single shots or 600 rpm are available. The Chain Gun also has the advantage of providing positive mechanical lift for the ammunition belt, instead of relying upon recoil of the gun's moving parts to actuate the feed. This, together with the precise control and inter-operation of the entire operating cycle, makes the Chain Gun one of the most reliable and smoothly-operating machine guns in existence.

Maremont Lightweight M60 Machine Gun

Manufacturer Maremont Corp., Saco, ME 04072, U.S.A.
Type Gas operated belt-fed machine gun
Caliber 7.62mm NATO
Barrel 22in (560mm)
Weight 18.98lbs (8.61kg)
Magazine capacity Belt fed
Cyclic rate of fire 550 rounds/minute

The M60 machine gun has been the U.S. standard infantry machine gun since the early 1950s, and while it has proven a reliable and robust weapon it is based on fairly old technology and is heavy and somewhat complicated. As a result the Maremont Corporation set about redesigning it to make it lighter and simpler and to take advantage of some things which have been learned since the M60 went into service.

The changes are, in themselves, relatively minor, but they have added up to a considerably improved weapon. For a start the bipod is now attached to the gas cylinder and not to the barrel, which means that the spare barrel no longer has to have its own bipod. The gas system has been simplified and provided with interlocking cylinder nuts, and the fore end has been done away with. Instead there is now a forward hand grip which makes the weapon much easier to manipulate from the hip and also

MACHINE AND SUBMACHINE GUNS

Above: The Maremont Lightweight M60 machine gun.
Below: The Brazilian Uru submachine gun, with silencer.

aids in steadying it when fired in the prone position. The foresight is fully adjustable for elevation and windage, so that each barrel can have its sight zeroed without having to move the rear sight; as a result, barrel changes can be carried out in the knowledge that the gun will shoot where it is aimed. There are also changes to the feed system to permit the gun being charged with the feed cover closed. The resulting weapon is slightly shorter than the M60 and some 4.2lbs lighter. It is currently under evaluation by the U.S. Army and by several South-East Asian countries.

Mekanika Uru

Manufacturer Mekanika Industria e Comercio Lda., Rua Belisario Pena 200, Penha, 21020, Rio de Janiero, Brazil
Type Blowback, selective fire
Caliber 9mm Parabellum
Barrel 6.89in (175mm)
Weight (empty) 6.63lbs (3.01kg)
Magazine capacity 30 rounds
Cyclic rate of fire 750 rounds/minute

This submachine gun was designed in Brazil in 1974 and after extensive testing by the Brazilian Army Ministry was approved for service with the Brazilian Armed Forces in 1979. It is currently being produced in quantity and will eventually replace the Beretta M12s with which the Brazilians are currently equipped. It has also been ex-

The Uru submachine gun field-stripped.

ported to other South American countries.

The mechanism is a simple blowback, the bolt moving in a tubular receiver and the magazine feeding from below. There is a tubular stock which clips on the rear end of the receiver, and the magazine housing is extended downwards to act as a front grip. There is a perforated jacket around the barrel which can also be used as a grip. The weapon has only 17 component parts and can be stripped without the use of tools in 30 seconds or less.

The manufacturers have produced a silencing kit which fits by removing the original barrel and replacing it with a combined barrel/silencer unit. It is claimed that this gives a good level of silencing with standard ammunition and is also capable of sustaining automatic fire. Another add-on kit is intended to convert the Uru to .22 rimfire caliber for use as a training weapon. This involves a new barrel and bolt, a weaker return spring and a new 12-round magazine, and the conversion can be done easily and quickly.

The South African Sanna 77, a refurbished CZ25 model converted to fire semi-automatic only.

Sanna 77

Manufacturer Dan Pienaar Enterprises Pty Ltd., South Hills, Johannesburg, Republic of South Africa
Type Blowback, semi-automatic
Caliber 9mm Parabellum
Barrel 11.3in (289mm)
Weight 6.2lbs (2.8kg)
Magazine capacity 40 rounds

The Sanna 77 is on sale in South Africa and is, strictly speaking, not a submachine gun since it has been modified so as to fire only in the semi-automatic mode. Dan Pienaar are said to be the manufacturers, but we suspect that they merely refurbish the weapons, modify them, and then sell them, since they are actually the elderly Czechoslovakian CZ25 submachine gun. These were used by the Czech Army in the early 1950s, and were also exported to several African and Middle Eastern countries.

The CZ was somewhat ahead of its time, being the first production weapon to adopt the 'overhung' or 'telescoping' bolt configuration, in which the face of the bolt is hollowed out so that much of the bolt actually lies ahead of the breech face when the weapon is fired. This system ensures a proper bolt mass to keep the rate of fire to manageable proportions but allows the weapon to be relatively compact, since the space required to accommodate the recoiling bolt is governed by that portion behind the breech.

The Sanna is of all-metal construction and has a folding metal buttstock. The magazine housing is incorporated into the pistol grip, and there is a safety catch behind the trigger which, when pushed sideways, locks both trigger and bolt. In addition, as with most submachine guns, the cocking handle can be shifted into a slot to prevent movement of the bolt.

'Scorpion' Machine Pistol

Manufacturer Czech State Arsenals
Type Blowback, selective fire
Caliber .32 ACP (7.65mm) (but see text)
Barrel 4.4in (112mm)
Weight 3.50lbs (1.59kg)
Magazine capacity 10 or 20 rounds
Cyclic rate of fire 840 rounds/minute

Like the Czech CZ58 rifle mentioned elsewhere this is not a new weapon but it deserves mention for two reasons; firstly because it is a unique miniature submachine gun, and secondly because it is appearing more and more often in the hands of terrorists and revolutionaries, largely because of its small size and concentrated firepower. In its original form it was of somewhat limited legitimate application; it was then increased in caliber to give it a wider military role, and it has since been

Above: The Czech Scorpion in .32 ACP caliber, a favorite weapon of terrorists. Below: A silenced version of the Czech Scorpion.

adopted and manufactured in Yugoslavia. (The two are easily distinguished, since Czech production has a wooden pistol grip and Yugoslavian models have plastic grips.) It equips various units of the Czech and Yugoslavian armies and has been exported to various African states with Communist connections. How these weapons find their way into terrorist hands is not for us to suggest.

The original Scorpion (or CZ61) is the .32 caliber model, and it was designed as a light weapon capable of being holster-carried by crews of armored vehicles, as a self-defense weapon. The small bullet is hardly a combat projectile, but as a last-ditch weapon for use by the crew of a stalled tank, it has some validity. The mechanism is a simple blowback bolt, and a change lever allows single shots or automatic fire. In either mode it can be fired one-handed, or the wire stock can be unfolded to allow its use as a shoulder weapon. It is unpleasant to fire from the hip since the empty cases are ejected vertically and usually hit the firer in the face.

The light bolt and weak recoil spring would lead to an unacceptably high rate of fire if left to themselves, and so a rate reducer is fitted into the pistol grip. As the bolt reaches the end of its rearward travel it is held by a catch; during the rearward movement the bolt trips a light plunger and drives it down inside the pistol grip, against a spring. This light plunger passes through a heavy weight and passes some of its energy to the weight, causing it to begin to move down. The plunger reaches the bottom of the grip and its spring sends it back, where it meets the descending weight and passes through it; this acts as a retardant to the plunger. Eventually the plunger reaches the top of the grip once more and releases the bolt catch, allowing it to go forward and fire the next round. This all sounds very time-consuming, but in fact it cuts the rate down to 840 rounds per minute, so the travel of the plunger is all over in about .0012 of a second.

Later models of the Scorpion were chambered for different cartridges; the CZ64 fires the .380 Auto (9mm Short) cartride; the CZ65 fires the 9mm Soviet (Makarov) cartridge; and the CZ68 is chambered for the 9mm Parabellum round. There has been little published about these variants and few have been seen outside Czechoslovakia. The CZ68 is, as might be expected, somewhat larger than the other models, to allow for the more powerful cartridge.

Singapore SAW Light Machine Gun

Manufacturer Chartered Industries of Singapore, Singapore
Type Gas-operated, automatic
Caliber 5.56mm (.223)
Barrel 20in (508mm)
Weight 9.65lbs (4.38kg)
Magazine capacity 20, 30, 60 or 100 rounds
Cyclic rate of fire 520 rounds/minute

Having successfully manufactured M16 rifles and M203 grenade launchers and then their own rifle (mentioned elsewhere in these pages) CIS of Singapore, moved by the U.S. Army's SAW program, decided to develop their own light machine gun, also calling it the SAW but in this case meaning 'Section Automatic Weapon'. Work began early in 1980, but this left them insufficient time to compete in the U.S. competition; nevertheless, they have completed their development work and the machine gun is now being evaluated by various military forces. Since it costs well over $1000 less than the new American weapon, it is likely that there will be a wide export market in the Far East.

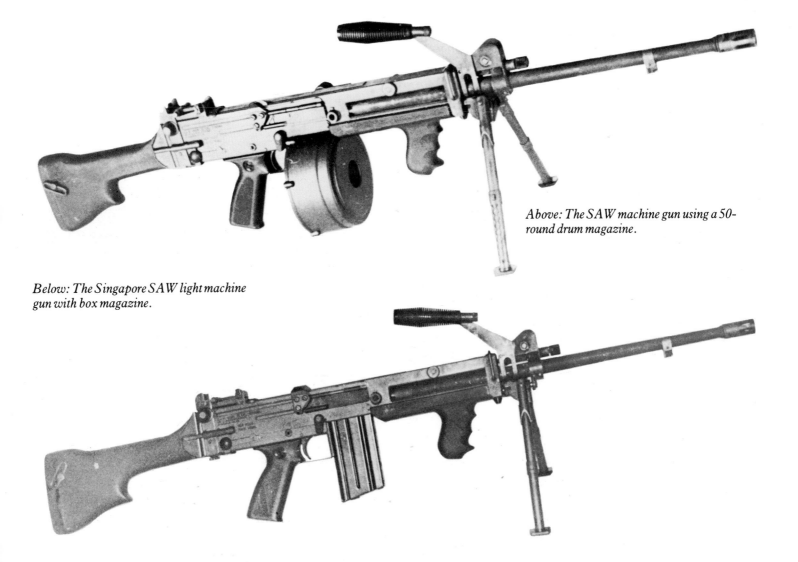

Above: The SAW machine gun using a 50-round drum magazine.

Below: The Singapore SAW light machine gun with box magazine.

Another view of the SAW with drum magazine.

The SAW is a fairly conventional gas-operated gun, using a piston to drive a bolt carrier which holds a rotating bolt. It fires from the open bolt position and only fires automatic – single shots are not possible except by careful taps on the trigger, the slow rate of fire helping here. The first model (Mark I) had a quick-change barrel which proved not to be very quick in practice, and it has been dropped. The Mark II uses a heavy fixed barrel capable of firing 500 continuous rounds without heat damage problems. The Mark III has a similarly heavy barrel but one which can be quickly changed.

There are various magazines; normal 20- or 30-round box magazine can be used, or a 60-round drum, or a special 100-round disposable plastic drum. With any of these the weapon can be fired from the shoulder or the hip under complete control. The sights are fully adjustable for windage and elevation and are graduated up to 1200 meters, a somewhat optimistic marking with 5.56mm ammunition. At ranges to 400-500 meters, though, it holds well on the target and is as accurate as any of its competitors. It will be interesting to watch the progress of this gun and to see if it is adopted by any military forces.

Center: One of several PK variations, this is the PKMT with electric solenoid firing gear, for installation in armored vehicles.
Above: The Soviet PK (Pulyemet Kalashnikova) squad machine gun, based on the Kalashnikov rifle mechanism but with modifications for belt feed.

Soviet PK Machine Gun

Manufacturer Soviet State Arsenals
Type Gas operated, belt fed, machine gun
Caliber 7.62mm Soviet Nagant M1891
Barrel 25.9in (658mm)
Weight 19.84lbs (9kg)
Magazine capacity 100, 200 or 250-round belt
Cyclic rate of fire 700 rounds/minute

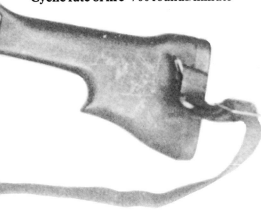

Since the 1920s the principal Soviet infantry machine gun had been a Degtyarev design, using a locking system based on flaps forced into notches in the receiver by the forward movement of the firing pin. But when the Kalashnikov rifle became the Soviet standard, it was thought advisable to develop a Kalashnikov-based machine gun, if only for commonality of parts and manufacture. As a result, the 'PK' series ('Pulyemet Kalashnikova') appeared in the mid-1960s and is now in universal use throughout the Warsaw Pact armies.

In fact, although the PK uses the same type of bolt carrier and rotating bolt as the Kalashnikov rifle, other parts of the mechanism have been 'borrowed' from other designs; thus, the feed system has been taken from the Goryunov machine gun, as has the method of changing the barrel; the method of using the gas piston to drive the belt feed mechanism comes from a Czechoslovakian design; and the trigger has

been taken from the older Degtyarev guns. One benefit of this is that the various parts should all be well understood by the troops and armorers, and the result is a useful weapon, but it would have probably been better had it been designed for a more modern, rimless, cartridge instead of the ancient rimmed round dating from 1891. Nevertheless, this is a good long range cartridge and it gives the weapon ample power to reach out with accuracy.

The PK is the Soviet Army's first 'general purpose' machine gun, a concept widely adopted elsewhere but so far resisted by the Soviets since they are reluctant to discard anything and had a vast collection of old medium machine guns to wear out before adopting the PK. The basic design has been parlayed into several versions, each slightly different and for a specific role; the PK is the basic gun on a bipod, the squad automatic; the PKS is the same gun but with a light tripod, making it the com-

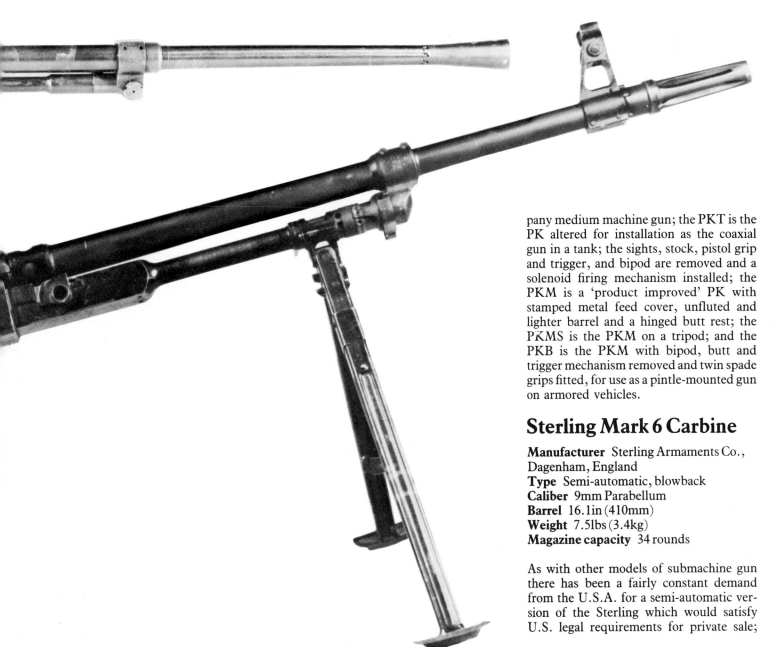

pany medium machine gun; the PKT is the PK altered for installation as the coaxial gun in a tank; the sights, stock, pistol grip and trigger, and bipod are removed and a solenoid firing mechanism installed; the PKM is a 'product improved' PK with stamped metal feed cover, unfluted and lighter barrel and a hinged butt rest; the PKMS is the PKM on a tripod; and the PKB is the PKM with bipod, butt and trigger mechanism removed and twin spade grips fitted, for use as a pintle-mounted gun on armored vehicles.

Sterling Mark 6 Carbine

Manufacturer Sterling Armaments Co., Dagenham, England
Type Semi-automatic, blowback
Caliber 9mm Parabellum
Barrel 16.1in (410mm)
Weight 7.5lbs (3.4kg)
Magazine capacity 34 rounds

As with other models of submachine gun there has been a fairly constant demand from the U.S.A. for a semi-automatic version of the Sterling which would satisfy U.S. legal requirements for private sale;

MACHINE AND SUBMACHINE GUNS

The Sterling Mark 6 carbine, a semi-automatic version of the well-known Sterling submachine gun.

there has been a semi-auto version of the standard Sterling for some years, for sale to police, but the barrel of this model is less than the legal U.S. length. The deficit has now been remedied by the development of the Mark 6 for sale in the U.S.A.

The Mark 6 uses the normal Sterling frame but has a 16.1in barrel, making it a legal 'rifle' or 'carbine' and thus permitting it to be sold commercially and used privately. The mechanism is such that only semi-automatic fire is possible, and it is not capable of being altered back to full-auto working except by major re-engineering. The stock may be folded, and the manufacturers supply an 8 inch dummy barrel so that this can be mounted for displaying the weapon.

The accuracy of the Sterling Mark 6 is good, bearing in mind the relatively poor ballistic shape of the 9mm bullet.

Steyr MPi 69

Manufacturer Steyr-Daimler-Puch AG, A-4400 Steyr, Austria
Type Blowback, selective fire
Caliber 9mm Parabellum
Barrel 10.2in (260mm)
Weight (empty) 6.46lbs (2.93kg)
Magazine capacity 25 or 32 rounds
Cyclic rate of fire 550 rounds/min

This submachine gun resembles the Uzi in some respects, but is a totally different and rather simpler design. It is currently in use by a number of armies and police forces throughout Europe and the rest of the world.

The receiver is formed from bent and welded sheet steel and is carried in the frame unit, steel with a moulded nylon covering. The magazine feeds in through the pistol grip, a convenient system in the dark, and the bolt is of the 'wrap-around' or 'telescoped' type in which the actual bolt face is well back within the bolt and much of the bolt mass is in front of the breech at the moment of firing. This system allows the maximum mass for the minimum bolt stroke and assists in producing a compact weapon. Cocking is performed by pulling on the carrying sling, which is attached, at the forward end, to the cocking knob. This,

at first sight, is open to abuse, but a bracket, welded to the top of the receiver, ensures that the cocking action can only be performed when the sling is held at right-angles to the receiver, on the left-hand side. The normal pull from the top of the weapon, as when slinging it over the shoulder, cannot move the cocking-piece.

There is a safety catch in the form of a cross-bolt above the trigger which locks the trigger when set to safe; it is a three-position bolt; when pushed across to the right, so that a white 'S' protrudes, it is safe; when pushed across to the left so that a red 'F' protrudes, it is set for automatic fire. There is also a half-way position in which single

The Steyr MPi69 field-stripped.

The Steyr MPi69 submachine gun, showing the sling anchored to the cocking lever.

shots are possible. This safety catch is a weak piece of design in my view since except by memorizing, it is impossible to know what the state is in darkness; it would be better to have one end ribbed or knurled.

The third position is, in any case, superfluous; with the selector set for automatic fire a light squeeze on the trigger fires a single shot, and this can be repeated as often as wanted. To fire bursts, a heavier squeeze is required. There is no need to reset the selector lever at all, and I can only assume that the central position has been put there as a safety feature during initial training, so that an over-enthusiastic squeeze will not produce a runaway gun. This two-stage trigger is also to be found on the Steyr AUG rifle, and takes some getting used to; I have not found it a hindrance to accurate shooting in the automatic mode.

The MPi 69 is easy to strip and reassemble, taking no more than 15 seconds in either direction for a trained soldier. Strictures on the safety and trigger apart, it is a well-designed, simple and robust weapon, and provided soldiers are trained to its peculiarities, a highly effective one.

The Semi-automatic version of the Uzi submachine gun, for commercial sale.

Uzi Semi-automatic Carbine

Manufacturer Israeli Military Industries, Tel Aviv, Israel
Type Blowback, semi-automatic
Caliber 9mm Parabellum
Barrel 16.1in (410mm)
Weight 8.5lbs (3.85kg)
Magazine capacity 25 or 32 rounds

The Israeli-developed and manufactured 'Uzi' submachine gun is probably one of the best-known modern weapons of its class. During its thirty years of military service many countries have bought it for their armies and even more for their police and security services. Undoubtedly many less well-connected gun buffs would like to have one for their collections, but the law tends to frown upon privately-owned machine guns; as a result IMI spent a good deal of time in redesigning the Uzi so that it became a repeater, firing single shots only, and yet was impossible to modify back into full-automatic form.

The resulting weapon came on the market in 1981 and the only visual difference from a service Uzi is the length of the barrel, some 6 inches longer than the military version. There are internal differences, within the receiver, which change the method of operation and which also prevent substitution of standard military components, so that it is impossible to swap parts and so change it back into a full-automatic weapon. In addition the mechanism is now altered so that the Uzi fires

from a closed bolt, instead of an open bolt; this makes good sense for a single-shot weapon since it helps accuracy, and there is no need to have the bolt stay open so as to allow cooling air to go through the barrel during pauses in firing.

The Uzi is built up from steel pressings and turnings, with grip and fore-end in black plastic. The folding steel butt is used, and stripping the weapon is extremely simple. The foresight is a post which is adjustable for windage and elevation for purposes of zeroing, and there is a special tool for this purpose. The rear sight is a simple two-position flip aperture with settings for 100 and 200 meters.

Although the 9mm Parabellum cartridge is not one which would instinctively commend itself to anyone searching for the ultimate in accuracy, it has to be said that this long-barrelled Uzi performs remarkably well, consistently making five-shot groups around one-and-a-half inches at 25 yards. As a home defense weapon it has an authoritative air and the accuracy to back it up, and when not in use the makers provide a dummy barrel of service length.

Wilkinson 'Terry' Carbine

Manufacturer Wilkinson Arms, Covina, CA 91724, U.S.A.
Type Blowback, semi-automatic
Caliber 9mm Parabellum
Barrel 16.187in (411mm)
Weight 7.125lbs (3.23kg)
Magazine capacity 30 rounds

This is another of the weapons designed to resemble a submachine gun but yet fall inside the U.S. regulations governing automatic and semi-automatic arms. The design originated in the late 1960s with a Mr J. R. Wilkinson and was produced as the 'J & R M-68'. He sold the manufacturing rights and the weapon was produced under various names, but it appears to have been made with scant regard for Wilkinson's specification and it was less successful than it should have been. After protracted legal manuvering, Mr Wilkinson regained control of the weapon, improved the design, and has now begun making it as the 'Terry', named after his daughter.

Mechanically the Terry is a simple blowback weapon, firing from a closed bolt by a hammer. Much of the barrel is concealed by the receiver, so the weapon looks more compact than some carbines, and the bolt surrounds the breech when closed so as to reduce the overall length. The barrel also has a three-pronged flash hider on the muzzle, concealed by a bell-shaped flash shroud which also acts as a rudimentary muzzle brake and reduces the recoil thrust. Aperture rear and post front sights are provided and the top of the receiver is dovetailed for telescope mounting.

The Terry is a well-made, reliable, and well-finished weapon, and relatively inexpensive compared to other weapons of this type on current offer.

Right: British infantrymen, armed with Sterling SMGs and FN rifles storm ashore in a training exercise.

The Wilkinson 'Terry' carbine, one of several private-venture submachine gun designs.

*The American M-60 machine gun in operation
during a training exercise in 1964.*

Left: Troops of the Royal Australian Regiment leap from a helicopter on South Vietnam in 1965. The lead man is carrying an Owen submachine gun while the others have F1 rifles (the Australian version of the FN-FAL). The american door gunner is armed with an M-60.
Below left: A soldier of the West German Bundeswehr with an MG3 machine gun.
Below: An RBY Mk1 light recce vehicle of the Israeli Army armed with a formidable array of four MGs.

Below: Frightened Vietnamese children huddle in a ditch under the protection of a US 1st Cavalry soldier armed with an M-16, during a battle near Da Nang in 1967.
Right: A soldier of the US 82nd Airborne Division checks his M-16A1 after dropping into Germany on a training exercise.
Below right: The M-16 was the standard US automatic rifle in the latter years of the Vietnam War.

Above: British troops armed with SLR rifles and a GPMG ford a river in Malaya.
Left: The Individual Weapon (IW) and Light Support Weapon (LSW) 4.85mm rifles developed by the Royal Small Arms Factory, Enfield, England.
Above right: Argentinian troops armed with FN FALs about to surrender at Port Stanley, Falkland Islands, 1982.
Right: British troops armed with SLRs and a Bren gun on exercise in Norway.

Below: Israeli infantry armed with Uzis and rifles.
Right: Uzis have been exported to a number of countries including West Germany as seen here.

Fine scroll engraving on a top quality English double-barreled 12-gage sporting shotgun, the 'Chatsworth' by W. and C. Scott.

SHOTGUNS

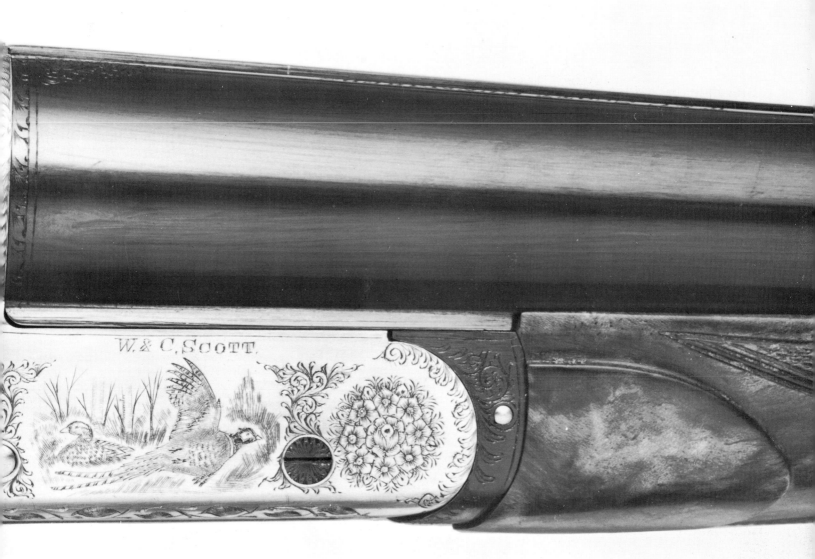

Astra Models 650 & 750 Shotguns

Manufacturer Astra-Unceta y Cia, Guernica, Spain
Type Superposed, single or double trigger
Gage 12
Barrels 28in (711mm)
Weight 7.34lbs (3.33kg)

Astra-Unceta are widely-known for their pistols, but rather less well-known outside Europe for their sporting guns, a state of affairs they are now seeking to remedy. Their home market has been satisfied by conventional single and double guns for some years, but they have now developed an over-and-under specifically for export.

The Models 650 and 750 differ in their trigger arrangement; the 650 has double triggers, while the 750 has a single trigger with a selector to permit firing either barrel first. Either can be had with automatic ejectors or with manual extractors. The barrels are bored to modified and full choke.

The gun is well-finished, with a walnut stock with pistol grip, and well-executed checkering on stock and fore end. The receiver is neatly roll-engraved, the fit of metal to wood is first-class, and the barrels are well polished and blued. The receiver body is somewhat deep, due to the use of bottom bolting, but this leaves ample room for the hammers and firing pins and the selective trigger mechanism, so that the component parts are robustly proportioned and easily reached for repair or adjustment. The firing pin holes in the standing breech have removable bushings. The barrels are surmounted by a ventilated rib with a gold bead front sight.

The Astra gun handles well and delivers consistent patterns. For its price it is a sound and reliable gun which should give long service.

AYA Model 25 Shotgun

Manufacturer Aguirre & Aranzabal, Eibar, Spain
Type Double, side-by-side
Gage 12
Barrels 25in (635mm)
Weight 6.25lbs (2.83kg)

AYA have a long and good reputation for the production of shotguns to a wide variety of specifications, ranging from 'working guns' to 'best guns', and their Model 25 is a classic side-by-side in the English tradition.

The walnut stock is straight, without a pistol grip, and is lightened by two longitudinal holes plugged at the butt end; both it and the short and tapering fore end are well finished and carefully checkered. The barrels are light and shorter than is usual, so that the principal weight lies in the centre of the gun and it balances well.

The action uses internal hammers and double triggers, and the smooth stock permits the hand to be moved rapidly to shift triggers between shots. The top lever opens the gun and sets the automatic safety, while the action of opening the gun cocks the hammers. As the gun is closed, so the ejectors are cocked and the double underbolt locks the gun firmly. The barrels are usually provided with modified choke on the right and full on the left, and these produce tight patterns.

These short, light, and centrally-balanced guns are not to everyone's taste; in broad terms this gun has been based on, if not copied from, the Churchill Model XXV of London, and Churchill had his own ideas on what constituted a good gun and on how to shoot it.

Benelli Auto-loading Shotgun

Manufacturer Benelli Armi SpA, I-61029 Urbino, Italy
Type Recoil-operated auto-loader
Gage 12 or 20
Barrel 25.6in (650mm); 27.6in (700mm)
Weight 7lbs (3.18kg)
(12-ga, 27.6in barrel)
Magazine capacity 3 or 4 rounds

The Benelli looks like any other automatic shotgun, but underneath the skin is a most unusual mechanism, much different to the usual long-recoil system pioneered by Browning and copied by almost everybody since then. It is well-known in Europe but a recent newcomer to the U.S.A. and deserves closer inspection.

The breech bolt of the Benelli is a two-

The Astra 750 over-and-under 12-gage shotgun.

part unit, the two being separated by a coil spring. Attached to the bolt head is a locking bar which trails beneath the bolt assembly and drops into a recess in the receiver so as to hold the breech closed during firing. When the shot is fired, the recoil drives the gun backwards; the bolt body's inertia causes it to remain stationary in space, so that it actually moves forward in relation to the rest of the gun. This compresses the spring and also holds the locking bar firmly down. This movement occupies the time during which the shot charge is passing up the barrel and leaving the muzzle, so that by the time the spring is fully compressed and the bolt body has stopped moving, breech pressure has dropped to a safe level. Now the spring reasserts itself, forces the bolt body back, and this lifts the locking bar from its recess. The complete bolt is now free to be driven back by the residual pressure inside the chamber, extracting and ejecting the spent case. The bolt's movement compresses a return spring and cocks the gun, after which the spring drives the bolt back, loading the next cartridge, the locking bar drops into place and the gun is ready again.

An interesting bonus of this system is that if cartridges with different loadings are used, the recoil force changes and so does the relative compression of the bolt spring, so that there is a self-regulating effect which gives fractionally greater delay in opening for heavier charges.

The Benelli is well-finished, with an aluminum lower section to the receiver, a steel upper section, and well-checkered walnut stock and fore end. The steel parts are highly polished and well blued, while the aluminum portion of the receiver is finished in matching black. The gun handles well and delivers a good pattern. Various choices of choke are available in the two barrel lengths.

The Spanish AYA 25 shotgun, a classic side-by-side design.

The Benelli Auto-loading shotgun uses an unusual two-part bolt mechanism.

Bentley Model 30 Shotguns

Manufacturer Squires, Bingham Mfg. Co., Marikina, Philippines
Type Slide action repeater
Gage 12
Barrel 30in (762mm) (but see text)
Weight 7lbs (3.17kg)
Magazine capacity 5 rounds

The Bentley is another trade name of the Philippine company of Squires Bingham, widely known in the East but relatively unheard-of elsewhere, a situation they are doing their best to remedy. The Model 30 is the basic term for three quite distinctly different models.

The 'Model 30 Standard' is a conventional hunting slide-action gun, rather long in the barrel but otherwise unremarkable. The length of barrel does give it a useful long-range capability, which may well be useful on its home ground. The stock and fore end are of figured Philippine mahogany, oil-finished, while the receiver and barrel are blacked and polished, the bolt showing an engine-turned finish through the ejection port. The action is normal slide, a tilting bolt locking into the roof of the receiver. The standard form of barrel is with full choke, but a 26 inch barrel bored improved cylinder or a 28 inch modified choke can be obtained to special order.

The Model 30 Skeet has the same mechanism but uses a 24 inch barrel, with a muzzle compensator and a special 'skeet choke' designed to get the optimum pattern at skeet ranges. The finish is to a higher standard than on the hunting gun, with a polished and varnished surface to the woodwork, a more hand-filling fore end, and checkering on pistol grip and fore end. This appears to be a very handy gun for rapid movement, and the muzzle compensator would diminish the throw-off and blast from such a short barrel.

The third model is somewhat specialized, the 'Model 30 Riot'. In general form this resembles the hunting gun, with plain stock and fore end (though with vertical ribbing to assist grip) but with a shorter 20in barrel which is cylindrical bored. This also has sling swivels on butt and magazine tube nose to permit it being carried slung.

All three Bentley guns are soundly made of good material and would appear to be good working guns in their particular roles.

Browning BPS Shotgun

Manufacturer Miroku Firearms Co., Kochi, Japan
Type Slide-action, single barrel
Gage 12
Barrel 24, 26, 28 or 30in (610, 660, 711 or 762mm)
Weight 7.75lbs (3.51kg) (28in barrel)
Magazine capacity 3 or 4 rounds

John Moses Browning designed his pump-action shotgun in the early 1890s and it went on sale under the Winchester name in 1893. Early in the century it was taken up by Fabrique Nationale of Belgium and sold in Europe under the Browning name. Now, for the first time, a pump shotgun is being marketed in the U.S.A. under the Browning name, though it differs in details from the original Browning design.

The BPS is an attractive gun, with well-polished walnut stock and fore end, with good checkering, and blued metal. The action is conventional enough, the breech locking into a barrel extension piece. The feed system is somewhat different in that there is a magazine cut-off actuated by a ring round the rear end of the magazine tube; this, when aligned with a letter 'S', shuts off the magazine feed and permits single-shot loading. When turned to align with a letter 'R' it permits normal slide-action loading. The object of this is to allow a cartridge to be unloaded from the chamber and a different type loaded, leaving those in the magazine undisturbed.

Various types of choke may be specified; all tend to be long, a style adopted in order to reduce the damaging effect of steel shot upon chokes. One result of this is that the shot patterns are perhaps less compact than might be expected from the choke description, a ballistic consequence of the longer constriction.

As can be seen from the data panel, there are a variety of barrel lengths available, and there are four grades of quality, so that with the three available degrees of choke there is something for everybody in this range.

Browning ST-100 Shotgun

Manufacturer Fabrique Nationale Herstal SA, Herstal, Belgium
Type Double-barrelled, superposed
Gage 12
Barrels 29.9in (760mm)
Weight 8.06lbs (3.65kg)

This is marketed as a 'Trap Gun' and in Europe is known as the 'Super Trap 80' model. It is unusual in that it is possible to vary the parallelism of the barrels so as to vary the placement of the patterns from each barrel.

The ST-100's barrels are not joined by a rib, as are most over-and-under guns, but are distinctly separated except for the breech lump and a band around the muzzles. About eight inches behind the muzzles there is a linking wedge between the barrels which can be adjusted into any one of five positions, so altering the set of the barrels and shifting the shot patterns. A table in the instruction book gives the theoretical

Top: The Browning BPS slide-action gun, manufactured in Japan.
Above: The Bentley Model 30 Standard slide-action gun from the Philippines.

Above: The Browning ST100 Super Trap gun has barrels whose convergence can be regulated.

differences, but practical tests show that while the sense of the shift follows the table, the exact distance may vary slightly.

This apart, the rest of the gun is conventional except for the ventilated rib which is attached by five supports and is capable of flexing, necessary because of the barrel adjustment feature. The single trigger is mechanically operated, rather than by inertia, to select the second barrel. The degree of choke can be selected from various options; the top barrel is always full, while the other can be had in steps from modified to full.

The gun delivers tight patterns from either barrel and the inter-barrel adjustment works well, though it needs to be checked by firing rather than merely set from the book figures. Finish is good, and this would appear to be keeping up the Browning standards of excellence.

CBC Combination Gun

Manufacturer Companhia Brasiliero de Cartouchoes, Sâo Paulo, Brazil
Type Rifle-shotgun combination
Calibers .30-30 and 20-gage
Barrels Shotgun: 28in (711mm)
Rifle: 26in (660mm)
Weights Shotgun: 6.78lbs (3.07kg)
Rifle: 8.28lbs (3.75kg)

This interesting and unusual weapon is the product of a company better-known for ammunition than for firearms, though it has considerable domestic sales of shotguns to its credit. The Combination Gun is a basic action to which either a 20-gage shotgun barrel or a .30-30 rifle barrel can be quickly mounted, and it seems to be an eminently sensible working weapon for anyone living in the wilds.

The basic action is a concealed hammer, similar to that of a shotgun and carried in a

The CBC Combination Gun, shown here with shot and rifle barrels.

simple receiver unit. To this the barrels can be attached by simply hooking the lump over the cross-pin and attaching the fore end by means of a spring latch. The result is tight-fitting, and the action can be dropped open for loading by pressing on a catch in the front of the trigger guard.

The rifle barrel is provided with a ramp front and adjustable folding leaf rear sight, as well as having standard grooves for mounting a telescope sight. The shotgun barrel has a simple front sight bead. One advantage of this sort of action is that it suits both right- and left-handed shooters equally well.

The shotgun delivers good patterns with consistency, while the rifle barrel is as accurate as most shooters would ask, giving three-inch groups at 100 yards from rest. Altogether this is a well-thought-out combination, practical and robust, capable of adequate accuracy, and remarkably inexpensive for what it gives.

Harrington & Richardson Model 176 Long Range Shotgun

Manufacturer Harrington & Richardson Inc., Gardner, MA 01440, U.S.A.
Type Single shot, hammer
Gage 10, 12, 16 or 20
Barrel 32in (812mm) or 36in (914mm)
Weight 10.04lbs (4.55kg)
(10-ga, 36in barrel)

The average shotgun is a handy weapon with 26 to 28 inch barrels, and this covers most of the day-to-day requirements of 95 percent of shooters. But there are those who demand something with the ability to reach

out and kill game at long ranges – wildfowlers, turkey hunters, vermin shooters – and this shotgun is designed for them.

There are, in fact, six variant models; the 10- and 12-gage are available in two barrel lengths, the 16- and 20-gage in 32 inch barrel length only. All barrels are full-choked and chambered for Magnum cartridges.

The guns are all simple but robust weapons, built for use and not for show but nevertheless well-finished. Stocks are hardwood with walnut finish and the metalwork is color case-hardened or blued. The action is a straight-forward exposed rebounding-hammer type with automatic ejection.

Firing the 10-gage is no work for the dilettante; it is a heavy and powerful weapon and the recoil is quite substantial, though not excessive unless one tries to fire several shots in rapid succession. The lighter gages are quite comfortable to fire since the weight, rather more than average for the gage, tends to soak up some of the shock. The full-choked barrels deliver patterns which are well-calculated for the long-range work envisaged by the designer. As the old saying goes, if this is the sort of gun you need, you need this sort of gun.

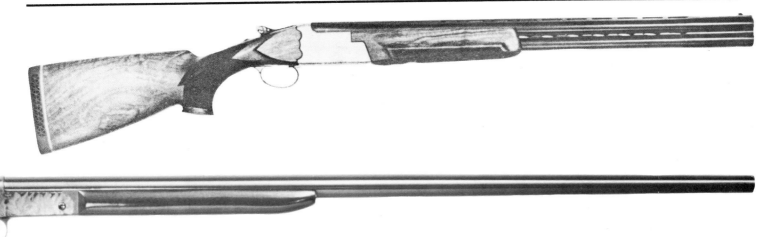

*Top: The IAB Premier Skeet gun from Italy.
Above: The Harrington and Richardson
Model 176 single shot Magnum gun in 10-
gage.*

IAB Premier Skeet Shotgun

Manufacturer Industria Armi Bresciane SpA, Marcheno, Italy
Type Superposed double, single trigger
Gage 12
Barrels 26.8in (680mm)
Weight 7.68lbs (3.48kg)

The IAB company is one of the younger Italian gunmaking concerns, numbers of which have begun to prosper in Northern Italy. There is a long tradition of fine metal-working and gunmaking in this region, and small companies have realized that they can aim for specialist areas of the market with high-class products and succeed where the big companies cannot compete. Over the past decade IAB have specialized in first-class competition shotguns and have a long string of international prizes to their credit.

The appearance of the IAB Premier Skeet is impressive; oiled-finish walnut of best grade, well-executed hand checkering, fine engraving on the receiver, and a high polish and blue on the rest of the metalwork allied with meticulous fit of the parts is indicative of the care this company lavish on their products.

The mechanism uses strikers, rather than hammers, and has an inertia-operated selector on the single trigger mechanism. This is fixed to fire the lower barrel with the first pull, then the upper, and the sequence cannot be changed. The gun is opened by the usual top lever which clears a single cross-bolt; dropping the barrels cocks the strikers, and closing the gun cocks the ejectors. The safety is manually operated.

The barrels are bored with what the makers call their 'enlarged skeet choke', a form of recessed choke in which the transition is very abrupt, with a step-form which acts as a trap for debris from the shot wads. This is not difficult to clean but it should be borne in mind, since a build-up of debris can play havoc with patterns. Patterning is extremely consistent at Skeet ranges, and there can be no doubt that this gun has earned its place in the competitive world.

Ithaca Model 37 Ultra-Featherlight

Manufacturer Ithaca Gun Co., Ithaca, NY 14850, U.S.A.
Type Pump action, single barrel
Gage 20
Barrel 25in (635mm)
Weight 5.06lbs (2.29kg)
Magazine capacity 4 rounds

The Ithaca Gun Company have been famous for their lightweight pump-action shotguns for almost fifty years, but in late 1978 they introduced an even lighter weapon, their 'Ultra-Featherlight', claimed to be the lightest pump-action shotgun in the world.

The ultra-lightness is achieved by the use of aluminum alloys for the receiver and trigger plate, while the butt and fore end are reduced in bulk and weight as much as possible. The mechanism is the standard type of pump or slide action in which working the fore end back and forth on the magazine tube actuates a rod which operates the breech block and cartridge lifter.

As is usual with Ithaca guns the finish is impeccable, with walnut stock and fore end nicely checkered, and with the slender barrel finished off by a ventilated rib with front bead sight. It can be obtained with various degrees of choke and patterns well with all of them. Recoil is noticeable, as might be expected in such a light gun, but not excessive. What is more prominent is the absence of momentum when following moving targets; heavier guns tend to follow better in these circumstances. But for those who desire a light gun and who take the trouble to master it, the Ithaca will give them everything they desire.

Kawaguchiya Model 250 Automatic Shotgun

Manufacturer Kawaguchiya Firearms Co, Tokyo, Japan
Type Gas-operated auto-loader
Gage 12
Barrel 26, 28 or 30 inches (660, 711 or 762mm)
Weight 7.31lbs (3.31kg) (28in barrel)
Magazine capacity 3 rounds

Most designers are happy to follow well-worn paths when producing new weapons, but occasionally there is one who spots a defect and tries to rectify it. The principal

The Ithaca Model 37, an exceptionally light weapon.

The Kawaguchiya Model 250 automatic shotgun, which has an ususual fore end arrangement to suit smaller hands.

defect with gas-operated shotguns is their excessive depth in the fore end, due to the need to fit in both the gas cylinder and the magazine tube, and guns of this sort have met some consumer resistance in the Far East where hands are rather smaller than elsewhere. Kawaguchiya have therefore made some alterations in an endeavor to produce a design with a more easily grasped fore end, and this has resulted in an interesting weapon.

The layout appears conventional enough except that the gas cylinder and magazine tube are side by side, with the gas cylinder offset to the left. The bolt is a three-piece unit, consisting of carrier, bolt and locking block, the latter locking into an overhead barrel extension in the usual way. On firing, gas passes into the cylinder and drives the piston back; in order to soften the operation, the piston rod is in two telescoping sections and carries a series of dished washers (or, more properly, 'Belleville Springs') which, as the rod sections are compressed, act as a shock absorber and transmit the piston stroke to the bolt carrier with reduced violence. The carrier moves back and, by cam action, withdraws the locking block, allowing the bolt to move back with the carrier. The hammer is cocked, a return spring loaded, and on the forward stroke the next shell is chambered and the bolt closed once more.

The mechanism can be easily dismantled and cleaned, and appears to be amply robust for its job. The gun handles well and shoots accurately, delivering good patterns. Finish is good, if plain, the walnut stock and fore end being lightly checkered and the aluminum receiver finished in polished black.

Lanber Model 844 Shotgun

Manufacturer Armas Lanber SA, Zaldibar, Spain
Type Double-barrelled, superposed
Gage 12
Barrels 27.56in (700mm)
Weight 7.62lbs (3.45kg)

The Lanber company are moderately well-known in Spain and Portugal but less known in the rest of the world, a situation they are now attempting to remedy by exporting their best grade gun.

The Model 844 is an over-and-under of conventional form using a single selective trigger; by moving a stud above the pistol grip the top or bottom barrel can be selected to fire first, whereupon a second pull of the trigger fires the other. There is an inertia mechanism within the lock which utilizes the recoil of the first shot to set the trigger for the second barrel.

The usual top lever breaks the gun and retracts the firing pins, and the action of opening the barrels causes the hammers to be cocked. The action of unlocking also sets the automatic safety which must be manually unlocked before firing again. The stock is of hardwood resembling walnut and is well finished with a checkered pistol grip and fore end. There is a ventilated rib carrying a bead front sight.

The Lanber is gracefully proportioned, comfortable to hold and shoot, and the metalwork is nicely engraved and polished. The top barrel is bored full choke and the lower bored modified choke; the patterns are not particularly tight, especially that of the lower barrel. On the whole the Lanber might be called an 'average' sporting gun, one suited to casual use rather than for sustained shooting, and within this limitation it represents good value.

Laurona Model 73 Shotgun

Manufacturer Armas Laurona SA, Eibar, Spain
Type Double-barrelled, superposed
Gage 12
Barrels 27.8in (710mm)
Weight 7.75lbs (3.52kg)

The Laurona company have been making shotguns for very many years, and they are somewhat idiosyncratic in their designs. Their Model 73 exhibits this trait in having twin single triggers, a system rarely found today. This is standard on the hunting gun, with an option of a single non-selective trigger; on the competition skeet and trap guns the single trigger is standard, with twin triggers as the option.

The twin trigger system, for those who have not met it, means that pulling the front trigger fires the bottom barrel; a second pull on the same trigger then fires the top barrel. Alternatively, pulling the rear trigger fires the top barrel first, and a second pull then fires the bottom barrel. The object behind this seeming superfluity is to permit the firing of a nominated barrel instantly without having to move a selector and firing the second barrel without having to shift to another trigger.

The barrels are bored with full choke on the upper barrel and modified choke on the lower, and both delivered tight patterns. A top lever opens the action, allowing the barrels to swing down and cock the hammers; closing the action cocks the automatic ejectors. The finish is good, the stock being straight-grained walnut with well executed checkering and the fitting has been carefully done.

The dimensions of this gun would seem to be best suited to the larger man; the frame and fore end are generously proportioned and the reach is somewhat long. The weight inhibits fast swinging but it helps to soak up the recoil and the Laurona is comfortable to shoot.

Leland Model 210 Shotgun

Manufacturer Union Armera, Eibar, Spain
Type Side-by-side double, hammerless
Gage 12, 16, 20 or 28
Barrels 26, 27 or 28in
(660, 685 or 711mm)
Weight 6.625lbs (3kg) (28in barrels)

Though made in Spain this takes its name from being imported into the U.S.A. by Leland Firearms of West Orange NJ; it is known under the maker's name in Europe. The Union Armera has been making shotguns for very many years and has a wide domestic market for all qualities of gun. The Model 210 is a basic side-by-side modelled on the English 'game gun' and it fits about half-way in the Union Armera catalog, retailing in the U.S. for about $1200.

The gun has an elegant appearance, using the English style of straight stock and splinter fore end. The wood is good quality walnut, hand-checkered and oil-finished, while the receiver and fittings are nicely scroll-engraved and color case-hardened. The side-plates can be removed, and the interior of the lockwork is polished and engine-turned. The fit of metal to wood is

The Spanish Lanber superposed gun.

Top: The Laurona 73, also from Spain, shows some originality in trigger design.
Above: The Leland Model 210, a traditional side-by-side gun of high quality.

Luigi Franchi SPAS Shotgun
Manufacturer Luigi Franchi SpA, I-25020 Fornaci, Italy
Type Automatic, combat-type
Gage 12
Barrel 19.68in (500mm)
Weight (empty) 7.05lbs (3.20kg)
Magazine capacity 8 rounds

very well done. The action is locked by a Purdey triple bolt, somewhat unusual nowadays, and there are automatic ejectors.

The standard gun is in 12-gage with 26-inch barrels having improved cylinder and modified choke; it is also possible to have the longer barrels with modified and full choke. The other gages noted are also available, and while the normal chamber length is 2.75 inches, 3-inch chambers can be specified at extra cost.

The Model 210 balances well, feels good, and delivers consistent patterns. The workmanship is good and most observers consider the gun represents value for money.

blacked and etched with a floral pattern.

The gun is well-balanced, allowing rapid movement when at the shoulder, and the recoil is, as usual with gas-operated weapons, damped down to an acceptable level. It delivers consistent patterns, and there is a choice of improved, modified or full choke available. For what you get, the Franchi is remarkably inexpensive, and with the company's reputation for workmanship, we would expect it to deliver flawless performance for many years.

Luigi Franchi are well-known for sporting shotguns of the highest quality, but their SPAS (Special Purpose Automatic Shotgun) series will be rather less well-known outside Italy. It was designed for police and military use and aims to be rather more efficient in that role than conventional civil shotguns which were designed with sporting use in mind and have been 'misappropriated' to police use. The firm claim that their design gives good accuracy with little training; instant hits in all kinds of employment; great firepower; the ability to launch grenades if required; and low maintenance.

Luigi Franchi Model 500 Autoloader
Manufacturer Luigi Franchi SpA, Brescia, Italy
Type Gas-operated auto-loader
Gage 12
Barrel 26in (660mm); or 28in (711mm)
Weight 7.15lbs (3.24kg)
Magazine capacity 5 rounds

The Luigi Franchi company is an old-established one with a high reputation for shotguns in Europe and elsewhere.

The Model 500 is a gas-operated auto-loader of conventional pattern, the bolt being locked to the barrel extension until freed by the action of the gas piston concealed in the fore end, along with the tubular magazine. The stock design features a flowing pistol grip which permits a rearward placement of the trigger hand, something which many shooters prefer, and the stock has rather less drop than is common. The finish is excellent, the stock and fore end in nicely-figured walnut with good hand checkering, and the aluminum receiver

The Franchi SPAS Model 12 gun with the butt folded; in this position the curved part can be hooked over the shoulder, the remainder of the butt passing under the arm, and it can be fired from the hip with one hand.

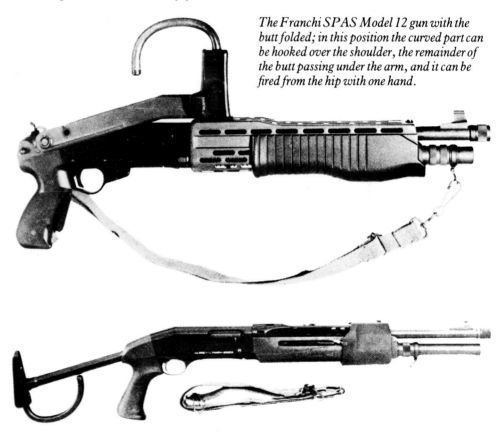

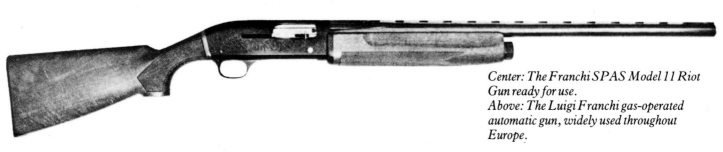

Center: The Franchi SPAS Model 11 Riot Gun ready for use.
Above: The Luigi Franchi gas-operated automatic gun, widely used throughout Europe.

The basic SPAS Model 11 is a short-barrelled semi-automatic shotgun with a folding butt which has been configured so that it can be locked under the armpit and allow the gun to be used one-handed. The receiver is of light alloy, while the barrel and gas cylinder have been hard-chromed to reduce the risk of corrosion. All the external surfaces are sand-blasted and phosphated black.

An unusual provision is for the gas cylinder to be shut off, converting the weapon to a slide-action repeater; the fore end can be unlocked to act as the reloading slide in this mode, which is designed for use with certain types of light ammunition which will not cycle the gas action reliably.

The barrel is cylinder bored and spreads a normal shot charge to about 900mm at 40 meters range, reducing the need for precise aiming. The automatic action will fire about four shots per second, and at this rate of fire, with standard buckshot loadings, it is possible to put 48 pellets per second into a one-meter-square target at 40 meters range. At this range the pellets have about 50 percent more striking energy than a .32 pistol bullet.

There is a wide range of ammunition available for security use, from buckshot and solid slug to tear gas rounds which fire a small plastic container of CS gas to 150 meters range. There is a launching attachment which fits the muzzle and which permits the firing of grenades to 150m range, and there is also a 'shot spreader' attachment which fits on the muzzle and breaks up the shot pattern to give much greater short-range spread, an option designed for indoor use.

The SPAS Model 12 differs slightly from the Model 11; it has an additional grip safety in the forward edge of the pistol grip, an improved and strengthened butt stock, and a reshaped fore end. The barrel is 40mm shorter but the complete weapon weighs almost exactly one pound more than the Model 11.

Perugini Emperor Shotgun

Manufacturer Perugini & Visini, Brescia, Italy
Type Double-barrelled, side-by-side
Gage 20
Barrels 27.68in (703mm)
Weight 6.59lbs (2.99kg)

England is always thought of as the home of the hand-built shotgun, constructed to the customer's requirements and preferences, but in fact this sort of service can be found in any European country if you look hard enough. Perugini and Visini are a small Italian company who export their hand-made guns all over the world, and although we have given specification figures above,

these merely apply to one particular gun; the customer can say what length of barrel, what weight, what chamber, what wood, what anything he wants, and Perugini build it that way.

The style is, not surprisingly, that of the classic side-by-side, and the actions are hammerless sidelocks with automatic ejectors. Single or double triggers can be fitted, as the customer wishes, and the barrels can be bored with any desired degree of choke. Fit and finish are flawless, the stock being of the finest figured walnut and the lock plates and furniture splendidly engraved. Observations upon the handling of the gun would be inappropriate; since each gun is made to measure a casual acquaintance with one cannot justify subjective criticism. Nevertheless, the balance and feel suggest that the person who fits it will have no complaints.

This sort of custom construction is not cheap, and the prices of such guns vary with the specification and the quality of the finish between five and fifteen thousand dollars.

Remington Model 870 Competition Shotgun

Manufacturer Remington Arms Co., Ilion, NY 13357, U.S.A.
Type Single shot, slide action
Gage 12
Barrel 30in (762mm)
Weight 8.81lbs (4kg)

The Remington Model 870 shotgun has been around for a long time and has built up a solid reputation for reliability, and using this model as the base the company have recently produced a highly specialized trap-shooting competition gun.

The Perugini Emperor is a traditional gun of the highest grade.

At first glance one would be excused for thinking that this is a slide-operated repeater, but it is strictly a single-shot weapon, with the breech bolt operated by the slide action. What appears to be the magazine tube is in fact the housing for an unusual gas-actuated recoil buffer. The object has been to combine the specified requirements of a competition gun with the reduced recoil of a gas-operated weapon, so that the trap shooter who is firing off long strings of shot through a sporting day will not suffer unduly.

The 'magazine tube' contains a gas piston which, instead of operating the breech mechanism, merely thrusts against a spring buffer, so transferring a portion of the recoil blow in a 'soft' manner. Tests against a ballistic pendulum might show that the actual recoil force delivered at the butt is very little reduced from an un-buffered gun – one cannot tamper with the laws of physics – but there is no doubt that the character of the felt recoil is changed to a less violent push against the shoulder.

The barrel is specially bored and choked for trap shooting, so as to reduce the chances of shot deformation and produce more consistent patterns. The stock has a straight comb, the fore end is well formed to fill the hand, and the ventilated rib is set higher than usual, all features which add to its optimization for trap work. Even the trigger has been carefully set up to deliver clean pulls at a relatively low tension.

This is, obviously, a weapon which fits into a tightly circumscribed area of shooting sport, but for those whose prime interest lies in trap shooting, the Model 870 is a very attractive and sensible package.

The Rossi 'Squire', an unpretentious working gun available in various gages and lengths.

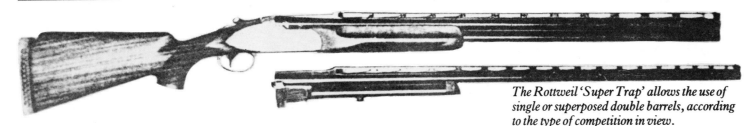

The Rottweil 'Super Trap' allows the use of single or superposed double barrels, according to the type of competition in view.

Renato Gamba 'London' Shotgun

Manufacturer Armi Renato Gamba SpA, Gardone Val Trompia, Italy
Type Side-by-side double, automatic ejector
Gage 12 or 20
Barrels 26.7in (680mm) or 27.5in (700mm)
Weight 6.62lbs (3kg) (26in barrels)

Renato Gamba build a number of grades of shotgun and the 'London' model is their top line; as the name implies, it sets out to duplicate the type and quality made famous by the London gunmakers, and it achieves this very well.

The 'London' comes in a traditional gun case, leather-covered and baize-lined, into which the dismantled gun and its cleaning gear fit neatly. The gun itself is elegantly finished with an English-style straight stock in European walnut, oil-finished, the case-hardened receiver is neatly engraved, as are the trigger guard, top lever and other components, the barrels are well polished and blued, and the fitting of metal to wood is excellent. The front trigger is hinged so as not to trap the finger on the second trigger during recoil, the firing pin holes are bushed, and the matted top rib is finished by a white metal front bead.

The stock has a slight cast-off and little drop, making it perhaps best suited to those small of stature. Fired with light loadings it is comfortable to shoot, but heavier loadings tend to punish the firer due to the low weight of the gun. Nevertheless, this low weight has its advantages when carrying the gun all day, and it is quick and accurate in coming to the shoulder and pointing.

Rossi 'Squire' Shotgun

Manufacturer Amadeo Rossi SA, Sâo Paulo, Brazil
Type Side-by-side double, hammerless
Gage 12, 20 or .410
Barrels 26in (660mm) or 28in (711mm)
Weight 7.75lbs (3.51kg) (12-ga)

Amadeo Rossi are a Brazilian company who, over the past fifteen or twenty years, have built up something of an export trade, particularly in revolvers. This hammerless shotgun first appeared in the 1960s and has recently been improved.

The 'Squire' is an unpretentious gun, designed to be used rather than admired. The stock and fore-end are of some local hardwood, plainly finished to resemble walnut and without checkering or decoration. The metal is well polished and blued, and the fit, though not to the highest standards, is perfectly serviceable. The mechanism of the lock is robust and the manufacturer's aim has been to produce a design capable of machine production and using as many interchangeable parts as possible. This at least has the virtue of delivering a sound gun at a reasonable price.

The 12- and 20-gage guns are well balanced full-sized weapons; the .410, as might be expected, is on a reduced scale and weighs rather less. We are, in fact, rather surprised that Rossi find it profitable to make a .410 gun since the current fashion appears to be moving away and to the 28-gage when a light weapon is required. Nevertheless, at whatever gage is chosen the Rossi functions reliably and shoots well, delivering consistent patterns to the point of aim.

Rottweil Super Trap Combination Gun

Manufacturer Deutsche Jagdpatronenfabrik GmbH, Rottweil, West Germany
Type Combination single or superposed
Gage 12
Barrels Single: 34in (864mm); double: 32in (812mm)
Weight 8.75lbs (3.96kg)

The phrase 'combination gun' means different things to different people; to workaday farmers it can mean interchangeable rifle and shotgun barrels, to upland shooters it can mean simply interchangeable barrels with different degrees of choke. But to International Trap competition shooters it means a gun which is specifically designed for their peculiar requirements and which can shift from a double over-and-under to a single barrel on call, so as to fit the various types of contest. On the face of it this sounds easy, but a look at this Rottweil gun shows that some careful thought and ingenious design is necessary to make a success of it.

The basic stock and receiver is no more than that; to it must be added first the barrel of choice and then the appropriate trigger unit. With the single barrel, there is (obviously) a single trigger; with the over-and-under set there is a selective single trigger, inertia operated and with a button which allows selection of the first barrel. The trigger units slip in and out and exhibit precise workmanship; the hammer coil springs are encased in telescoping steel tubes for alignment and protection, and all metal surfaces are polished clean of tool marks.

Each barrel set has a ventilated rib which stands well clear to avoid heat mirages, and the single barrel has a short balance tube beneath it so that whichever barrel is fitted the gun always weighs and balances the same. The same fore end will fit either barrel set. The stock and fore end are in satin-finished French walnut with excellent hand-checkering, while every metal surface is immaculately finished. The bores are hand-honed, test-fired, and re-worked if necessary at the factory in order to produce absolutely flawless patterns. The result of this careful hand fitting shows up in its performance, which is beyond criticism; it also shows up in the price, currently in excess of $5000.

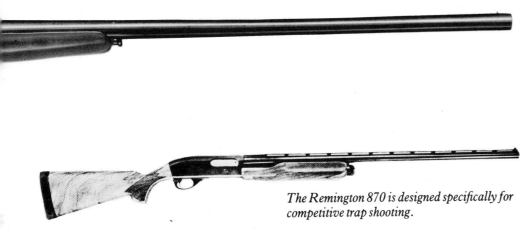

The Remington 870 is designed specifically for competitive trap shooting.

Ruger Over-and-under Shotgun

Manufacturer Sturm Ruger & Co. Inc., Southport, CT 06490, U.S.A.
Type Superposed, single trigger
Gage 12 or 20
Barrels 12-ga: 26in (660mm);
20-ga: 26in (660mm) or 28in (711mm)
Weight 7.06lbs (3.20kg) (26in barrels)

The Sturm Ruger company have been well-known for their handguns for some thirty years, but in the late 1960s they began work on a shotgun design. First shown in prototype form in 1971, it has been progressively developed and perfected and the first guns, in 20-gage, were sold in 1978. Now a 12-gage has been added and premium grade models were anticipated by 1983.

The Ruger uses some patented design features, notably the positioning of the locking bolt between the bore axes so as to obtain a low-set profile, and the inertia-locked single selective trigger mechanism. This can be set to fire either the upper or lower barrel first. There are rebounding hammers and a hammer interruptor which guard against accidental discharge when the weapon is cocked and set to safe; when set to fire, the hammer interruptor is only moved by positive action of the trigger.

The barrels are accurately fitted to the breech end monobloc, into which go all the ejector mechanism and the trunnions which form the barrel pivot. There is a ventilated rib with glare-free top surface and a brass sight bead at the muzzle end. The stock and fore end are of fine American walnut, well figured and neatly hand-checkered and with a soft lustrous finish.

The Ruger may be obtained with various degrees of choke; practical tests indicate a very high degree of consistency in boring and good tight patterning. The whole gun is 'of a piece', elegant and well-balanced, and looks like becoming a popular and respected sporting gun.

Top: The Ruger Over-and-Under 12 gage, which has 2¾in chambers, field-stripped.
Above: The elegant Ruger 20-gage with 3in chambers.
Top right: The open breech of the Ruger 12-gage.

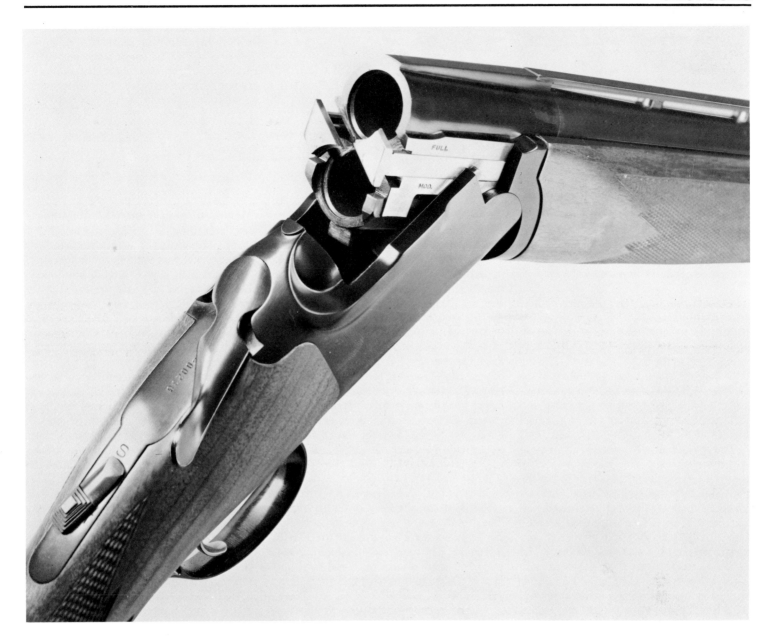

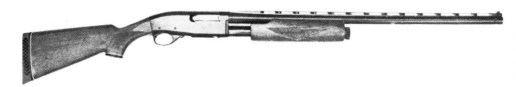

Left: The SKB M-7300 slide-action gun, made in Japan for export to the U.S.A. Below: The SKB 'ultimatic' automatic shotgun is gas-operated with a self-regulating method of operation.

SKB M-7300 Slide Shotgun

Manufacturer SKB Arms Company, Japan
Type Slide action repeater
Gage 12 or 20
Barrel 26, 28 or 30in (660, 711, or 762mm)
Weight 7.5lbs (3.40kg)
(12-ga, 28in barrel)
Magazine capacity 4 rounds

The SKB company are one of the few concerns outside the U.S.A. who find it profitable to manufacture pump-action shotguns, since this mechanism is less widely used in the rest of the world. Having done so, the obvious tactic is to sell it in the U.S.A., and SKB have built up a substantial following by producing a reliable and well-finished weapon at an economical price.

The M-7300 model comes in a variety of barrel lengths and choke options to suit most requirements; all guns are chambered for 3 inch cartridges and will handle shorter loadings. The stock is of close-grained walnut, neatly checkered and with a shiny finish, while the aluminum receiver and steel barrel are blacked and polished. The action is conventional, the bolt locking into a recess in the barrel extension and controlled by the slide action of the fore end. The tubular magazine holds four shells, and a plastic plug is provided to reduce this to two shells for those areas in which this is a legal requirement.

The barrel is topped by a ventilated rib carrying a fluorescent orange sight bead. It is possible to purchase spare barrels of different length or with different choke and interchange these without the need for individual fitting. The gun is handy and smooth in action, delivers a consistent pattern, and performs very reliably.

SKB Ultimatic XL 900 Shotgun

Manufacturer SKB Firearms, Kochi, Japan
Type Single-barrel, gas-operated, semi-automatic
Gage 12 or 20
Barrel 28in (711mm)
Weight 7.75lbs (3.51kg)
Magazine capacity 4

For some years the SKB company produced shotguns for sale under the names of importers and other manufacturers, but

they have now begun exporting under their own name, and their 'Ultimatic' is their top-line automatic gun.

The SKB uses the usual method of gas operation; an annular piston surrounds the magazine tube and fits into a gas cylinder beneath the barrel. A piston rod attached to the gas piston operates the breech block which locks into a recess in the barrel extension. Two types of 12-gage barrel are available, one for 2¾ inch cartridges and one for three inch; the former has two ports leading to the gas cylinder, the latter one port, so automatically regulating the amount of gas to the requirement of each load. The 20-gage uses the same barrel for either length of cartridge and regulates the gas by an adjustable valve.

The barrel carries a ventilated rib with a bead foresight; three lengths of barrel are available, each having a different choke. The 26 inch barrel has improved cylinder, the 28 inch modified or full and the 30 inch full choke. The receiver is of aluminum and is etched with decorative scrollwork and hunting scenes. The stock is of walnut, checkered and finished in a plastic varnish.

The SKB is comfortable to shoot, with the low recoil characteristic of gas-operated automatics, patterns well and is a reliable and well-proven model.

Smith & Wesson Model 1000 Shotgun

Manufacturer Howa Machinery Co. Ltd., Nagoya, Japan
Type Gas-operated auto-loading
Gage 12 or 20
Barrel 26, 28 or 30in
(660, 711 or 762mm)
Weight 7.5lbs (3.40kg) (28in barrel)
Magazine capacity 4 rounds

Smith & Wesson, long famed for their revolvers, surprised a great many people when they came into the shotgun business in the late 1970s, though they did it the easy way by having the gun built for them in Japan rather than turning over their normal production lines.

The finish is well up to Smith & Wesson standards; the butt and fore end are in figured walnut, with a polyurethane finish and neat checkering, while the barrel,

'Manufactured in Japan to S&W Specification' according to the legend thereon, is blued and polished. The receiver is in light alloy, blacked and with elegant engraving.

The 26 inch barrel, intended for Skeet shooting, can be had with improved cylinder boring; the longer barrels offer modified and full choke options. All deliver good patterns with consistency. The action is smooth and the perceived recoil is the usual soft thrust, made even softer by a pressure compensator and floating piston in the operating system.

The Auto-loader was followed by a slide action gun, the Model 1000P, which followed the same lines and indeed uses many of the same components as the auto-loader but having a steel receiver. Then came the 1000S, a special auto-loader for Skeet shooting which added a form of muzzle compensator and a special recessed choke to deliver optimum patterns. This is built to a somewhat higher specification, with such refinements as a contoured trigger, balance weights and fluorescent front bead, and commands a higher price. But whatever the shooter's need, one of these S&W guns will satisfy it with high quality and reliability.

Valmet Model 412 Shotgun

Manufacturer Valtion Kivaarithedas, Jyvaskyla, Finland
Type Double-barrelled, superposed
Gage 12 or 20
Barrels 27.75in (705mm)
Weight 7.75lbs (3.51kg)

We have chosen to give the specifications for a shotgun above, but in fact this weapon forms a component of the 'Valmet 412 Shooting System', something quite unique.

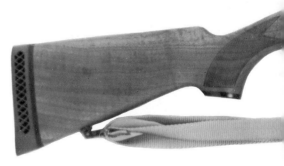

In brief, it is an action body to which four different butts can be fitted at the rear end and an enormous variety of over-and-under barrel combinations at the front. These range from double shotgun barrels of various gages and lengths to shotgun/rifle combinations or double rifles, again of various calibers and lengths. The shot barrels are in 12 or 20 gage, to various degrees of choke and various length; the rifle barrels of the combinations run from .22 Hornet to 9.3mm×74R, and the double rifles can be obtained chambered for most calibers from .243 Winchester to .375 Winchester. In addition it is possible to obtain chamber adapters which will allow .22 rimfire to be fired from various of the rifle calibers.

The Valmet can be purchased as an outfit or it can be bought as a single weapon and then expanded by acquiring fresh sets of barrels as the need arises (or the pocket allows). They can be simply fitted to the action, though it is perhaps wiser to have the initial fit checked by a gunsmith to ensure that all is well. The barrel assemblies are all monoblocs, the breeches being bored from a solid block of steel with the barrels then fitted into the front end. The shotgun barrels have a continuous rib joining them and a ventilated rib above, with a bead foresight. The combination guns and double rifles have an adjustment at two points on the barrels so that the two may be regulated to shoot to the same point of aim. This is a very valuable feature since it means that the regulation can be altered when changing, for example, from factory to hand-loaded ammunition.

The shotguns can be fitted with selective

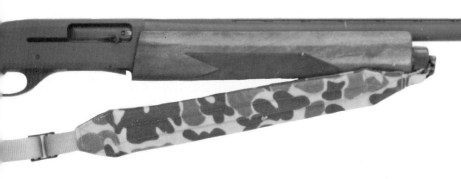

Center: The Valmet 412 'Shooting System' resembles a superposed shotgun but can have various combinations of rifle and shot barrels.
Left: The Smith & Wesson Model 1000 Waterfowler with sling attachments.

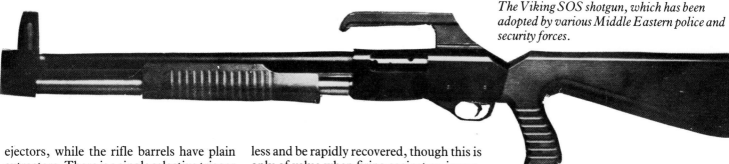

The Viking SOS shotgun, which has been adopted by various Middle Eastern police and security forces.

ejectors, while the rifle barrels have plain extractors. There is a single selective trigger with a push-button inset which selects the first barrel to be fired. The stock is of good quality walnut, well checkered and finished, and the finish on the metalwork is excellent. The Valmet system is extremely good value for money and it offers a degree of versatility which is not approached by any other maker at this time.

Viking Arms SOS Shotgun

Manufacturer Viking Arms Ltd., Harrogate, England
Type Slide action repeater
Gage 12
Barrel 24.25in (616mm)
Weight 7.43lbs (3.37kg)
Magazine capacity 7 rounds

The shotgun has evolved into certain well-known shapes over the years, and the appearance of something new comes as a shock to most people. The Viking gun is designed along the lines of the modern assault rifle, with a 'straight-line' stock and a carrying-handle-cum-sight unit which requires an equally high-set foresight. The makers suggest it as a 'defense' gun rather than as a purely sporting gun, and I have little doubt that the appearance of this weapon on some European shoots would result in a rapid request for the bearer to leave.

But leaving visual impressions aside, the Viking is a well-made weapon with certain definite 'plus' points. It has an unusually large magazine for a slide-action gun, and since the barrel is cylinder-bored it makes a good gun for firing solid slugs. The sights assist in this, though they are not capable of being adjusted without the aid of a gunsmith. As a trap gun or as a sporting gun the shape takes some getting used to, and it does not come to the shoulder as easily or smoothly as a traditional shape, though doubtless practice would improve this.

The straight-line configuration helps to control recoil, the gun appearing to jump

less and be rapidly recovered, though this is only of value when firing against an immobile target. There is the possibility that the gun would be attractive to police or security forces; it is certainly reliable and accurate, simple to dismantle and maintain, all features making it attractive for service use, and it is comparatively inexpensive. We understand that an optional butt of conventional form will be available in the near future so that it will be possible to convert it into a more normal-looking pump gun for 'social' occasions.

Viking Suhl Shotgun

Manufacturer Viking Arms Ltd., Harrogate, England
Type Side-by-side double, non-ejector
Gage 12
Barrels 28in (711mm)
Weight 6.56lbs (2.97kg)

Suhl, in Thuringia, was once the heart of the German gunmaking industry, the address featuring after many famous names. It now lies in East Germany and the famous names have either departed or have been swallowed up by impersonal state-controlled cooperatives named after Communist heroes; this shotgun is made in Suhl, but I have been unable to determine by whom, and I have therefore listed the English agent as the manufacturer.

In an age when manufacturers vie with each other to make more and more luxurious products at higher and higher prices, the Suhl shotgun comes as a welcome surprise; it is an unpretentious 'working gun', with no concessions to elegance. The walnut stock has a half-pistol grip, the fore end is machine-checkered, but the finish is good and the fit of the gun to the stock is excellent. The action is a double-bolted box-lock, color case-hardened and without decoration, but it works smoothly, the trigger pull is crisp and consistent, and the whole action is tight and sound.

The barrels are bored quarter and three-quarter choke on Continental standards, closer to half and full-choke to western

ideas, but the patterns are good and consistent. It handles well, the stock being cast-off for right-handed shooting, and gives the impression of a no-nonsense gun which will stand years of hard use.

Winchester Model 23 Shotgun

Manufacturer Olin-Kodensha Co., Tochigi, Japan
Type Double-barrelled, side-by-side
Gage 12, 20
Barrels 26 or 28in (660 or 710mm)
Weight 7.18lbs (3.25kg) (12-ga with 28in bbl)

Introduced in 1980 this was the first side-by-side production Winchester shotgun for twenty years and it is manufactured by a subsidiary of the Winchester group located in Japan.

It is a conventional double gun produced in one grade, Winchester's 'Pigeon Grade', with selective ejectors, single trigger and a ventilated rib with fore and mid sight beads. The action is a box-lock with double underbolt locking, and the trigger can be selected to fire either barrel by moving the safety tang sideways. Once the first barrel has been fired, the trigger automatically resets for the second barrel. There are safety interruptors in the lock which prevent the gun being fired unless the trigger is properly pulled, so preventing accidental discharges in the event of a loaded gun being dropped. There is an automatic safety which is set as the gun is broken open.

The barrels are for three inch shells and the choke varies with the length; 26 inch barrels have improved cylinder and modified chokes, while 28 inch barrels have modified and full. Finish inside and out is first-class, the barrels blued, the action grey, and the stock of high-grade American walnut, though the shiny plastic varnish finish may not be to all tastes. The lockplates are tastefully decorated in a scroll and leaf pattern.

The Winchester handles well and shoots comfortably, though the patterns do not appear to be as tight as might be expected from the choke designations. In spite of this it kills cleanly and proved to be a solid performer in the field.

The Winchester Model 23, made in Japan, the first Winchester side-by-side for many years.

The muzzle of the Franchi SPAS 12, a 'law enforcement' shotgun.

Combat Shotguns

The past two or three years have seen a sudden resurgence of interest in the shotgun as a possible military weapon, and there is every possibility that the next year or two will see some quite remarkable designs appearing on the market, designs, which may show some spin-off to the commercial and sporting areas.

There is, of course, nothing new about shotguns in military service, but their use tends to come and go in cycles. Shotguns were commonly carried by US troops in the Indian Wars and were also prominent in the Philippines campaigns against the Moros in the 1890s. They then disappeared from sight until the Mexican Intervention of 1916 when General Pershing outfitted his cavalry with shotguns. When Pershing went to France to command the US Expeditionary Force he quickly realized that shotguns were the ideal trench weapon and several thousand were rapidly procured and issued.

To the Europeans, shotguns were sporting weapons and their employment in a military situation was decidedly unsporting. The Germans lost no time in complaining of the barbarous weapon now being used by the Americans, and threatened to shoot any shotgun-bearing prisoners out of hand, the stock response of the Germans to any new weapon which confronted them. For their part, the Americans merely pointed out that shotguns had a long history of military employment, that there were no international agreements prohibiting their use, and that, in fact, during a prewar conference on the rules and usages of warfare the Germans had been given the opportunity to outlaw any weapons they wished and had failed to do so. And if any AEF men got shot the AEF would take appropriate action. That was the end of that, though the German press continued to complain until the war ended.

Trench warfare probably saw more practical application of shotguns than had any previous combat, and several things became apparent. Firstly the classic 'side-by-side' sporting gun was virtually useless as a combat weapon; it was too long and too slow to reload. Sawing the barrels down to make the handling more convenient helped, but didn't do anything to the reloading and rate of fire problem. But the slide-action shot- gun was a common commercial product by that time and so the US Army bought several thousand short-barrel riot guns, modified to accept a bayonet and sling.

The next problem to appear lay with the ammunition. The conditions in the trenches were probably the worst which could be imagined for shotgun ammunition, based, as it was, on a cardboard shell case. The trenches were invariably wet, and the dampness soon got into the cardboard and swelled the cases until they would stick in the gun's action. It was here that the slide-action gun showed its superiority over automatic guns, since when a case stuck, extra exertion on the slide would generally free it, whereas the automatic had no reserve of power and jammed solid. The only long-term answer to this was to adopt brass-cased shells.

After the war the Trench Gun M1917, as the issue shotgun was known, went into store and it was reissued after Pearl Harbor to the US Marines, who used it to good effect in the South Pacific. It was rarely seen in Europe, since the mobile warfare there gave little scope for its employment.

Belgian police carry FN-Browning slide-action 12-gage guns while checking traffic.

As a military weapon the shotgun is at its best in close-quarter fighting, such as obtains in the jungle, in trenches or in street fighting. And its next employment in any numbers was by the British in the Malayan Confrontation against Communist guerrillas in the 1950s. The British military had never used shotguns nor ever contemplated their use, but the Malayan Police used them and soon showed the military how valuable they were in ambushes and jungle combat. The British Army purchased several thousand Browning and Remington automatics and various makes of slide-action guns and, in true British style, set about making a careful analysis of their effectiveness and drawing up tactical instructions, based on this analysis, to make them even more effective. The subsequent report which was produced has been instrumental in guiding military thinking about shotguns ever since.

Broadly speaking, the effectiveness of a shotgun is governed by its ammunition, and the ammunition has almost always been whatever was commercially available, since few armies have ever made careful studies of shotgun ammunition ballistics. The most generally-favored shell is the 'SG' or '00 Buck' loaded with nine lead balls each .33in diameter and weighing 130 to the pound. These have good penetrating power at ranges up to about 50 yards, but after that the velocity falls off and the spread is such that it becomes possible to miss a man-sized target quite easily. For this reason the British experimented with various types of buckshot loading with more pellets of smaller size; but while

Right: The combat shotgun in use; a 12-gage slide action gun resting on camouflage net, one of the weapons of a South West African Defense Force patrol operating against SWAPO terrorists along the Namibia-Angola border.
Below: Ithaca 37 Stainless handgrip 12-gage gun with 8-shot magazine.

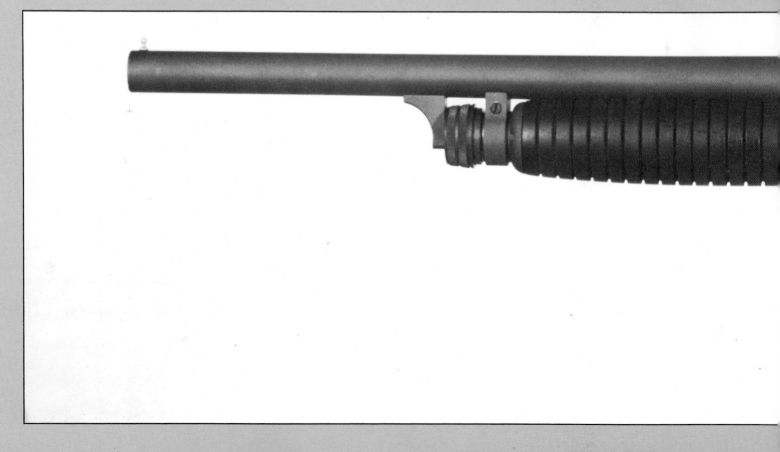

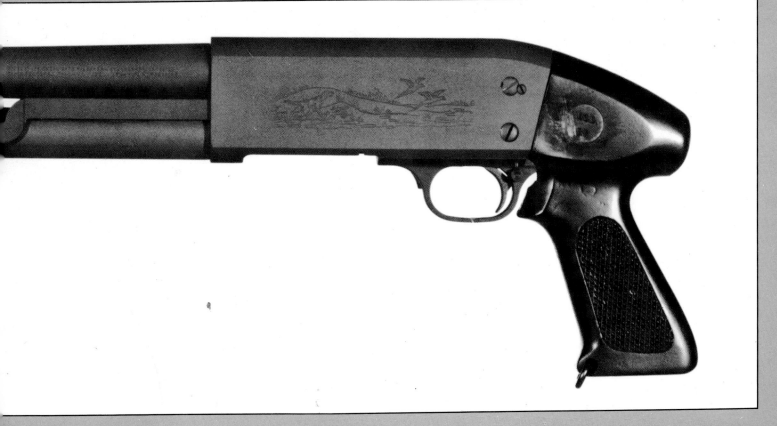

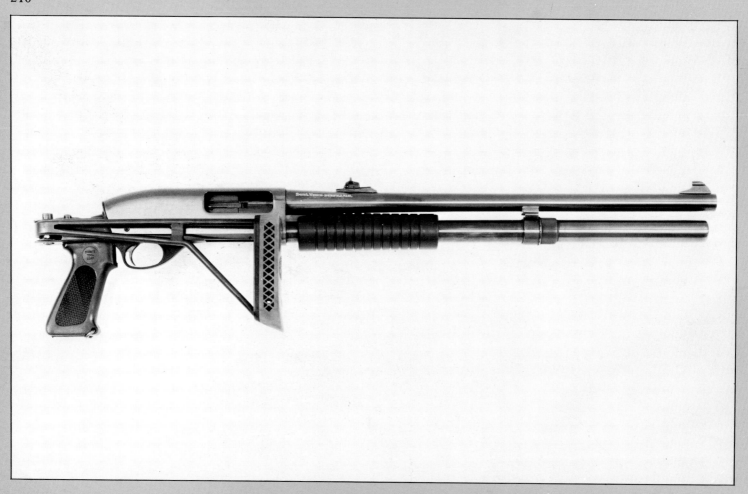

reducing the size of pellet allowed more to be loaded and thus improved the chances of a hit because of the improved spread pattern it provided, the reduction in size made them less effective at the target.

The US forces in Vietnam in the 1960s also used shotguns, basing their employment upon the knowledge gained in the Pacific during World War Two but largely ignoring the British studies in Malaya. As is usually the case, after three or four years of combat they came up with recommendations and suggestions which more or less paralleled the British conclusions, so that the two sets of reports reinforce each other and became the foundation of most of the subsequent development which has taken place.

Two facts have been made apparent by these various practical experiences; firstly that commercial ammunition is not much use in a military environment, and secondly that

Above: Smith & Wesson M3000 12-gage, fitted with a folding stock, makes a compact weapon for carrying in police and military vehicles.

the standard tubular magazine used with automatic and slide-action shotguns is totally impractical in combat. One of the significant features of military rifles is that they can be reloaded very rapidly; the bolt is opened and a clip dumped into the magazine or a charger stripped in, or the magazine simply removed and a full one attached. Whatever the system reloading a full magazine is a matter of a few seconds simple work. With the tubular magazine shotgun, the picture is very different; here the individual shells have to be

Right: Another view of the folding-butt version of the Smith & Wesson M3000 12-gage gun.
Below: The Smith & Wesson M3000 12-gage gun in standard form.

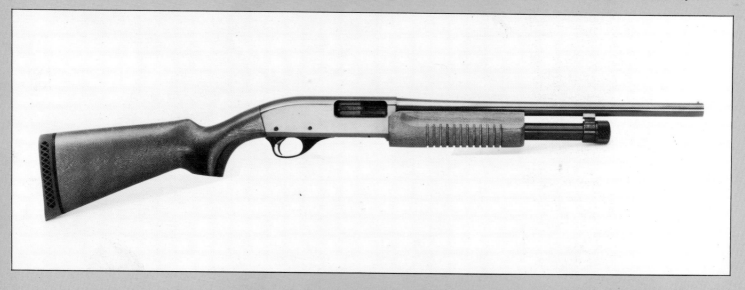

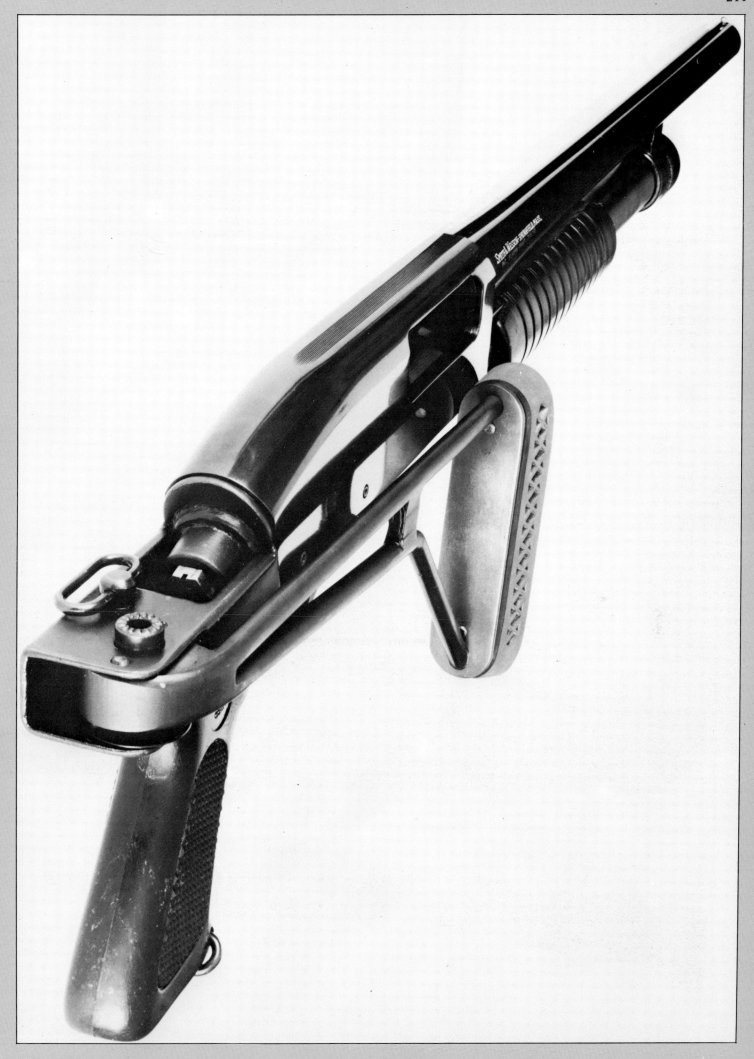

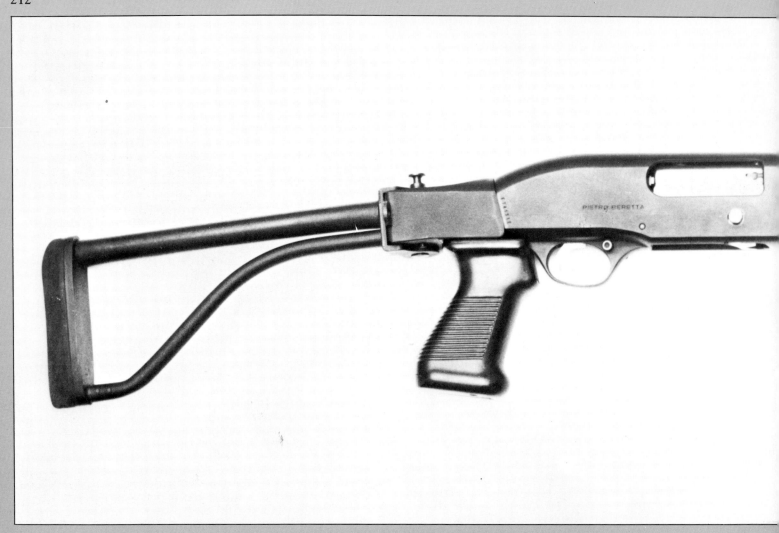

The Beretta RS-202-P is designed for police and security use.

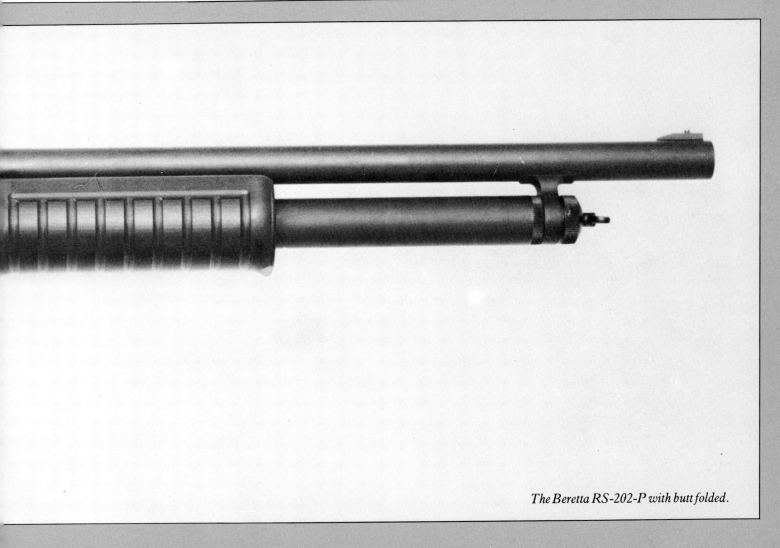

The Beretta RS-202-P with butt folded.

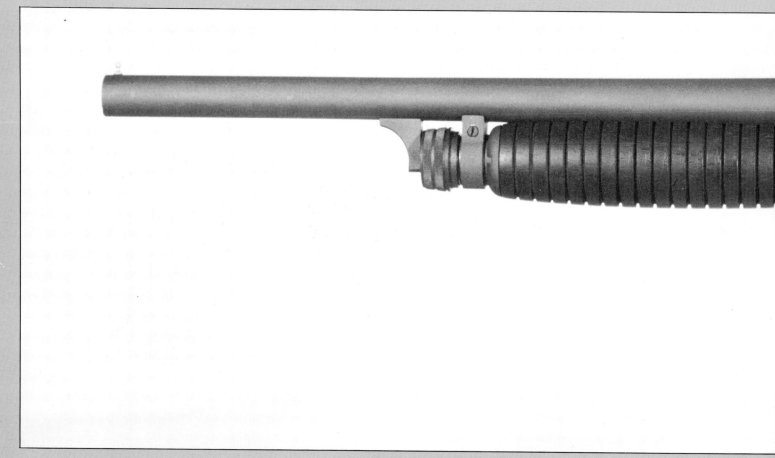

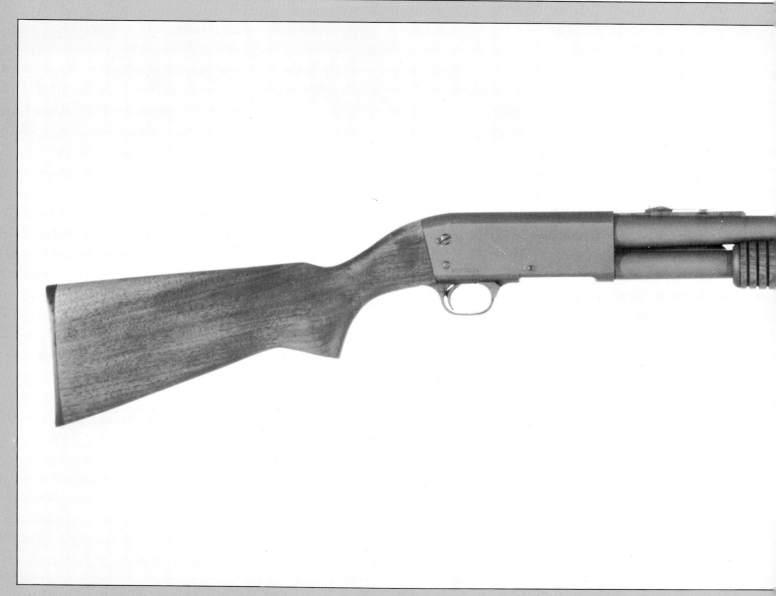

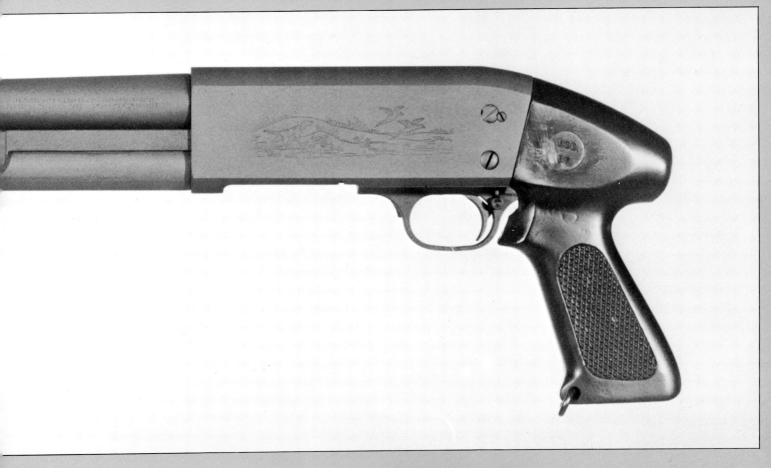

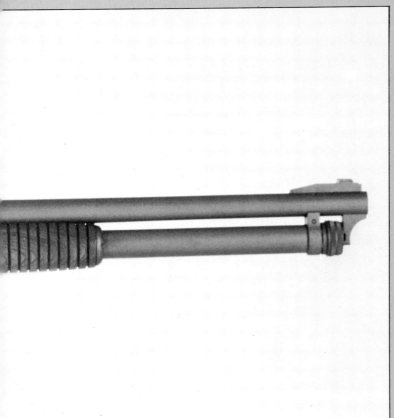

Above: The Ithaca 37 'Handgrip' gun is specially designed for police use and is provided in stainless or Parkerized finish to withstand the rigors of all-weather duty.
Left: The Ithaca 12-gage 'Deerslayer' Police Special gun uses the high-precision 'Deerslayer' cylinder-bored barrel in order to fire rifled slugs with the utmost accuracy.

loaded in one at a time, a slow and fiddling procedure at the best of times and not one to be encouraged in the middle of a fire fight.

One solution – not really a solution, more an evasion of the problem – has been to make tubular extensions to the standard magazines so as to increase the number of shells carried and so cut down the need for reloading so often. This is satisfactory so far as it goes, but it really doesn't solve the basic problem. Pre-packed tubes of shells, which can be slid into the magazine from the front end, have been suggested and tried, but this, again, is impractical; how can a combat soldier carry a relatively delicate reload tube which is all of two feet long without damaging it?

The obvious solution is a box magazine, just like those used with rifles. But here the awkward contours of the shotgun shell cause problems. Loading a rifle or pistol cartridge from a box magazine is relatively simple, since the rounded or pointed nose of the bullet, directed to a shaped loading ramp, steers the cartridge into the breech quite reliably. But the squared-off end of a shotgun shell is a more difficult article to persuade in the right direction, and the cardboard of the shell casing is too easily deformed should it meet any obstacle.

The final question raised by the experiences of the 1950s and 1960s was that of reliability. The commercial shotgun is a very fine article and has been raised to a high degree of perfection, but the fact remains that it was never envisaged as

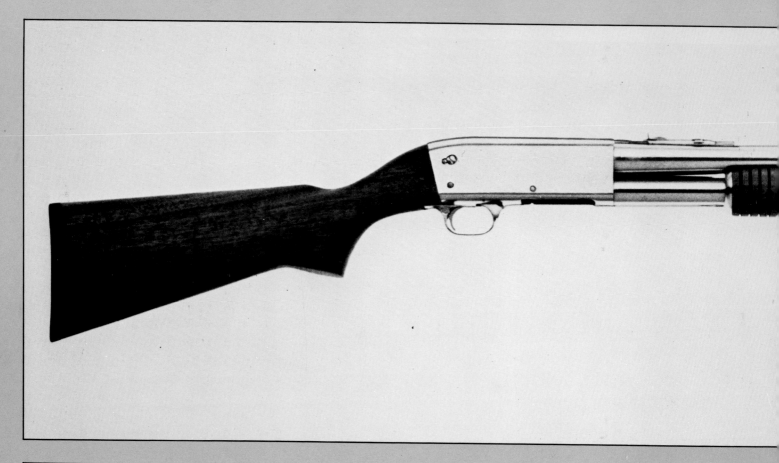

Top: The Ithaca Deerslayer Police Special is also available in a chromed weather-resistant finish.
Above: The basic Ithaca 'Military & Police' 12-gage slide gun is a utilitarian weapon designed to stand up to strenuous use.

a military weapon by its designers and therefore its reliability in a military environment is, by military standards, poor. Slide-action guns are perhaps an exception to this, because the riot-type weapons are very simple and robust, but they still fall short of the degree of reliability assumed for military rifles. Automatic weapons, on the other hand, are comparatively delicate and no sporting automatic has ever survived a military acceptance test, nor is ever likely to. This is something which soldiers have had to accept, together with accepting the burden of a much higher maintenance load, the need for greater care in day-to-day cleaning and inspection, and the provision of a high percengage of spare parts.

The answer, of course, was to ask manufacturers to develop weapons with military employment firmly in view, weapons which would be more robust and reliable. But development costs money; shotgun development was entirely in the hands of commercial firms who were governed by the need to show a profit at the end of the year and could not shovel huge sums of money into development programs which, if successful, would result in small military orders which would never pay the development costs. Several companies showed an extremely cooperative spirit in beginning development programs, but when it was obvious that no government backing was going to appear, and that the market was not worth the endeavor, all these programs came to a halt.

But that was in the late 1960s, in the aftermath of Vietnam and all the political unpleasantness which followed in its wake. Since then the wheel has turned through another cycle and the combat shotgun has made another appearance. And this time there seems to be a greater willingness to put money into development and a greater likelihood that military aid will be forthcoming both in funding such development and in providing a market for the weapons developed.

Strangely, considering that we are contemplating what is

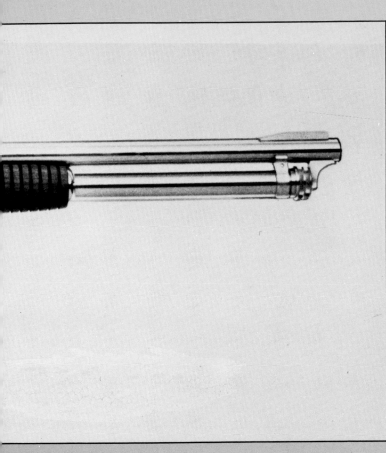

basically an infantry weapon, the US development in this field is being performed under Naval auspices. The Joint Services Small Arms Program (JSSP) has set up an investigation aimed at providing a 'more capable, rugged and versatile replacement for the combat shotgun' and the program is being managed by the Naval Surface Weapons Center at Dahlgren, Va. The NSWC comes into this area by virtue of its having been deeply involved in developing a combat shotgun for the Marine Corps and for US Naval SEAL teams in the late 1960s.

In 1968 Carroll Childers, an employee of the US Naval R&D Unit, Vietnam, began looking at ways of improving the firepower of SEAL teams and Marine reconnaissance units, and developed a 50-round magazine for the M16 rifle which was successful. He then turned to shotguns and in 1970 produced a slide-action shotgun with a box magazine. He had solved the problem of feed by taking the shells out of the magazine backward, then transferring them up, into the chamber, by the normal mechanism used with tubular magazines. Not only did he develop a box magazine but he actually managed to make staggered-column magazines

Below: In an attempt to use more effective ammunition, shotguns are being shouldered aside by larger-caliber weapons such as this 38mm Hawk Engineering MM-1 grenade-firing revolver.

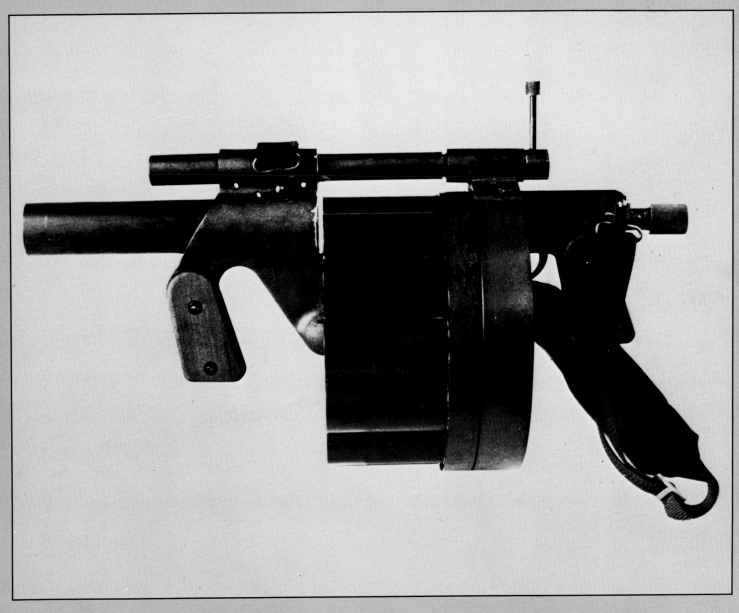

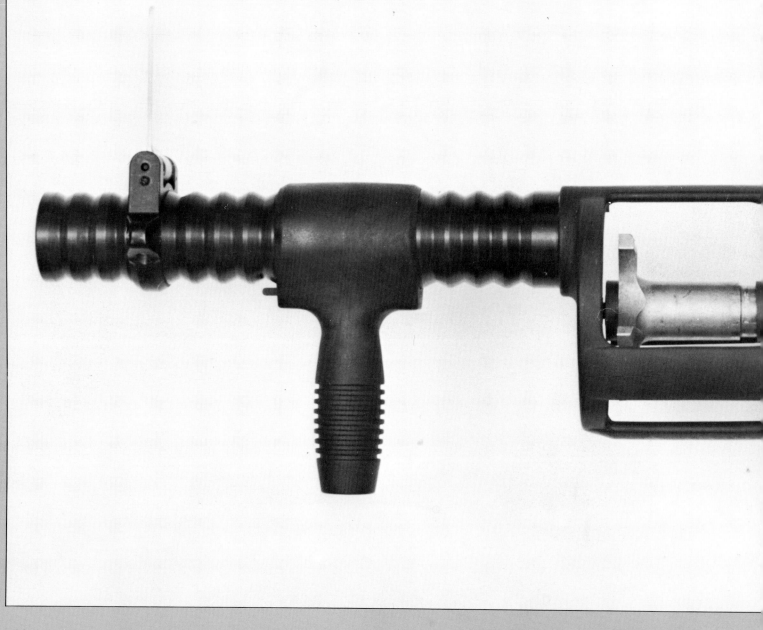

which would take 10 or 20 rounds, the first time such a magazine had ever been achieved for shotgun ammunition. Unfortunately, just as he perfected the design, the decision to withdraw from Vietnam was taken and development was stopped, so the Childers-Dahlgren shotgun never saw the light of day.

Undeterred, Childers now turned to developing a more purpose-built weapon, a full-automatic 12-gage magazine or belt-fed shotgun. This, as might be imagined, demanded some flights of imagination before it could be made to work, but Childers' design used a blow-forward mechanism in which the barrel moved away from the stationary breech-block after firing, allowing the fired case to be extracted, and was then returned by a spring to chamber the next shell. Known as the 'Special Operations Weapon', the gun could spew out 200 rounds a minute, truly formidable firepower.

An additional feature was that it could be opened and

Above: The British ARWEN anti-riot gun which was intended to replace the single-shot type of gun with a 5-shot revolver. In 37mm caliber it is now being developed as an infantry patrol and anti-ambush weapon.
Right: This Smith & Wesson Model 210 riot gun is typical of the single-shot weapon capable of firing tear-gas.

hand-loaded with extra-length shells containing special loadings, and Childers envisaged flare, incendiary, CS gas and anti-armor loads, as well as a high-explosive fragmentation anti-personnel cartridge which would duplicate the affects of the existing M40 grenade launchers. However, innovative as the idea was, it, too, fell under the Vietnam withdrawal cutback, and the idea was shelved.

To return to the present day; it is this involvement in the Childers designs which has led the JSSP to pass the shotgun program to Dahlgren, and it can be assumed that Dahlgren have reached into their files and have put some of the 1970s

The ARWEN reduced to its component parts; barrel on the left, action body on the right, cylinder housing in the center. The bolt is above the pistol grip and the five-shot sprocket feed is detached. The entire weapon is of alloy and plastic and is surprisingly light.

experience to good use. But the demands are such that the term 'shotgun' is somewhat less than complete, and so the new program is aimed at producing a 'Close Assault Weapon System' or CAWS.

CAWS is anticipated to be a gas-actuated weapon, fed from a top-mounted 10- or 20-shot magazine, offering the option of left- or right-handed shell ejection. It is possible that full-automatic fire will be provided, but this appears to be left to individual designers and is not, apparently, a firm demand. One thing which has been specified, though, is a recoil-reducing muzzle brake or similar device, since it is envisaged that the ammunition will be considerably more powerful than standard shotgun shells.

Indeed, it is the ammunition which is at the heart of the CAWS concept. The primary round will be what is officially termed 'an improved 12-gage shotshell', but the improve-

ment will have to be fundamental and considerable, since the demand is for better lethality and area coverage and an effectiveness against personnel *at ranges of 100 to 150 meters.*

Precisely how manufacturers intend to go about producing this long range lethality is currently a close-guarded secret, but we would expect to see shot pellets made of something rather more effective than lead, probably depleted uranium or a tungsten alloy, which would give excellent sectional density and carrying power, leading to minimal loss of velocity. But this will also need to be propelled by a somewhat higher charge than usual, and hence the demand for a recoil reducer. Many people will doubtless suggest flechettes, those finned darts which were extensively used in artillery shells in Vietnam and also in loadings for the M40 grenade launcher. These have been tried in rifle and shotgun loadings, but, in truth, they are much less efficient than most people imagine. All projectiles relying upon their kinetic energy, be they bullets, shot or flechettes, have to have a specific degree of momentum before they can do any damage, and that momentum is a combination of their weight and velocity. You can throw a heavy bullet slowly or a

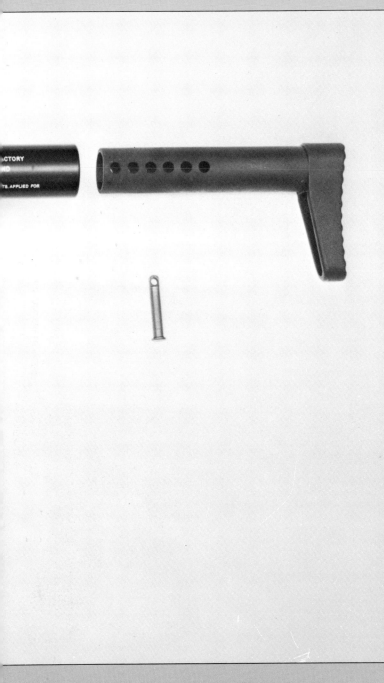

at 300 yards range. For those familiar with anti-armor munitions, the obvious answer to this appears to be a hollow-charge shell which would rely upon explosive energy to punch a hole in the target, but from the published statements it appears that a 'long rod penetrator' is contemplated. This means using kinetic energy, the projectile being a long and slender dart of extremely hard material such as depleted uranium or Stabiloy. It also means delivering the penetrator to the target at high velocity, and it would appear that the only method likely to achieve this is to adopt the discarding sabot configuration, which is discussed in greater detail elsewhere in these pages. No wonder the specification asks for a recoil reducer.

Requests for Proposals, the formal demand for ideas, have been sent out to various manufacturers, and by the time this book is published development contracts will have been placed with manufacturers to produce prototype weapons. four companies have expressed willingness to work on the project; the AAI Corporation, the Ithaca Gun Company, Pan Associates, and Heckler & Koch of Germany. The Olin Corporation are working on anti-personnel ammunition development, and the Vought Corporation has done some work on anti-material rounds. So far the only physical result made public has been a prototype weapon mock-up shown by Heckler & Koch at the 1982 Ausa Conference in Washington, but the exhibitors were reluctant to discuss any details of the weapon.

Outside the USA any development going on is being kept well concealed at present. The only comparable weapon which has been revealed in public is the British 'ARWEN', which stands for 'Anti-Riot Weapon, Enfield'. At 37mm caliber this is perhaps somewhat large to be considered a small arm, but its projected employment is so close to that of CAWS that it is a valid comparison.

ARWEN was developed, in the first place, purely as an anti-riot gun to shoot plastic 'baton' projectiles and CS gas pellets. The existing guns of this type are all single-shot weapons, and experience in riots showed that the pause while the firers reloaded was often sufficient to permit a rioter to appear, throw a bomb or take a shot, and vanish again. ARWEN was developed as a five-shot revolver capable of delivering several shots in quick succession or of being able to snap off a quick second shot when the unwary rioter put his head up. It is a highly effective weapon, and new ammunition developed to accompany it is extremely accurate. But the idea of a multiple-shot anti-riot weapon was unacceptable to British politicians who felt that it gave the military an unfair advantage against their enemies, so ARWEN is forbidden to the British Army. It is, we gather, selling quite well to overseas police and security forces unhampered by such considerations of politeness.

But the British Army have seen more than an anti-riot application; with a caliber of 37mm there is sufficient room inside a projectile to put some useful combat loadings, and therefore development of high explosive-fragmentation, smoke, illuminating and anti-armor projectiles is going forward, with the idea of developing ARWEN as an infantry squad support weapon. It will be interesting to compare the eventual results of the CAWS and ARWEN programs when they are made public in a few years time.

light bullet fast, as long as Mass×Velocity comes out at a respectable figure. A shotgun firing 00 Buckshot can produce the desired combination, but the extremely light flechette (about 8 grains weight is normal) needs a very high velocity in order to deliver a sufficiently lethal effect. Nevertheless, flechette loadings have been produced by several firms in the past and were used with some reasonable results in Vietnam. There is reason to believe that there is a sufficient mass of information on flechette performance which would allow development of an effective round, bearing in mind that technology has made some steps forward since these original loadings were developed some twenty years ago. Certainly, one advantage of the flechette is that it will range to a greater distance than simple pellets.

But more important than the improved shotshell is the 'family of ammunition' which is proposed for CAWS. This, according to a recent US Army statement, is likely to include an explosive-fragmentation projectile, a tactical tear-gas cartridge, and, most important of all, an 'anti-material' projectile which should be capable of penetrating at least 1¼ inches of armor plate, and possibly as much as three inches,

INDEX

Acknowledgments

The author and the publishers would like to thank the following for their help in the preparation of this book: David Eldred who designed it, Richard Nichols and Bridget Daly who helped with the editing and Ron Watson who prepared the index. The majority of the illustrations were provided by the manufacturers and our thanks are due to them. Additional material was provided by the organizations listed below.
Armi Renato Gamba 25
Australian Army 182
Fabrique National Herstal 10, 143
FFV Ordnance Division Sweden (Mars) 6
Foto Zanoni 37, 88
T. J. Gander 124
C. Handley Smith 208
Heckler and Koch 167, 168
Ian V. Hogg (Sturm, Ruger Inc.) 12, 16, 73, 144
Hughes Helicopters Inc. 169
Robert Hunt Library 186
Imperial War Museum (Fowler) 132
Keystone Press Agency 179
Ministry of Defence (Mars) 186, 187
Renaldo S. Olive 170
Ramta Div. IAI Ltd. (Mars) 182
Royal Small Arms Factory (Mars) 22, 186
Soldier Magazine (Mars) 24
Steves Photography Inc. 57
A. C. Kranzmayr Steyr 46, 154
Steyr-Daimler-Puch (Mars) 17, 26
United Press International 184
US Army 185
Weller and Dufty 5